E. E. (Elizabeth E.) Flagg

Holden With Cords, or, the Power of the Secret Empire

A Faithful Representation in Story of the Evil Influence of Free-masonry

E. E. (Elizabeth E.) Flagg

Holden With Cords, or, the Power of the Secret Empire
A Faithful Representation in Story of the Evil Influence of Free-masonry

ISBN/EAN: 9783337030896

Printed in Europe, USA, Canada, Australia, Japan

Cover: Foto ©ninafisch / pixelio.de

More available books at **www.hansebooks.com**

HOLDEN WITH CORDS

OR THE

POWER OF THE SECRET EMPIRE.

A FAITHFUL REPRESENTATION IN STORY OF THE EVIL INFLUENCE OF

FREEMASONRY

BY E. E. FLAGG,

Author of "Little People," "A Sunny Life" Etc.

CHICAGO, ILLINOIS,
EZRA A. COOK, PUBLISHER,
1883.

Entered according to Act of Congress in the year 1883,

By EZRA A. COOK,

In the office of the Librarian of Congress at Washington, D. C.

PUBLISHER'S PREFACE.

The educating influence of stories—both for good and evil—is everywhere recognized. The vile anecdotes of the bar-room and saloon debauch the conscience worse than the liquor they drink does their bodies.

It is notorious that it is neither the most eloquent or worthy politician, but he who can give the most sensational illustrations, that stands the best chance of election.

The popular legends and fables of a nation indicate and largely determine the character of the people.

Masonic writers have not been backward in the use of legends and narratives to bolster up that institution.

Albert G. Mackey, the most influential and extensive Masonic writer of this country is the author of a book entitled "THE MYSTIC TIE, or Facts and Opinions Illustrative of the Character and Tendency of Freemasonry." Of course the object of the work is to show by what Masonry *has done* for men, its practical value, and such chapter headings as "Freemasonry Among Pirates," "Masonic Courtesy in War" and "The Soldier Mason," show the object of the author. Such stories have doubtless led many to join the order, that by its mystic power they might be safe among pirates and other outlaws, little thinking they were at the same time obligating themselves to shield these outlaws from deserved punishment.

But the power *for good* of narrations illustrative of God's dealing with individuals and nations must not be overlooked, for this forms a large portion of God's Word, and Christ himself employed narratives and parables with great power in his teachings.

Bunyan's beautiful allegories have shown many the blessedness of " walking with God," and the influence of " Uncle Tom's Cabin " in showing the people the abominations of human slavery can scarcely be overestimated, because it was a true picture of that iniquitous system. Like the volume before the reader it was a recital of facts, with but enough of the garb of fiction for a covering.

For ample proof of the accuracy of the sketch of the abduction and murder of Wm. Morgan and the trials that followed, the reader is referred to the " Broken Seal," by Samuel D. Greene, and to the " History of the Abduction of Capt. Wm. Morgan," prepared by seven committes of leading citizens of the Empire State. And for the story of Mary Lyman's wrongs the pamphlet entitled " Judge Whitney's Defense," furnishes ample material. All of these may be had in pamphlet form by addressing the publisher of this work.

After reading the aforesaid pamphlets the reader will certainly be ready to exclaim, " Surely facts are stranger than fiction," and will be able better to see *how* the thousands of our land can be thus HOLDEN WITH CORDS of secret iniquity. THE PUBLISHER.

CONTENTS.

Chapter.		Page.
I.	My Grandfather's Advice...	11
	Mackey Asserts that Masonry is a "Religious Institution," Note 1..	12
	Chase says "Masonry has nothing whatever to do with the Bible."..	12
	Morris tells the "Allurements" of the Lodge, Note 3...............	12
	"Masonry unites men of every country, sect and opinion, Note 4..	12
	Grandfather's Masonic Experience in a French Prison...............	13
	"Secrecy has a mystic binding almost supernatural force," Note 5..	14
II.	The "Common and Profane" Discussing Freemasonry..........	19
III.	A Mysterious Book—Chambers of Imagery......................	25
	Initiation "a death to the World and a resurrection to a new life" Note 6	29
	Mackey Hints at the Stripping for Initation, Note 7.................	29
	Taking the Entered Apprentice Oath.................................	30
	"The importance of secret keeping," Note 8.........................	31
	"The shock of enlightenment," Note 9...............................	32
	"The social hour at high XII," Note 10..............................	33
IV.	A Talk with My Grandfather.......................................	34
	"This surrender of free-will to Masonic authority is *absolute*," Note 11	34
	"Masonry is a religious institution," Note 12........................	35
	"The dignity of the institution depends mainly upon its age," Note 13	36
V.	Preparation for a Journey—Passed and Raised."................	38
	"It is the obligation which makes the Mason," Note 14.............	38
	"Entered Apprentices are possessed of very few rights," Note 15 ..	45
VI.	An Evening with Rachel..	47
	"Do you suppose the Good Samaritan was a Freemason?"...........	49
VII.	A Certain Man went down from Jericho..........................	53
	"A violent blow on the head that knocked me senseless from the saddle"...	59
	"The horseman had flung himself off and was listening to my tale"	57
	"Don't go to maddening me with any of your grips and signs"....	59
VIII.	Mrs. Hagan's Opinion of Elder Cushing...........................	60
	"Honest Ben Hagan"...	61
IX.	Mr. Hagan tells what he knows about Masonry..................	67
	"Placing a drawn sword across the throat," Note 16.................	72
	Treason and Rebellion not Masonic Offences, Note 17...............	73
	"I promised to help a companion in any difficulty, right or wrong"..	74
X.	A Masonic Murder—Success and Return Home.................	76
XI.	More Talk with My Grandfather—A Modern Pan..............	87

CONTENTS.

CHAPTER.		PAGE
XII	A FEW MASONIC PUZZLES	98
XIII.	MASONIC BONDAGE.—SAM TOLLER'S AFFAIRS	107
XIV.	A DECLARATION OF INDEPENDENCE—NOT OF '76.—SAM TOLLER MISSING	115
XV.	THE SPRING OF 1826.—SAM TOLLER.—"COMING EVENTS CAST THEIR SHADOWS BEFORE"	126
XVI.	AN ADHERING FREEMASON INCAPABLE OF ENTIRE LOYALTY TO HIS WIFE.—A LODGE QUARREL.—JACHIN AND BOAZ	134
XVII	LUKE THATCHER.—RUMORS.—MASONRY IN ITS RELIGIOUS ASPECTS	144
XVIII.	THE GATHERING STORM	152
XIX.	A NIGHT IN BATAVIA	162
XX	AN EXCITING SCENE	176
XXI.	THE MYSTERIOUS CARRIAGE	187
XXII.	MARK RELATES HIS MASONIC EXPERIENCES	197
	"The *ties* of a Royal Arch Mason," Note 23	200
	"Libations are still used in some of the higher degrees," Note 24	200
	"That vail of mystery—that awful secrecy," Note 25	200
	"The Ancient Freemasonry that was practiced in the Mysteries," Note 26	203
	"The Worshipful Master himself is a representative of the sun," Note 27	203
XXIII	AN EVENING IN THE LODGE	207
	'The Ancient Mysteries,'' Note 28	210
XXIV.	FREEMASONRY'S MASK REMOVED.—SILENT ANTIMASONS.—THE CIRCUIT PREACHER.—RACHEL FINDS PEACE.—HE GIVETH HIS BELOVED SLEEP	217
XXV.	MOVING.—THE MASONIC OBLIGATION REMOVED.—THE WARFARE BEGINS	229
XXVI.	THE FALL OF 1826.—OUR JOURNEY.—FREEMASONRY VS. JUSTICE	238
XXVII	THE SWORD OF DAMOCLES	249
XXVIII.	MASONRY REVEALED.—SAM TOLLER'S MASONRY.—THE MYSTERY OF OAK ORCHARD CREEK	257
XXIX.	SUNDRY HAPPENINGS	267
XXX.	MASONIC SLANDER.—THE ENGAGEMENT.—RATTLESNAKE CORNER	275
XXXI.	NEW SCENES AND OLD FACES	286
XXXII.	THE MYSTERY OF INIQUITY	294
XXXIII.	AUGEAN STABLES	301
XXXIV.	ONE MORE UNFORTUNATE	308
XXXV.	MASONRY PROTECTING MURDERERS.—VOX POPULI, VOX DEI	317
XXXVI.	SOME EXAMPLES OF MASONIC BENEVOLENCE AND MORALITY	333
XXXVII.	HISTORY REPEATS ITSELF	348
	"Masonry is strong enough to spread its protecting wing over the vilest criminal"	349
XXXVIII.	UNDER THE JUNIPER TREE	360
XXXIX.	A FORETASTE	369
LX.	THE VICTORY OVER THE BEAST	376
	"I would not wish to enter Heaven with one honorable scar the less"	379
	"Will you be the slaves of the lodge, HOLDEN WITH CORDS of secret iniquity?"	384

INTRODUCTION.

For clothing fact in the garb of fiction the writer deems no apology necessary, having only followed in so doing the universal fashion of the day; but in order to establish between author and reader a sympathetic understanding from the outset, it has seemed both proper and needful to give some of the reasons which lead to the writing of this volume.

Once in their past history has God in His providence placed before the American people a great moral issue that could be neither shirked, nor ignored, nor met half way. In vain statesmen compromised, in vain pulpit and press cried "peace, peace!" when there was no peace. God continually sent "prophets and righteous men," who kept that one issue sternly before the popular mind, and in many cases sealed the truth they spoke with their blood. The sequel we all know. The question God had been asking the American nation so many years in the terrible, relentless logic of events, was forced upon us at last—but it was at the point of the sword. Shall the lesson be in vain?

It would seem as if God intended America to be the great moral battle field for the world. In her freedom from priestcraft and kingcraft; in the sacred traditions that cluster about her past and the bow of promise which spans her future she occupies a vantage ground in such moral struggles impossible of attainment to a people fettered, as are the nations of the Old World, with the remnants of feudalism, and bowed down with centuries of oppression, and toil, and ignorance. To America, the pole star of the world's liberties, their eyes are looking with longing desire. In every great question that agitates us, which affects the freedom of our government and the stability of our institutions, they have a vital interest. Shall the simple, hardy, honest emigrant escaping from the despotisms of Europe, find enthroned on our shores the more hopeless despotism of the Secret Empire, with its Grand Masters and Sir Knights and Sublime Princes, its Kings and Prelates and Inquisitor Generals, its secret cliques and rings and combinations? This is one phase of the question which the sons of Pilgrim and Revolutionary sires will be called upon at no distant day to answer, and whether the shadow on the dial-plate of human freedom is to go forward or backward in the next generation depends in no small degree on the readiness with which they wake to the danger and their right understanding of a subject fraught with such far-reaching consequences to themselves and their posterity.

Thus it will be seen that the writer would have found in motives of mere patriotism more than sufficient excuse for desiring to embody in a living dramatic form a true picture of the Masonic system both in its past history and its present revival. From the Morgan tragedy, unlocked at last by the sworn testimony of that great Christian statesman, Thurlow Weed, to the closing scenes of the book, not a single incident of importance has been introduced which cannot be easily verified, the writer allowing no artistic considerations to blunt the force of that mightiest of weapons against error—the simple, unvarnished truth.

INTRODUCTION. 9

But weighty as is this reason—and let the reader judge for himself if indifference to such facts as are here presented is compatible with sincere love of country—another and even higher reason was the primary force which first urged the writing of these pages.

For again God is calling the American people to face a second great moral issue, greater than the first inasmuch as the evil we are now called upon to combat is not merely local and sectional but national; not merely national but world-wide. Slavery was a foul excrescence requiring the surgeon's knife; secretism is a subtle poison which, if not speedily erradicated from our body politic will make "the whole head sick and the whole heart faint." Again God is commanding, "Proclaim liberty to the captives," for though slavery exists no longer there is a system of spiritual bondage in our midst, a fettering of mind and conscience worthy of the darkest days of priestly tyranny. And every church, every individual Christian, who through dread of agitation, fear of stirring up strife or mere lazy indifference countenances this great evil or refuses to bear witness against it, has the fearful guilt to answer for of forging those fetters anew.

More than all, Masonry is a religion, and as there can be but one true religion in the world any more than there can be but one true God, it follows that it is either a false religion or else for eighteen hundred years the hopes of humanity have centered about a cunningly devised fable of a certain Divine Man who came on earth, died for sinners, and rose again to be their eternal Friend and Intercessor—which was all quite unnecessary if Daniel Sickels, a distinguished Masonic writer, is correct when, in speaking of the Master Mason, he says: "We now find man complete in morality and intelligence, with the stay of RELIGION added, to insure him of the protection of the Deity and guard him against ever going astray. These three degrees thus form a perfect and harmonious whole; nor can we conceive that anything can be suggested more which the soul of man requires."—*Sickel's Monitor*, p. 97. Believing devoutly "in one Lord and Saviour Jesus Christ of whom the whole family in Heaven and earth is named," the writer felt called of God to show the anti-Christian character of the Masonic system, but at the same time it is hoped that the reader will recognize in the portraits of Leander's grandfather and Anson Lovejoy a desire to do justice to the many good men who have been and still are caught in the snare of the lodge. In truth, throughout the writing of this volume two classes have been kept continually in view as especially needing enlightenment—Masons and non-Masons; the former being in nine cases out of ten actually the most ignorant of the real nature and designs of the institution to which they have sworn away their liberties and their lives.

These, in brief, are the author's reasons for presenting this work to the public, in the hope that many honest and candid minds both in and out of the lodge may be lead thereby to a still farther investigation of its character and claims.

"For every one that doeth evil hateth the light, neither cometh to the light lest his deeds should be reproved. But he that doeth truth cometh to the light that his deeds may be made manifest that they are wrought in God."

E. E. F.

CHAPTER I.

MY GRANDFATHER'S ADVICE.

I HAD just attained my majority. If this sounds like an abrupt as well as egotistical way of beginning a story, to people who do not care to waste their time reading long parables, it will at least have the merit of simplicity and directness, while as respects the second charge the very fact just stated is sufficient answer. I *was* egotistical. I thought a great deal more of myself than the world did, or was ever likely to.

But, as I said, I had just attained my majority. My grandfather, seated tranquilly in his favorite corner, felt it incumbent on him to give me some advice. It was very good and excellent advice, of the same general sort that is always given to young people, and I need not repeat it here, except to say that counsel very like it may be found in certain old-fashioned moral essays called the Proverbs of King Solomon.

"Now, Leander," said my grandfather, laying down his pipe for a final and solemn winding up, "you will be a useful and honored man if you strictly obey these rules. It is like the law of gravity, or any other great principle in nature. You cannot disregard them without suffering the consequences and making your friends suffer with you. But I am going to speak of something else. You are the right age now to become a Freemason, and I am of opinion that it would be an excellent thing. No one can be a good Mason without a belief in God[1] and the Bible,[2] and strict attendance to his moral duties, so that it developes and trains a sense of moral obligation in its members from the outset. Then there are, of course, other advantages,[3] though I don't want you to get the habit of always looking at the worldly side of everything. We are immortal souls and should remember that this is not our final abiding place. Still, it is proper to use all right means for advancement in life, and becoming a Mason will be a great help to you, Leander, now that you are just about to start in business for yourself. All the members of the fraternity will be bound to consider your success as their own, and should you ever travel, or be taken sick away from friends, you have only to give the necessary sign and any true Mason will minister to your wants like a brother.[4] Now I have a story to tell at this point that

---

NOTE 1.—"The truth is, that Masonry is undoubtedly a religious institution—its religion being of that universal kind in which all men agree, and which, handed down through a long succession of ages from that ancient priesthood who first taught it, embraces the great tenets of the existence of God and the immortality of the soul; tenets which by its peculiar symbolic language, it has preserved from its foundation, and still continues to teach in the same beautiful way to teach. Beyond this for its religious faith, we must not and cannot go."—*Mackey's Masonic Jurisprudence*, page 95.

NOTE 2.—"Blue Lodge Masonry has nothing whatever to do with the Bible. It is not founded on the Bible; if it was it would not be Masonry; it would be something else."—*Chase's Digest of Masonic Law*, page 207.

NOTE 3.—"The allurements to unite with the Masonic fraternity partake of the nature of personal advantages. It were folly to deny that while the applicant is willing to *impart* good to his fellows, he expects equally to *receive* good." * * * "The prime advantages derived from a connection with Blue Lodge Masonry may be summed up under three heads, viz: relief in distress, counsel in difficulty, protection in danger."—*Morris's Dictionary; Art., Advantages.*

NOTE 4.—"Masonry unites men of every country, sect and opinion."—*Morris's Dictionary; Art., Brotherly Love.*

happened—let us see—over twenty years ago, and I don't know but as much as twenty-five. I guess it was, for you wasn't born then, Leander. Well, well, 'Life's an empty show,' as the hymnbook says."

My grandfather sighed and took a pinch of snuff.

I had heard the story before but was not averse to hearing it again. I am afraid the idea of any moral or religious benefit to be gained by taking the step he so strongly advised did not impress me very deeply. But on the other hand the idea of joining a fraternity, all the members of which would be bound to help me on in life, I *did* find especially agreeable, for reasons that need not now be stated.

"At the close of the last century," began my grandfather, "French cruisers, as you know, were greatly troubling our commerce. I was captain of the 'Martha Ann,' and the deck of a stauncher, trimmer vessel I never trod. I shipped with a good crew, tried and able seamen; so, getting all things together, I was calculating by the help of Providence to have a pretty prosperous voyage. The idea of being captured hardly entered my head till we *were* captured, ship, cargo, crew and all by a French frigate that swooped down on the 'Martha Ann' like a hawk on a chicken. We were carried to the nearest French seaport and thrown into prison, a vile, close hole where we nearly smothered. The place must have been some old fortress, I think, for there were slits in the wall like port holes, only so high from the ground that we had to make a ladder of each other's shoulders when we wanted to look out. We could catch a glimpse of the water and the ships, and though the sight used to make us so homesick that half of us cried like babies, we all wanted to take one turn in looking. I tell you, Leander, I felt a thousand times worse for my poor men than I ever did for myself."

I did not doubt this statement in the least. My dear grandfather had the kindest heart that ever beat in mortal bosom. His very silver snuff-box reflected the benevolence of his face like a radiator.

"One day," he continued, "a military officer visited the prison. I believe he was some sort of General Inspector or something of the sort, and it flashed through my mind that very possibly he was a Mason. Without stopping to think I gave the sign of distress, to which he promptly responded. And now do you wonder that I rate highly the advantages of joining such an institution—a universal brotherhood as wide as the world? For remember, he was as ignorant of English as I was of French. Only his vow* as a Mason could have led him to take the smallest interest in my fate. Yet from that hour my condition was entirely changed. New and roomy quarters were given me, a new suit of clothes, good food and considerable freedom—everything in short but the privilege of writing home to my family and friends. But the condition of my poor men weighed on my heart. I tried hard and used every means in my power to exert my influence as a Mason

---

NOTE 5.—"Secrecy has a mystic, binding, almost supernatural force, and unites men more closely together than all other means combined. Suppose two men, strangers, traveling in a distant country, should by some accident be brought together for a few brief moments, during which they happen to be the involuntary witnesses of some terrible deed, a deed which circumstances demand shall remain a secret between them forever. In all the wide world only these two men, and they strangers to each other, know the secret. They separate; continents and oceans and many eventful years divide them; but they cannot forget each other, nor the dread mystery which binds them together as with an iron chain. Neither time nor distance can weaken that mighty bond. In that they are *forever one*. It is not, then, for any vain or frivolous purpose that Masonry appeals to the principle of secrecy."—*Sickel's Ahiman Rezon,*, p. 63.

in their behalf, but it was of no use. They had to remain six months in that wretched prison, destitute of every comfort, till finally the difficulties were settled between our government and the French, when we were all set free."

"But I can't see why this officer, whoever he was, was not bound by his Masonic oath to heed your appeal in behalf of the poor sailors," I said, rather inconsequently, as my grandfather proceeded to show.

"*They* were not Masons. We must draw a dividing line somewhere. Because a general rule sometimes bears very hard on a particular case it doesn't follow that the rule is not good. To allow outsiders to share its benefits would only end in the destruction of the order. Nothing could be plainer. But then Leander, if you don't care to join just yet I won't urge it. There's plenty of time."

My grandfather evidently thought he had said enough, but his sudden lapse into a tone and manner, seemingly half indifferent, by some curious law of contraries produced more effect on me than his former earnest strain.

"I don't want to put off doing anything that would really be an advantage to me," I said.

My grandfather looked gratified.

"I'm glad to hear you say so, Leander. Procrastination is a bad thing. It has ruined the prospects of many a young man before now. If a thing is right and proper to do, nothing is gained, but sometimes a good deal is lost by delay."

My grandfather shook the ashes from his pipe and said no more, while I suddenly remembering some neglected farm duties, to which the moral reflections he had just uttered were certainly very *apropos*, took my hat from its peg and hurried out.

It was the spring of 1825. It was also the spring time of the Nineteenth century, ushered in for the Old World in fierce storm and conflict, for us of the New in comparative peace and quiet, though the year 1812 had left scars on our prosperity not wholly effaced, while there was even then in the atmosphere of the times, at least for those who had ears to hear, " a sound as of a going in the tops of the mulberry trees "—a stir of contending moral forces, of great questions to be answered, and great issues to be met—*how* answered and how met, ye brave souls who have stood so nobly for God and right, even in the very darkest hour of wrong's seeming triumph, tell us!

In our small wilderness community, with few books and fewer newspapers, we knew little and cared less for the differing issues of the day, but there are always some souls who seem to be electrically responsive to the times they are born into, and such a one was my second cousin and nearest neighbor, Mark Stedman. To a slightly built frame was coupled one of those ardent, longing, religious souls that are ever striving after unattained—the world says unattainable—ideals.

He had taught our district school two winters, but in the summer he worked on his father's farm. Astronomy and theology were his favorite studies. They fed his love of the sublime and the mysterious, while they ministered to the deepest cravings of a nature at once reverent and speculative; ready to follow Truth to the world's ends, but afflicted with a certain moral near-sightedness that made him just as ready to follow Error when she aped Truth, though in never so clumsy a fashion.

It was, as I have said, a period of suppressed stir and ferment in the intellectual and religious life of the country—a breaking away from the old forms of thought, a cutting loose from the anchor of the old creeds, and the subtle influence of the times could not fail to reach a soul so sympathetic and intense as Mark Stedman's, though with an effect a good deal like new wine in old bottles.

How we ever became close friends may puzzle the reader. I can give no better explanation than the facts previously stated, that we were cousins and near neighbors, with this important addition, I was affianced to his sister Rachel.

Of course the sagacious reader will at once perceive why my grandfather's advice was so peculiarly palatable. It was my ambition—a very pardonable one certainly—to give Rachel a comfortable home at the outset, and almost any stepping stone to success I felt warranted in mounting, unless it involved doing what was really mean or dishonorable. And *that*, one thought of Rachel, and the noble scorn that would flash from her black eyes if she knew it, had the power to stop me from on the instant.

This being the case I was blessed with something like a double conscience. Her approval or disapproval, like a final verdict from the Supreme Bench, carried with it no possible chance of appeal. Yet with all her stern sense of right she was a most gentle creature, pitiful to a worm, careful of everybody's feelings, and ready to show kindness to the most degraded human being.

I had no thought of entering the lodge without first talking over the subject with her. I felt that her practical good sense would be quick to see the advantage of such a step, and being by this time fully persuaded that it was entirely and solely for her sake that I contemplated taking it, I was naturally not unwilling that she should be cognizant of this fact.

But on paying my customary visit at the Stedman's I found only Mark at home, seated on the back stoop with a book and a piece of paper before him on which he was drawing some complicated diagram by the failing sunset light. Rachel was spending the afternoon with a neighbor and had not yet returned.

It was so warm and pleasant I declined his invitation to go in, but took a seat beside him on the stoop, and after a little preliminary talk, rather absently sustained by Mark, whose soul was in his beloved calculations, I began upon the subject just now uppermost in my thoughts.

"Mark, I'm thinking of joining the Freemasons. My grandfather strongly advises it, and when all is considered I am not sure but it would really be as he says, the very best thing I could do."

Mark chewed a spear of grass in silence. But his abstracted manner was entirely gone, and I could see that my communication had for some reason roused an unusual degree of interest, though he waited full three minutes before replying.

CHAPTER II.

THE "COMMON AND PROFANE" DISCUSSING FREEMASONRY.

"WELL, Leander," he said at last, "what is your principal reason for wishing to join the Masons, anyway?"

"The idea of some practical benefit to me, of course. Their influence will help me on in my business, and be a great advantage now that I am just starting in life."

"I beg your pardon; but such a reason seems to me very low and unworthy. Motives of mere selfish interest ought not to be the chief ones to sway men of principle and conscience when making any important decision; especially when it regards joining an institution whose character and antiquity ranks it only next to the church itself. Even you, Leander, would shrink aghast from the thought of joining the church for any such reason as mere worldly benefit."

I listened in some amaze, for Mark in his earnestness was twirling and twisting the piece of paper on which he had drawn his half-finished diagram, into a shapeless quid between his thumb and finger—a forgetfulness which evinced as nothing else could have done, that our subject of talk was, for the moment at least, of supreme and absorbing interest.

"I know Masonry claims to be very old and to teach morality and religion and all that sort of thing," I said at length. "But the fact is, you and I belong to two different sets of beings. I am of the earth, earthy. I'll frankly own up to it. And you are—well, somewhere between heaven and earth most of the time, and I guess a little nearest heaven of the two. After all, I don't understand this fuss about motives. If two roads lead to the same place, what great difference does it make which one I take? Though I don't join with an especial eye to these moral and religious considerations that you seem to think so much of, I suppose I shall get the benefit of them just as much as those who do."

"I am not so sure of that, Leander. Do gold and jewels lie on the surface of the ground for men to pick up at their will? And is truth, which is more valuable than topaz or ruby, to be gained at less cost? Doesn't it make all the difference in the world whether a man sets out to search for gold, or hunt for blackberries? If you join the lodge for mere worldly advancement you will probably get what you seek, but its higher and grander benefits, as they formed no part of your motive in entering, will not in all likelihood ever be yours."

"For pity's sake, Mark, why don't *you* join?" I asked, banteringly. "Does the Papal doctrine of supererogatory merit prevail in the lodge? I hope so. I am sure it would be very convenient for me and other poor sinners, for a few members like you scattered here and there would cover up all our shortcomings."

"Leander, don't make a joke of serious things. I can't bear to have you. The fact is I have been thinking over the matter for a long time—ever since I had a talk with our minister, Elder Cushing. You know I never could see my way clear to join the church. I hope I am a Christian, but I never had the assurance. I am sorry for my sins, but I was never visited with those deep convictions that others feel. And while these evidences are lacking I simply don't *dare* approach the Lord's table for fear I may eat and drink unworthily, and so bring down on my head the guilt of unpardonable sin. I told him just how I felt, and he said that perhaps, on the whole, it would be better to wait till my evidences grew clearer. And then he began to talk about Masonry, how it was the oldest and most venerable of institutions, sanctioned by the good and great of every age. Religion's strongest ally, teaching the most sublime principles of virtue, so that it was really like a kind of vestibule leading into the church itself. He strongly recommended me to join it as a kind of preparatory step. I have put it off for a good while, but I don't mean to any longer. Now you know my reasons, Leander, for becoming a Mason."

It is said by Christ that "the children of this world are in their generation wiser than the children of light." Even in this case I was a good deal wiser than Mark Stedman. But I made no audible comment except a low whistle under my breath which would bear any interpretation he chose to put upon it.

"Have you told Rachel?" I finally asked.

"No, but I have been meaning to; I hardly know why I haven't."

The fact was I enjoyed more of Mark's confidence than his sister did. His poetical, mystical nature was apt to shrink from the touchstone of her clear common sense. The very closeness of their near relationship, allowing as it did no vantage ground of distance from which to view each other, was in their case what it very often is—a bar to mutual understanding.

At that moment Rachel's light step parted the orchard grass. The gold and crimson had faded from the sky and in its place was the more heavenly glory of the eventide. There was the pale sickle of a young moon overhead and a few stars had begun to tremble faintly out of the blue. She came forward with her bonnet untied and falling backward, and her brown cheek glowing with youth and health. Ruth might have looked thus hastening home from the harvest fields of Bethlehem.

"I thought I heard my name spoken," she said, as she came up. "What is the confab about, pray?"

"We were talking about joining the Masons. What do you think about it, Rachel?"

Rachel took her bonnet entirely off and twirled it by the string a moment before she replied.

"I don't think anything about it. Why should I? In the first place I know nothing about it, and am never likely to. That is reason enough for keeping my opinions to myself. But I don't mind telling both of you that there are things about Masonry which I neither like nor understand. What is the need of secrecy, for instance? I should not have to ask that question about a band of thieves, or even a handful of patriots who had met to plot the overthrow of some tyrant such as we read of in history. But in a time of peace and a land of freedom what is the use, as I say, of secrecy?"

"I suppose good can work in secret as well as evil," said Mark. "Indeed, I asked Elder Cushing this very question and he reasoned something like this: that the mysteries of Masonry, like the mysteries of religion, were too sacred to be openly exposed to the gaze of the common and profane, who would not be benefited thereby, and for whom such things would only make sport. Even the white stone and the new name were secret symbols used in heaven."

"Well," said Rachel, turning upon him rather sharply, "as nature made me a woman I suppose I am one of the common and profane in the eye of Masonry and Elder Cushing. How could he draw any such parallel? Religion opens the door freely to male and female, rich and poor, bond and free. I never did get any good out of our Elder's sermons and I am afraid I shall get less now. But that brings me round to the next point. Isn't it rather hard that women are excluded? Don't we need its moral and religious teachings as much as men do? Are we never placed in circumstances of trial or danger when the succor and help that you say every Mason is bound to give his distressed brothers would be very grateful?"

"But, Rachel," I said, "men vote and make the laws. Women are excluded from our legislative halls, but you don't complain of that. If our laws are made by only one sex they are framed in the interest of both, one as much as the other. And so, though women cannot be Masons, they get all the real benefits of the institution when their husbands and brothers join."

My experience had not then shown me their falseness. I was telling Rachel only what I actually believed.

She was silent a moment and then with a little laugh in which amusement seemed to blend with a suppressed doubtfulness, she turned to go into the house, only saying as she did so—

"I won't presume to dictate in a thing I know nothing about. I dare say it is all right. It must be if such a good man as your grandfather thinks it is. He is a better man than Elder Cushing—a great deal."

Rachel did not open her lips again on the subject and steadily evaded all efforts on my part to resume it.

CHAPTER III.

A MYSTERIOUS BOOK—CHAMBERS OF IMAGERY.

IT WAS accordingly arranged that Mark Stedman and I should present ourselves as candidates for admission into the lodge, which was at that time one of the most flourishing institutions of our little village. Not only did the minister belong to it, but the senior deacon and many church members, to say nothing of others, who, though of that carnal world which, according to St. John, "lieth in wickedness," were yet pew owners, and in their way pillars of respectability and influence.

The preaching of Elder Cushing was on this wise. He often gave us excellent moral homilies and sometimes equally excellent resumes of Israelitish history, in which he lashed severely the sins of the chosen people and their countless backslidings into idolatry, from Aaron's golden calf down to the sun worshipers seen by Ezekiel in the temple. The young people meanwhile, seated in the galleries, laughed and whispered, and wrote notes to each other, while their elders slept comfortably in the pews below. But into his sermons, Christ Jesus, the Hope of all nations, the Sin Bearer for a ruined world, if He entered at all, came only "as a wayfaring man who turneth aside for a night."

Under a preaching that had so little to say about the great Head, it must be owned that the church in Brownsville needed considerable propping up, and might well be congratulated that so efficient an "ally" stood at her elbow; for the meeting house and the lodge, as if to symbolize their friendly relations were only separated by the main street of the village, and stood not a stone's throw apart.

Perhaps the meekest sheep would have its thoughts if the shepherd persisted in feeding it on thistle; and I cannot blame Rachel if in her young uncharitableness, craving for spiritual food that should satisfy a hungered soul, hardly knowing herself what she wanted, only knowing that she never got it, she often said sharp things of Elder Cushing.

My initiation into the lodge preceded Mark's by his own desire. As for me I was quite willing to take the entering step first and alone, and was only amused at Mark's request. "Of course so many good men would never join it if it wasn't all it claims to be," he said, apologetically, making use of that time-honored argument, which I believe has, at one period or another, buttressed up every evil thing under the sun. "But the thought troubled me of assuming solemn obligations whose nature I can know nothing about beforehand. It really makes me tremble. Supposing I couldn't conscientiously take them?"

"Don't distress yourself, old fellow," I returned carelessly. "Your conscience is just like a new shoe—always pinching. When I've crossed the Rubicon you'll pluck up some courage, I hope."

And poor Mark, meeting with no sympathetic understanding of his peculiar difficulties, either from Rachel or me—for she would not be drawn into another discussion of the subject by the most artfully framed attempt to throw her off her guard—betook himself to the barn, where a dozen gentle-eyed moolies, his special pride and care, stood ready for milking. Not a creature on the farm but would come at Mark's call. And in their dumb trust and confidence I have no doubt he found some comfort, if nothing else. They, at least, never misunderstood him.

I must state here that my younger brother, Joe, had been improving his leisure time for several days in poring over an old book which he generally contrived to shuffle out of sight when anybody approached. I thought it beneath my dignity to be unduly curious in Joe's affairs, but one night—the important one of my initiation into the lodge—seeing him occupied in his usual manner, I inquired, as I consulted the glass and ran my fingers through my hair several times to be sure I was all right, what book he had there.

"Maybe I'll lend it to you when I'm done with it," was Joe's evasive answer.

When I turned round Joe was innocently paring an apple, but the book was gone: a faculty of suddenly and completely disappearing, as if the earth had opened and swallowed it up seeming to be one of the most remarkable properties of the volume.

"I dare say it is some foolish dream book. If it is, Joe, you'd better throw it into the fire and not be spending precious time in this way."

"It ain't a dream book," said the indignant Joe, in response to this brotherly counsel. "It's a Bible story, now; ain't it, Sam?"

The person appealed to nodded his head and blinked

one eye alternately at Joe and me like a quizzical owl, but made no other reply.

Sam, by the way, was a kind of village "ne'er do weel" who only worked when he felt like it; and as his feelings in this respect were about as little to be depended on as the weather, his services were not in much demand among the farmers round, except at particular seasons of the year when help was scarce. But my grandfather, in the kindness of his heart, often hired Sam Toller when nobody else would; and thus Joe, who rather took to the shiftless, kindly fellow, had as much of his society as he liked.

"Going now, Leander?" asked Joe, as my hand was on the latch.

"Yes; its about time. Why?"

"Oh, nothing. Only take care you don't get too much light. 'Taint healthy. It blinds folks sometimes."

As this enigmatical advice was only a specimen of many mysterious hints dropped by Joe, I paid no attention to it, though after closing the door I was very certain I heard a smothered guffaw from Sam.

My first view of the lodge room was not calculated to impress me with any undue sense of solemnity. Our meeting house, bare, homely, barnlike structure though it was, I never entered without feeling in some dim way that there was a wide difference between it and all secular places. Here tobacco juice defiled the floor, while the atmosphere was unmistakably pervaded with a strong smell of Old Bourbon. But as this was before the era of the temperance reform, when even ministers drank their daily glass (or more) as a matter of course, it is to be hoped the reader will conceive no unreasonable prejudice.

Except as regarded the obligation to secrecy, which I naturally thought must imply a secret of some importance to keep—else why the obligation?—and the equally natural idea that the ceremonies of initiation into an order coeval with the building of Solomon's temple must be conducted with at least some degree of corresponding dignity, I had not the dimmest guess of what was to follow.

To the question whether " unbiased by friends, uninfluenced by worldly motives, I freely and voluntarily offered myself a candidate for the mysteries of Masonry," I gave, though rather falteringly, the expected affirmative. Had I not been strongly " biased " by my grandfather's wishes? and had not Mark Stedman told me that my motives in entering were altogether unworthy? Though I had none of Mark's religiousness, I had been brought up in good old Puritan fashion, and a double falsehood right on the very threshold of my Masonic career did not look to me like a promising beginning.

I am an old man now, but I blush to-day at the thought of a half-nude, blindfolded figure,⁶ with a rope around his neck waiting for the lodge door to be opened to "a poor blind candidate '"—poor and blind enough.

NOTE 6.—"There he stands without our portals, on the threshold of this new Masonic life, in darkness, helplessness and ignorance. Having been wandering amid the errors and covered over with the pollutions of the outer and profane world, he comes inquiringly to our doors seeking the new birth and asking a withdrawal of the veil which conceals divine truth from his uninitiated sight. * * * There is to be not simply a change for the future but also an extinction of the past, for initiation is as it were a death to the world and a resurrection to a new life."—*Mackey's Ritualist*, pages 22-23.

NOTE 7.—"PREPARATION. There is much analogy between the preparation of the candidate in Masonry and the preparation for entering the Temple as practiced among the ancient Israelites. The Talmudical treatise entitled "Beracoth" prescribes the regulations in these words: 'No man shall enter into the Lord's house with his staff [an offensive weapon] nor with his outer garment, nor with his shoes on his feet, nor with money in his purse."—*Mackey's Ritualist*, page 42, *Art. Preparation.*

Heaven knows! "who had long been desirous of receiving and having a part of the rights and benefits of this worshipful lodge, dedicated to God, and held forth to the holy order of St. John, as all true fellows and brothers have done who have gone this way before him."

Of course the Masonic reader is privileged to skip these details. They are only intended for the "common and profane" outsider—to borrow Elder Cushing's phrase, so highly resented by Rachel; and as they are not pleasant to me in the retrospect, I may be excused for wanting to abridge them as far as is consistent with a graphic account.

Suffice it to say, that after answering in an equally foolish manner a variety of foolish questions—or rather having them answered for me, I was made to kneel in front of the altar with my left hand under the open Bible, and my right on the square and compass, there to take the oath, with the customary assurance that it "would not affect my religion or my politics."

Up to this time I had been simply dazed and confounded. The wide difference between my imaginings and the reality had almost roused in me the indignant suspicion that instead of being regularly initiated I was being made the victim of a practical joke. *Now* the real thing was to come; and comforted by thinking that the Ultima Thule for which I had embarked on the unknown sea of Masonry was at last in plain sight, I went through the first part calmly and steadily.

"I, Leander Severns, of my own free will and accord, in presence of Almighty God and this Worshipful Lodge of Free and Accepted Masons, dedicated to God, and held forth to the holy order of St. John, do hereby and hereon most sincerely promise and swear that I will always hail, ever conceal and never reveal any part or parts, art or arts, point or points of the secret art and mysteries of Ancient Freemasonry which I have received, am about to receive, or may hereafter be instructed in, to any person or persons in the known world, except it be to a true and lawful brother Mason, or within the body of a just and lawfully constituted lodge of such; and not unto him or unto them whom I shall hear so to be, but unto him and them only whom I shall find so to be after strict trial and due examination or lawful information.

"Furthermore I promise and swear that I will not write, print, stamp, stain, hew, cut, carve, indent, paint or engrave it on anything movable or immovable, under the whole canopy of heaven, whereby or whereon the least letter, figure, character, mark, stain, shadow or resemblance of the same may become legible or intelligible to myself or any other person in the known world, whereby the secrets[8] of Masonry may be unlawfully obtained through my unworthiness."

But when I came to the closing part: "To all of which I do most solemnly and sincerely promise and swear, without the least equivocation, mental reservation, or self-evasion of mind in me whatever, *binding myself under no less penalty than to have my throat cut across, my tongue torn out by the roots and my body buried in the rough sands of the sea at low water mark, where the tide ebbs and flows twice in twenty-four hours; so help me God, and keep me steadfast in the due performance of the same,*" I stopped short in horror and dismay.

NOTE 8.—"The importance of Secret-keeping is made the ground-work of all Masonic degrees.—*Morris's Dictionary, Art. Secret-Breaking.*

Bind myself under penalties so horrible? Never. Not for the secret of the philosopher's stone.

Shocked and horrified I was going to refuse decidedly to go on, when a thought of my absurd condition, kneeling there blindfolded, haltered, with only a shirt and a pair of drawers, the former with the front folded back, one leg and one arm bare, one shoe off and one shoe on, to vary slightly the classic rhyme of "my son John," rushed upon me with a horrible sense of the ludicrous. And after that one moment's hesitation I swallowed my scruples and took—God forgive me!—the Entered Apprentice oath.

Then came, in Masonic phrase, the " Shock of Enlightenment,"⁹ by which I was curiously reminded, as I had been several times before, in the course of the ceremonies, of Joe's mysterious hints. I heard the Worshipful Master repeat that passage which stands on the threshold of Holy Writ, alone in its majesty, like a sublime archangel, set to guard the portals of eternal truth, "*And God said, Let there be light, and there was light.*" I heard a confused uproar all around me like Pandemonium let loose. The bandage fell from my eyes, and giddy and faint I staggered to my feet to listen to a short semi-moral, semi-religious, semi-mystical address from the Worshipful Master, receive my lambskin apron, and be presented with the three Masonic jewels, " a listening ear, a silent tongue, and a faithful heart," which though not used in exactly the

---

NOTE 9.—"In Masonry by the Shock of Enlightenment we seek humbly, indeed, and at an inconceivable distance, to preserve the recollection and to embody the idea of the birth of material light by the representation of the circumstances that accompanied it, and their reference to the birth of intellectual or Masonic light. The one is the type of the other, and hence the illumination of the candidate is attended with a ceremony that may be supposed to imitate the primal illumination of the universe."—*Mackey's Ritualist*, page 34.

manner intended, I have had considerable occasion for since, as subsequent chapters will show.

It was all over. I was a regular Entered Apprentice in a lodge of Free and Accepted Masons.

I went home " clothed," but not in my " right mind." My senses were in a whirl and my head ached terribly, which was no matter for special wonder considering the fact that in our lodge, as in most others at that time, " refreshment "[10] had followed very close on "labor," and contrary to my usual habit I had taken more than was good for me.

As I felt in no mood to encounter the rasp of Joe's tongue, I was much relieved to find him in bed and asleep. But his evident inkling into lodge room matters was a puzzle. With the resolve that on the morrow I would get Joe's secret out of him if bribes or threats could do it, I crept silently into bed, not desiring to waken Joe if I could help it, and went to sleep like "one of the wicked," without saying my prayers.

NOTE 10.—" By the term 'refreshment' is symbolically implied the social hour at high xii., when the members of the lodge are placed under charge of the Junior Warden, who is strictly enjoined to see that they do not convert the purposes of refreshment into intemperance and excess."—*Morris's Dictionary, Art. Refreshment.*

CHAPTER IV.

A TALK WITH MY GRANDFATHER.

A CALM review of the whole subject next morning only confirmed me in my wondering bewilderment. If *this* was Freemasonry, great indeed were its mysteries; and feeling that my unassisted faculties were quite powerless to comprehend them, I concluded to have a talk with my grandfather, as being the only person near me eligible to such communications. For even now I began to feel the galling bond" of lodge slavery. I could not tell my perplexities to Mark Stedman, my bosom friend from boyhood, and though in his case the embargo on our free speech was likely soon to be removed, between Rachel and me how was it? How must it be in the years to come, when we should sit by our own hearthstone? Freedom to talk on every other subject, but as regarded this, a black, bottomless gulf of silence, which one of us *could* not cross, and the other *dared* not.

I did not want to start the conversation, and fidgeted about some time, hoping my grandfather would begin.

NOTE 11.—"That this surrender of free-will to Masonic authority is *absolute*, (within the scope of the landmarks of the order) and *perpetual*, may be inferred from an examination of the emblem (the shoe or sandal) which is used to enforce this lesson of resignation."—*Morris's Dictionary, Art. Authority.*

I must stop to state that, owing to his age and infirmities he had not for some years attended any meetings of the lodge.

"Well, Leander," he said at last, pushing his spectacles back over his forehead, "when are you intending to take the other degrees?"

"I don't believe I shall ever take them at all."

My grandfather pushed his spectacles farther back and looked at me with mild surprise.

"That won't do, Leander. To get the full benefits of joining the order you ought certainly to become a Master Mason. That's far enough; as far as I ever went myself. I don't think much of these higher degrees they are perpetually tacking on nowadays. They are what Papist ceremonies are to religion; innovations that can only work mischief. These new-fangled, upstart degrees are invented to tickle shallow minds. They are like mitres, and red hats, and triple crowns, just made to puff up human vanity, nothing else under the sun. Masonry, pure and simple, is a divine institution, and doesn't need any of this artificial bolstering up."

"To tell the truth, grandfather," said I, waiving a branch of the subject in which I did not feel interested. "I am disappointed in the whole thing. It isn't what I thought it was. I don't understand it."

"Of course you don't," answered my grandfather, placidly. "It isn't intended to be understood at first. Knowledge must come by degrees. I never met with a

---

NOTE 12.—"All the ceremonies of our order are prefaced and terminated with prayer because Masonry is a religious institution and because we thereby show our dependence on, and our faith and trust in, God."—*Mackey's Lexicon, Art. Prayer.*

man yet who understood the first chapter of Genesis."

"But," said I, making a desperate rush to the real point, "I don't like the way in which the oath is put, and don't quite like the idea of taking an oath at all; but if I could take it as in a court of justice, erect, with my eyes open like a man, and none of those horrible penalties at the end, I should make no objections to it."

"You feel something as I did, Leander," was my grandfather's unexpected reply. "There are things in Masonry that I never could understand even to this day, that I never could bring myself to quite like. But we must remember that it is a very ancient[13] institution, founded in very different times from these, so naturally there would be things about it that don't accord with our ideas now. Why, I find it just so with the Bible, Leander. There are things in the Old Testament that I never could quite reconcile in my own mind with the New: the wars of the Jews, for example, and David's praying for vengeance on his enemies. But then I don't give up my Bible. I know it is all right, and that is enough for me. And just so with Masonry; I take what I do understand, and let the rest go."

Oh, my dear grandfather! was there ever a simpler, truer soul than thine caught in the coils of "the handmaid?"

I felt my objections unconsciously melting before such simplicity, such kindness and candor, as snow

---

NOTE 13. — "From the commencement of the world we may trace the foundation of Masonry. Ever since symmetry began and harmony displayed her charms our order has had a being." *Webb's Monitor*, page 1; *Sickels's Ahiman Rezon*, page 14; *Sickels's Masonic Monitor*, page 9. 'A belief in the *Antiquity* of Masonry is the first requisite of a good teacher. Upon this all the legends of the order are based. The dignity of the institution depends mainly upon its age, and to disguise its gray hairs is to expose it to a contemptuous comparison with every society of modern date."—*Note by Robert Morris*, page 1, *Webb's Monitor.*

melts under a spring sun. After all, could there be inherent evil in Masonry when such a man as he, upright, benevolent, doing his duty to God and his neighbor, so far as he knew it, saw none? If the reader is tempted to ask the same question, let me in return put to him another: In the days when human slavery lay like a pall over our land, were there no apologists for the terrible system, as kind, as candid, as Christian as was my grandfather?

Joe, contrary to my expectations, had not tried to annoy me with any of his mysterious inuendoes; and, acting on the wise old adage, to let "sleeping dogs alone," I concluded that it would be best on the whole to let him enjoy his secret unmolested. That he had overheard the talk of some careless Masons who had neglected to "tyle" their doors properly against "cowans and eavesdroppers" seemed the most probable way of explaining it; and, truth to tell, I shrank from a contest with Joe in which I was very likely to come off second best.

I was much more troubled to think what I should say to Mark, especially as I saw him just then crossing the fields, and knew that though he had come ostensibly on some errand of the farm, his real object was to have a talk with me. And so it proved.

"Mother wants to know if Uncle Severns has got a setting hen he'd like to part with. One that she put some eggs under the other day is flighty, and keeps leaving her nest."

We went out to the barn together and a hen of the desired proclivities being duly selected, Mark, holding his captive fast, turned to me with an expectant— "Well?"

CHAPTER V.

PREPARATION FOR A JOURNEY.—"PASSED AND RAISED."

"WHAT do you want me to tell you?" I asked.

"None of the secrets, of course; but I thought you might give me some general idea of the nature of the obligations without disclosing anything."

"That's exactly what I can't do," I answered, promptly. "The obligations" themselves are a part of the secret."

Mark's countenance fell perceptibly. He stood still for a moment, softly stroking the brown feathers of the hen, which gently pecked at his hand and gave sundry low, pleased cackles in response to his rather abstracted caresses. Then with a sudden brightening of his face he looked up and said:

"Anyhow, you can tell me one thing. Are you glad or sorry you have joined the lodge?"

He had put the test question. I might have shirked it by some cowardly evasion, but I thank God—him alone, for it was no courage of mine—that I never thought of doing so.

"Mark," I answered, "when a thing is done and there is no going back, regrets are not of much use. But I want to tell you now that Masonry is not in the least what I thought it was, and when you come to find

---

NOTE 14.—"It is the obligation which makes the Mason."—*Morris'* Dictionary. Art. Obligation.

out what it really is you will be more disappointed than I am, because you expected more. And this is about all I am able to tell you."

"But then," said Mark, after an instant's thought, "you must remember that you have only taken the first degree; perhaps that is the reason it disappoints you. If we judged everything by its beginning our judgments would be very partial and biased, and lead us to utterly wrong conclusions in the majority of cases."

Though the more I thought about it the more repugnant grew the idea of letting Mark, with his nervous system as finely toned and delicate as a woman's, enter the lodge without any notion of the ordeal he must pass through. How could I utter a syllable to warn him, with the iron grip of that terrible vow binding me to perpetual silence? And what added to my perplexity, I did not feel prepared, since that talk with my grandfather, to call the system evil, and entirely evil. I had only taken the first degree, as Mark said, and it was not impossible that by going farther and deeper into it I might find my previous impressions entirely altered; for I felt much as Rachel did, that my grandfather, though an untaught layman who had followed the seas most of his life, in his simple-hearted goodness actually stood on a far higher level of Christian attainment than our formal and perfunctory Elder.

Let the reader bear in mind that at this period Masonry was a power that, according to one of its own orators, " stood behind the sacred desk, sat in the chair of justice, and exercised its controlling influence in executive halls." a factor of unknown quantities that entered more or less into every problem of the day, social or political, and he will understand one reason why it was so seldom denounced as a moral evil. True, some exceptionally bold spirit here and there had the courage to protest, but his witness generally fell powerless between the horns of two opposing dilemmas; for either he was or was not a member of the lodge, obliged in the one case to withhold his real reasons for denouncing it, because those reasons were themselves a very important part of the secrets his oath required him to keep; or, on the other hand, forced to base his opinions of the system almost wholly on the little he could see of its outside workings.

While I was thinking what to say to Mark, Joe's inseparable companion, Sport, a brown and white puppy of no species in particular, ran in and began to smell frantically about the floor, then giving one joyous yelp and bark dashed into a corner behind me, and tearing away the hay, disclosed Joe himself in his retreat, which, to do him justice, he had chosen for purposes of privacy rather than eavesdropping. For among other inconvenient traits incident to his age and disposition, he had a habit of shirking any irksome or unsavory task about the farm by absenting himself in the manner above described. And thus he had overheard all our conversation.

I regret to say that I immediately collared Joe with the intent to give him a shaking, but as Mark, who had much the same liking for him that he might have felt for a mischievous monkey, good-naturedly interposed in his behalf, I finally released the young gentleman, after darkly promising that " he would catch it another time."

Mark went off with his hen under his arm, perplexed, curious and dissatisfied. I must confess that it was a relief to me to have our conversation broken off. At the same time it was plainly evident that I could not guard my Masonic jewels any too carefully from the unscrupulous Joe.

At that moment Sam Toller, pitchfork in hand, looked in at the barn door.

"Yer gran'ther wants ye, Leander, right off."

"Do you know what for, Sam?" I asked, rather surprised at this sudden summons.

"Wall, I couldn't say for sartin. May be he's got some news to tell you. He kinder looked as though he had. And, come to think on't, I saw the postman leave suthin' about an hour ago."

Sam's Yankee faculty for guessing, and generally guessing right, whether it concerned the weather, or the crops, or human doings in general, was seldom at fault. It was not in the present instance.

My grandfather held a certain land claim in western Pennsylvania, and the important news was this: There was now an opportunity for selling the land at a great advance on the original price, so great indeed as almost to make our fortune, as fortunes went in those primitive times. Furthermore, as doing business by correspondence was slow, troublesome and unsafe, our present perfect mail system being then in embryo, and as there were also sharpers in the land in those days, human nature being much the same in 1825 that it is in 1882, it seemed highly necessary that some member of the family should go in person to negotiate the sale.

My grandfather adjusted his spectacles at exactly the right angle, and gave the letter one more careful and deliberate reading. Then he folded it up and turned to me.

"*You* must be the one to attend to this business, Leander; I see no other way. I've always calculated on giving you and Rachel something to start with when you are married, instead of leaving it all to you in my will, and this'll come very handy now. It's something of a responsibility, I know, to put on young shoulders, and if you were like Mark Stedman, with your mind in the clouds half the time, I shouldn't feel easy to trust you. Not but what Mark is as good a fellow as ever breathed, and knows enough to be a minister, only when it comes to doing business it needs a level head."

My grandfather's decision was ratified in a solemn family council held at dinner, when the subject was discussed in all its phases and bearings, the only opposing voice being my gentle widowed mother's, who saw only danger and death for me in the enterprise.

"O, I can't let Leander go!" she cried. "He will certainly be killed by the Indians."

"Poh!" said my grandfather. "What are you thinking of, Belinda? There are no Indians about there now. He will be in a sight more danger from painters and rattlesnakes. Not that *I* ever saw rattlesnakes anywhere else as thick as I've seen 'em right here in this very township. Why, I remember when we first came here a party of us went out and killed twenty in one afternoon."

Whereupon Sam Toller—for in true democratic fashion master and servant eat at one table—proceeded to match this story with another which I will not mar by trying to repeat. Sam was renowned far and near for his snake stories. While nobody could relate tougher ones, he had the true artist instinct, and knew just how to mingle fact and fiction so nicely that it was impossible to tell where the one began and the other left off. Even my grandfather listened with indulgent interest, but my mother gave rather absent attention, and as soon as Sam finished started a fresh cause for alarm.

"There are worse things than painters or rattlesnakes. What if he should be robbed and murdered coming home?"

"Belinda," and my grandfather spoke gravely and solemnly, "this business has got to be attended to. I hate to have Leander go, but there seems to be no other way to do. He is the staff of my old age, but there is One in whose keeping I can safely trust him."

And Miss Nabby Loker, my mother's prime minister in all domestic affairs, and despotic, as prime ministers are apt to be, put in her word of consolation.

"After all, Mrs. Severns, I wouldn't worry. If anybody is foreordained to be killed, staying at home won't help it any, and if they are foreordained to die a natural death, why, it'll be so even if they go to the world's ends. There's a sight o' comfort now in that doctrine. I wonder folks don't see it more. It makes you feel so easy like to know that everything is all decreed beforehand."

As my grandfather leaned towards Methodism, his ideas of free grace and Miss Loker's rigid Calvinistic interpretation of the Divine decrees often came in conflict; but now he offered no word, either of contradiction or comment, but sat with his gray head bowed in silent reverie: possibly prayer. It may have occurred to him that even so stern and forbidding a doctrine might be a refuge to the troubled soul in hours like this. There are times when it is good to feel that underneath God's love and tenderness is an infinite knowledge, embracing all our future life, our down-sittings and uprisings from the cradle to the grave, and even beyond into that dim eternity which bounds all mortal vision.

Rachel took the news very quietly. Like all self-contained natures her feelings showed very little on the surface.

"It is your duty to go, Leander, and that settles it. I am sorry your poor mother feels so worried. She exaggerates the dangers. I have no doubt you will come home all safe and quite a hero."

"And then?"—

I looked up at Rachel questioningly. She understood me, for a little wave of color rushed over cheek and brow. But there was not a shade of coquetry about Rachel. In her sweet, pure nature there was no room for such a thing.

"As soon as you get home, Leander;" she quietly answered.

And so our wedding day was fixed. It was to be the sixteenth of September—Rachel's birthday.

Sam Toller duly spread abroad the tidings of my projected journey, in which the whole village took a decided interest not at all strange under the circumstances.

As my grandfather was liked by every man, woman and child—and I might safely add the very dogs in Brownsville—everybody was full of good wishes and kindly advisings, given in the hearty, neighborly fashion of rural communities, where the weal and woe of the individual is considered part and parcel of the whole.

Among others who came in to talk over the important matter was Deacon Brown, a man of much influence, both in the church and out of it. Not only was our village named for him, and its every post of trust and honor filled by him at various times, but he had been twice elected to the State Legislature.

Being an enthusiastic Mason himself, when the talk turned, as it naturally did, on the length and possible perils of the journey, he at once adverted to my having lately joined the fraternity as a particularly good thing at this juncture.

"Only he ought to take the two upper degrees before he starts; decidedly, he ought to."

"You are quite right, Deacon," answered my grandfather: "I have told him myself that to get the full benefits of belonging to the order he must go as high as the Master Mason's[15] degree. You must urge it on him. The words of a man like you, now, might have a good deal of influence with him."

The Deacon was used to such gentle, unconscious flattery from his townsmen and turned to me with a fatherly smile.

"You must listen to your grandfather, Leander. You are not at liberty to neglect such an important duty; such a shield against all manner of unknown perils. You owe something to your friends if you don't to yourself. Why, nobody knows or ever can know how many lives Masonry has saved," he added, waxing enthusiastic over his pet institution. "I've heard of even pirates and highway robbers that respected the Masonic sign and, when it was given, treated those they had been laying out to rob and murder like brothers. But I don't mean," explained the worthy Deacon with a

---

NOTE 15.—"Entered Apprentices are possessed of very few rights, * * are not permitted to speak or vote or hold any office; secrecy and obedience are the only obligations imposed upon them."—*Mackey's Jurisprudence*, p. 159.

sudden remembrance of the possible interpretation which un-Masonic ears might put upon this statement, " that a lodge would ever take in such characters, knowingly. Even the church cannot always keep out unworthy members, so I have no doubt some have joined the Masons who became robbers and pirates afterwards, and yet had enough of conscience left not to dare violate their oath."

Remembering the awful nature of that oath, as it had been imposed on me, I found no difficulty in believing that it might have acted as a restraint on Captain Kidd himself, had that worthy ever joined the fraternity, of which I was doubtful.

As the highest Masonic authority gravely holds out, among the various inducements of the order, its power " to introduce you to the fellowship of pirates, corsairs and other marauders," let not the innocent-minded reader conceive any ill opinion of Deacon Brown for doing the same thing; nor think it strange that, urged by him and entreated by my grandfather, who was not quite willing to leave his favorite grandson to the shield of Omnipotence alone, I consented to take the upper degrees and was duly " passed and raised " to the Sublime Degree of a Master Mason, with all the privileges appertaining thereunto—among them that of consorting on brotherly terms with " the pirates and corsairs " aforesaid.

CHAPTER VI.

AN EVENING WITH RACHEL.

I WAS going to take the journey on horseback; and Major, a fine, fleet, spirited animal raised on the farm, was the one selected by my grandfather as best fitted in qualities of speed and endurance to bear me successfully on the expedition.

They all gathered round to say "Good-bye," and see me off—the dear home faces transfigured with the love and tenderness of parting. Even Joe, though he had so often been an aggravating thorn in the side of his more sedate elder brother, now looked almost manly in his new gravity and soberness. So much so that I bent down and whispered to him, as he stood giving Major a farewell pat:

"Dear Joe, I hope I shall come back all safe, but if I don't—if anything happens to me—take good care of our mother and grandfather. Don't let them want for anything, but be their prop and stay instead of me."

"Oh, Leander, don't talk in that way!" sobbed Joe, who was as warm-hearted as he was provoking. "I want to tell you now before you go off, I'm real sorry for all the mean, aggravating tricks I've played off on you, and I want you to forgive me."

Forgive Joe! Yes, until seventy times seven! Nor

was it any check on the freeness and fullness of my forgiveness that I knew very well Joe's repentance would last as long as my absence by the calendar, and not a day longer.

I had bid good-bye to Rachel the night before. What we said I will not write here, for I am afraid the reader will not be interested in our lover's plannings for the future, or all the little things as important to us as the bits of straw to nest-building birds, which, with provident New England forecast, Rachel was already beginning to gather together in reference to our future home, and now showed me with a pretty pride in her own economy and thrift. There was an old arm chair that she had stuffed and covered with her own fingers, till it was the perfection of coziness and comfort; a stand bought at a bargain, which would be just right to hold the family Bible; and such stores of linen table cloths and towels of her own weaving, wonderful to behold in their exquisite fineness and whiteness.

Yes, Rachel and I loved each other with that pure, honest love, which I am afraid is not as common now as it ought to be, but which, whenever I see it, makes me feel as if a flower from Eden had suddenly blossomed in my path. Yet Eden had its serpent.

There was one subject avoided by both of us with a kind of instinct. I had advanced to the third degree in Masonry only to find my first experience repeated; to be disappointed and astonished at the infinitessimal smallness of the secrets revealed, and bewildered with the general mixture of solemnity and puerility which characterized the ceremonies. But I had come to the conclusion that so long as I was fairly in, with no prospect of getting out, I would make the best of it by reaping all the advantages I possibly could from my connection with the order. My self-satisfaction, however, was much disturbed by Rachel's negative disapproval, which I felt, like a kind of Mordecai in the gates, that would neither bow down nor do homage.

"You must see, Rachel," I said, with the hope of getting her to say something favorable, "that my joining the Masons is a very good thing now. I may be placed in circumstances where I shall need assistance that no mere stranger, uninfluenced by any such tie, would be likely to render."

Rachel took a moment to consider, and then, instead of giving me any direct answer, turned around with the rather startling inquiry:

"Do you suppose the Good Samaritan was a Freemason?"

"What an idea, Rachel!"

"I don't see anything so very strange about it. Didn't Elder Cushing tell us when Uncle Jerry died, and had that great Masonic funeral, that Masonry was many hundred years older than the time of Christ? Didn't he tell us that John the Baptist and ever so many others, way back to Hiram and Solomon, were Masons? So the Good Samaritan might easily have been one, only I am certain he wasn't."

"Why not?" I inquired, curious to see by what style of reasoning she would prove her point.

"Just because our Savior holds him up as an example of the purest benevolence for all mankind to imitate, which he certainly never would have done had there been any tie between the Samaritan and that poor wounded Jew, other than just their common humanity; for then it would not have been benevolence, but a mere sense of honor or duty, or some such thing, quite different from charity. Don't you see?"

I did see, and for the first time felt a little vexed at Rachel's clearsightedness. I had been rather fascinated, to tell the truth, with the brotherly love, so strongly inculcated among lodge duties,—the only thing about Masonry, by the way, which had as yet very much commended itself to either my conscience or common sense.

"It seems to me, Rachel, you are straying wide of the subject," I said, impatiently. "Why do you evade a plain question? I only asked if you did not think it a good thing under the present circumstances."

"Oh, I dare say," answered Rachel, indifferently, as if she did not care to discuss the subject. And then she went and stood at the window a moment, silently gazing out at the starlit sky.

A vein of mingled poetry and humor, bubbling up in all manner of unexpected ways and places, gave to Rachel's character a sort of piquant charm. I think now she resembled as much as anything a New England huckleberry pasture, rich with every kind of wild, sweet, homely growth—hardhack and sweet fern and blackberry vines full of sharp little briars, all tangled in together.

"Now, Leander," she said, suddenly pointing up to the sky, "I am going to give you something to remember me by. I shall choose a star and call it mine, and whenever you see it shine out you must think, 'That's Rachel's star.' But which shall it be?" And she stood in a pretty, reflective attitude, with upraised eyes, scanning the airy vault. Then she clapped her hands gleefully.

"There, I have it!" she exclaimed. "Don't you remember when we were children, coming home from school hot and thirsty, we used to think the water at the Widow Slocum's was better than anywhere else, for no earthly reason than because she always gave it to us in a new tin dipper, so bright we could see our faces in it? Thinking of that has put it into my head what I will choose—the constellation of the Dipper. It has such a housewifely, practical sound, too; just the thing."

And Rachel laughed her sweet, low, musical laugh, in which, as I had now forgotten my momentary vexation with her, I could not help joining. But she suddenly sobered, and turned away from the window with eyes suspiciously bright in the star gleam.

"Sometimes I have thought it wrong for me to pray," she said, "because I am not a Christian; but I *shall* pray—that God will guard you from every danger, and I think he will hear me, though I am not 'a believer,' as they call it. But oh, I wish I was! I think I might be one if I had somebody to tell me how. I tried to talk with Elder Cushing once, but what he said to me might as well have been so much Hebrew. It was all about 'saving faith,' 'sanctification' and 'assurance,' and such things that I could not understand in the least, or see how I could ever make them have any practical connection with my homely, actual, every-day life. I suppose these things are really necessary before one can be a Christian, but they seem to me as far off and as hard to reach as the very stars shining up there. Of course, it is not really so, or else nobody could be a Christian. I suppose the fault is all in me—that I might have them if I would. But it seems to me that I *am* willing, and all I want is to find somebody that knows how to begin low down, and teach me as they teach the primer to little children."

While nothing in my own heart answered to Rachel's longings, I was touched by the pathos in her cry, and felt something like indignation at Elder Cushing's utter inability to help her. For what right had a man to stand where he did and yet have no word of heavenly counsel that a simple, honest soul like Rachel's could appropriate to her spiritual needs? When she asked for bread—when, in the humility of her soul-hunger, she would have been glad of the very crumbs of Gospel truth—why did he give her a stone?

It is but fair to say that Elder Cushing had no direct intention of thus mocking her needs; no thought of bringing down on himself the old prophet's terrible denunciation, "Woe to the idle shepherd that leaveth the flock." But did he never sorrow in secret over his fruitless, barren ministry? Was he satisfied that while the lodge grew and prospered the church received next to none into its fold? Did no thought cross his mind that, professed minister of Jesus Christ though he was, he served at a strange altar—that he even took of its unhallowed fires, and in the very temple of Jehovah offered profane incense in praise of another God?

I dare not say.

Long years ago Elder Cushing went where mortal judgment has neither right nor the power to follow him; but let the "foolish shepherds" of a later day heed these words of warning from another plain old prophet:

Thus saith the Lord God, Behold I am against the shepherds, and I will require my flock at their hands.

CHAPTER VII.

A CERTAIN MAN WENT DOWN FROM JERICHO.

THE parting fairly over, my spirits went up like the barometer before a clearing nor'west wind. The going forth like the hero in a fairy tale to seek my fortune had a pleasurable excitement that buoyed me up through the first part of the expedition, and made me insensible to most of the discomforts and fatigues which a journey of any length in those days almost necessarily involved.

But I had never any difficulty in obtaining a night's shelter even when tavern accommodations failed me, as they often did in that new, sparsely settled country; for among the rough but kindly farmers, hospitality was the rule and its opposite the exception. Thus the first part of my journey was utterly devoid of those situations in which the Masonic rites and privileges with which I had been lately invested are peculiarly valuable; and a certain pride and self-respect, the result of my New England birth and breeding, kept me from claiming them when there was no urgent call for so doing.

Near the Ohio boundary I stopped at a cabin situated in the middle of a small clearing, but with no sign of any other human habitation near, to inquire my way, of which I felt doubtful. Dogs, little and big, rushed out as I rode up, barking defiance in various keys, from the shrill yelp of the smaller curs to the deeper and more threatening bass of their leaders; but an old man sitting on a log outside, smoking his pipe, came forward and hospitably dispersed the dogs with an oath here and a kick there—all but one, who seemed to be a privileged character, a cross between the bull and mastiff breed, and as surly as the captain of a regiment of Bashi-bazouks.

The whole place was repulsive—its owner no less so. Rum-soaked, tobacco-soaked, he was the very picture of a hoary-headed old sinner; I could not bear to look at him.

"Fine beast, that o' yours," he said, admiringly, eying my horse, "but looks kinder jaded. Been far to day?"

"Quite a piece," I said, feeling disposed to be laconic. "Can you tell me if I am on the right road to Lundy's Settlement?"

"Lundy's Settlement? Ye ain't reckonin' to git thar to-night?"

I answered in the affirmative, feeling that I should infinitely prefer spending the night out of doors with Major tethered to a tree than accept his hospitality, which, however, he did not seem to offer.

"I say, Matt," he called out, stepping back and speaking to some one within the cabin. "Here's a man wants to go to Lundy's Settlement. You kin tell him about it I reckon." And in answer to this appeal "Matt" came out; but as our conversation was mingled on his part with profane expletives, many and various, I shall not record it here, only to say that it was extremely unsatisfactory, for while possessing entire knowledge of the whole local geography of that region, he ingeniously evaded giving me any direct information regarding the points on which I most desired to be enlightened. He was a younger man than the other—young enough to be his son, and of equally sinister expression. Indeed the relationship between them was apparent at a glance.

"He kin git thar to-night, dad," said the worthy, finally, and tipping a sly wink in the old man's direction as he spoke. "There's a way through the woods, only its kinder lonesome. Git out thar, *you!*"

This side remark, I must explain, was not addressed to me, nor to the paternal relative, but to the canine Bashi-bazouk, who was smelling viciously about Major's BONES. By putting a few more questions I found that the "way through the woods" was a bridle path that would lead me out near the river, on the other side of which the settlement lay, and decided to take it without more ado.

"Just follow the road you come on, straight along till you come to a blazed tree—its a big butternut. Turn in thar and keep along till you come to the river." was the gist of the directions given me as I rode away, which being so plain and simple seemed hardly to admit of mistake, especially as I found without any difficulty the "blazed" tree which was to be my guide to Lundy's Settlement.

Innocent readers of more civilized regions and times may need to be informed that the number of "blazes" on a tree—that is, where the bark is chipped off—also their peculiar position on the trunk, whether horizontal or perpendicular, formed a system of directions for the use of the traveller as important for him to understand as the language on the regular signboards in more civilized parts.

For a while I trotted on in good spirits. But the woods grew denser, the shadows longer, and I halted and looked about me with a feeling of disheartening doubt. Could I have possibly mistaken the way?

I was about to move on when the woods to one side of me crackled sharply. Several masked men sprang out, and before I could turn for defence or parley I received a violent blow on the head that knocked me senseless from the saddle.

* * * * * * *

When I awoke to consciousness the stars were shining. At first I did not try to move but lay in a kind of stupor, feeling curiously indifferent to all that had happened. But as my senses slowly returned the whole terror of the situation rushed upon me like a great wave. The robbers had not only taken my faithful horse and my trusty pistol, but had also taken every cent of money I had about me.

I tried to sit up but fell wearily back with a groan of pain, wondering if there was anything left for me to do but lay there, desolate and forsaken, in those wild, unknown woods till death found me. But suddenly my heart leaped with a new sense of hope. As I gazed blankly upward I could see shining down upon me, still and clear, the constellation of the Dipper—Rachel's chosen sign. O Rachel, bright, merry, housewifely Rachel! What was she doing now? Working some pretty knicknack for the happy home that perhaps would never be ours? drawing the needle in and out with bright visions of the future? "O Rachel, Rachel," I moaned; and then, echoing in my heart like an angel's voice, I hear again her tearful words said on the eve of our parting: "I shall pray that God will guard you from every danger, and I think he will hear me."

I felt strangely comforted! The awful terror passed from me, and in its stead came a restful, soothed feeling almost like a child on its mother's breast. And the hours of the night wore on, and still I lay there watched over by Rachel's starry sign that paled as the dawn approached like a beautiful hope lost in its own fulfillment.

The east grew pearly gray, then flushed to roseate. All about me was the stir of awakening life. I roused myself to one more effort, and found I could walk, though with great pain and difficulty, for among my other injuries I had suffered a dislocation of the ankle bone, which was the result of falling from my horse when the sudden attack of the ruffians felled me to the ground.

As I limped groaningly along, being obliged to sit down and rest at such frequent intervals that I made small progress, the welcome sound of a distant gallop struck my ear. It was coming nearer, and I shouted, "Helloo!" with all the strength of voice I could muster.

"Helloo!" was answered back, and in an instant the horseman had flung himself off and was listening to my tale in much wonder and indignation. He wore the common, rough, backwoodsman's dress, and his black hair and beard seemed totally unacquainted with razors or barber's shears; but he had very pleasant features, lit up by an expression of unconscious, almost childlike goodness, that I secretly felt to be rare, and was attracted to accordingly.

"Confound the mean, horse-stealing rascals," he burst out at last. "I ain't swearing, stranger, though my woman would say I was. It must have been Dick Stover's where you stopped. I always suspected him and his sons of being in with that gang, but never could get the proof. They directed you right the opposite way from the settlement, and then gave information whereabouts to lay in wait for you as you rode along. I now see it all as plain as a church steeple."

I may as well stop to explain that I had suffered at the hands of a noted gang of horse-thieves, the impunity with which they committed their outrages being chiefly due to the fact that they had secret accomplices scattered here and there through the settlements.

"If the folks in these parts don't get stirred up a trifle now, my name ain't Benjamin Hagan," continued that modern representative of the Good Samaritan. "But let me help you mount my beast, and we'll get home as quick as we can. You look as though you wanted a little fixing."

Grave as was the situation, it occurred to me with some sense of amusement that I was pretty thoroughly "fixed" already, being now in circumstances of sufficient distress to give me an undoubted claim on the charity of any Masonic brother, for it may not be known to the general reader that the style of dress, or rather undress, imposed on every lodge candidate and duly described in a prior chapter, is really an object lesson, the lodge being much given to this peculiar method of instruction; and the reasons therefore, Masonically considered, are as follows: "That, being an object of distress at the time, it was to remind the candidate if he ever saw a brother in like situation to contribute liberally to his relief."

Mr. Hagan's connection with the fraternity I felt to be a rather doubtful point, but I remembered that among the other bits of disinterested advice given me before leaving home, I was told that it was always best to determine, by putting a direct question at the outset, whether or no the person on whose charity I might happen to be thrown was a Mason. And this question I accordingly put. But instead of answering me at once, Mr. Hagan stared with something between a frown and a smile, and then put the return interrogatory:

"Be you one?"

"Yes," I answered, rather faintly.

"Then, stranger, I will give you some advice. Don't go to maddening me with any of your grips and signs, for I tell you beforehand, I ain't responsive."

And having thus delivered himself, Mr. Hagan's face resumed its usual serenity of expression, as he helped me to mount, and then led the horse by the bridle for about half a mile, till he reached a neat, substantially built log cabin, the front almost covered with flowering vines, where "his woman," a gentle, dove-like being, who used the Quaker thee and thou, stood ready, as soon as the case was explained to her, to lavish upon me every motherly care.

And sorely, indeed, I needed it. Fever set in, the result of my wounds, and for several days ran high.

CHAPTER VIII.

MRS. HAGAN'S OPINION OF ELDER CUSHING.

"AM glad thee is feeling better, friend Leander. Will thee try some squirrel soup? It will be nice and nourishing for thee."

This remark was addressed to me by Mrs. Hagan, one day after I had made considerable progress on the road to convalescence. Dressed in the regulation gray of her sect, with a snowy handkerchief pinned across her bosom, and on her head the daintiest Quaker cap, which could not quite confine the bright hair that waved and rippled over her forehead with most un-Quaker like freedom, my hostess was a charming woman, as fitted to adorn a palace, had Providence seen fit to place her in one, as her own log cabin home.

During my sickness I learned considerable about my host and his wife. They were both communicative in the easy, simple-hearted fashion which naturally begets confidence in return. Already I had told them all about Rachel, and my engagement to her, to the great delight of the worthy couple, the history of whose own courtship and marriage I will now proceed to relate.

Mr. Hagan was born in Virginia, and on the death of his father came into possession of considerable property, of which a number of negro slaves formed the most valuable part. On a visit into the bordering State of Pennsylvania, he fell deeply in love with a fair young Quakeress, who, though her family were decidedly against her marrying outside the pale of Friends, seemed disposed to smile upon his suit. But on one point she stood firm. Educated to believe that human slavery was a horrible system, replete with wrong, and the grossest injustice, she utterly refused to countenance it so far as to marry a slaveholder. And as fourteen years of service were as nothing to Jacob for the love he bore to Rachel, so the value of his human chattels were to honest Ben Hagan as the small dust of the balance compared to the priceless jewel of such a woman's affection. Like the merchantman in the parable he sold all he had and bought it.

As was natural with a man of his intense convictions it was but a step from ceasing to be a slaveholder to becoming an ardent Abolitionist, and Mr. Hagan, by his fierce denunciations of the system, soon made himself so unpopular with his neighbors that he was finally glad, for more pressing reasons than poverty— for after freeing his slaves there was not much left of the father's patrimony—to leave Virginia and buy a tract of land in one of the wildest portions of western Pennsylvania. But the woman who had urged him to this step for conscience' sake was not the one to shrink back from any personal sacrifice it might involve. Cheerfully she accepted all the hardships and privations of that rough border life, while her Quaker thrift and management told in the long run. Children were born to them, and a fair degree of comfort and prosperity now bless their simple, God-fearing lives.

itinerant Methodist preacher, whose services at camp-meetings were in great demand, as before his stentorian voice and fervid eloquence his simple, excitable hearers bent like a field of corn before the reaper's scythe; and his gentle Quaker consort supplemented his labors most efficiently, for their seemingly opposite faiths, producing no discord in their lives, caused no separation in their work. Her "inner light," and his "witness of the Spirit;" her Quaker simplicity of speech and his Methodist fervor, blended together in delightful harmony like the different parts in a psalm tune; though the unregenerate man within him would sometimes crop out in a mild expletive—for which she always reproved him with a gentle, "I am surprised at thee, Benjamin."

As I was sipping the squirrel soup, delicious in its rich flavor and exact seasoning, Mrs. Hagan took out her knitting and began to engage me in a talk about Rachel, which brought out among other things the story of her spiritual difficulties to which she listened with silent though intent interest.

"Has thee no minister in thy midst?" she finally asked.

"O yes; Elder Cushing. He is considered a good preacher, I believe; but Rachel doesn't like him very well, and he never seemed to help her any."

"Hath he helped others?"

I thought a moment and then was obliged to answer, bluntly but frankly, "I never heard of his converting anybody."

"Then am I to understand that thee never has any revivals in thy midst, no seasons of refreshing from the Lord?" gravely pursued my interlocutor.

"A few join sometimes—by letter from other churches mostly. Now and then somebody makes a profession, but that's rather an uncommon thing."

Mrs. Hagan's needles clicked very fast for a moment, and I began to hope she had asked me all the questions she was going to,—at least on this particular subject; for not having thought much about it before I did not feel qualified to give her strictly accurate information.

Finally she dropped her knitting and turning round to me inquired,—

"Is thy minister a good man?"

"Nay, friend Leander," she added, seeing that I was really too much astonished to make an immediate reply, "thee need not look so surprised at my question, for if thee will turn to the Bible thee will learn how the priests under the ancient covenant sometimes wrought evil in the sight of the Lord. There must always be offences, but woe unto that man by whom the offence cometh; and a double woe if he be set for a watchman of Zion. But I desire to think no evil of thine Elder. It may be in the people. What more can thee tell me about him?"

"He is thought a good deal of by other ministers, and some of his sermons have been printed; mostly Masonic addresses, delivered at funerals and other special occasions. He stands very high in the order, and has taken fifteen or more degrees. I really don't know as I can think of much of anything else to tell you about him," I added, apologetically, for I could hardly suppose she would be satisfied with such a brief and bare description of Elder Cushing's ministerial character and qualifications.

But she answered quietly, "Thee has no need to say more, for thee hath said quite enough to show me why he has no help for thy friend. 'Can the blind lead the blind?' He hath need to be taught himself, and how should he teach another?—taught the same lesson that my husband learned five years ago this very night, when the Spirit of the Lord came upon him mightily, and so convinced him of sin in the matter of being a Mason and joining in their false worship, that he came out from among them forever, and bore testimony to their evil works."

She spoke with slow, solemn, almost rhythmic cadence, as she generally did when under the influence of strong feeling. And much as I wondered at her words, I wondered more at the speaker—this fair, spiritual woman with her strange dual life; one part all earthly and practical, filled with the rough, homely duties of a borderer's wife, while the other took such hold on the divine and the heavenly that she seemed almost like one who moved and had her being among the eternal realities of the unseen world.

During my illness she had often beguiled me of weariness and pain, by relating to me some of her "experiences," which, as I think of them now in the light of a maturer understanding, appear to have been the result of a mighty faith acting unconsciously on one of those rare natures in which the practical common sense of the worker goes hand in hand with the poetic mysticism of the idealist and dreamer.

Once when lost in the woods she had prayed for guidance and seemed to hear angel voices directing her steps. At another time when her husband was prostrated by a slow wasting sickness in which neither medicine nor doctors proved of any avail, after a season of prayer by his bedside she had seen in a vision an elderly man of grave appearance, who, bidding her to "be of good cheer," put into her hand a certain root with directions how to make a medicine from it for her sick husband; which directions she at once on awakening from her trance proceeded to follow with such good results that he soon began to recover.

Of course nothing could be easier than for the skeptically inclined to demonstrate to a nicety that Mrs. Hagan was altogether mistaken and deceived; that the angel voices were mere figments of a bewildered fancy, and her knowledge of the root which proved so efficacious a remedy, instead of being supernaturally imparted by a divine messenger, had dropped in her childhood from the lips of some old Quaker nurse, but being too young at the time to give it any heed, it had lain dormant and forgotten until memory, wrought upon by a sudden crisis, had delivered up the secret in this visionary guise. But, after granting the truth of any theory like the above, there remained much the same difficulty that thoughtful minds experience after hearing the Bible miracles explained away on the most approved materialistic basis; for her whole life and character, sublimated as they were by a habit of most frequent and exalted intercourse with the Eternal, presented in itself a phenomenon more wonderful than any of her dreams and visions.

"My husband desires to have a talk with thee on this subject before thee leaves us," she said, rising to take away the empty bowl. "I fear thee will never see thy horse again, but thee must not feel uneasy about pursuing thy journey. Means will be found for so doing when thou hast gained sufficient strength. The robbers have been pursued, thee knows, but without success. It was hoped the capture of Dick Stover and his sons would break up the work of the gang in these parts, but they received warning in time to flee the settlement. But there is Benjamin, now."

And she hurried off to greet her husband, and attend to certain housewifely duties incident on his home-coming.

CHAPTER IX.

MR. HAGAN TELLS WHAT HE KNOWS ABOUT MASONRY.

"I HOPE if the rogues ever are caught—and there's small chance of that, for they are miles over the border by this time, and safe in some of their haunts, most likely—they'll be hung without benefit of judge or jury," remarked Mr. Hagan, whose soul chafed within him at the easy escape of the desperadoes.

"Does thee know what thee is saying, Benjamin?" mildly inquired his wife, this outburst rather shocking her peaceful non-resistant principles, as savoring quite too much of that spirit of vengeance inherent in "the natural man." "It is an awful thing to send any poor soul before its Maker without giving it any time for preparation."

"I know that, Mary, and I would be the last man to counsel violence if the law could be depended on. But now about Dick Stover. Who gave him and his sons warning? and how did it happen that the sheriff at the time the writ for their arrest ought to have been served was away and couldn't be found till there had been plenty of time for them to make tracks out of the settlement? When sheriffs, and juries, and the very judges on the bench are in league with thieves and murderers, honest men had better take the law into their own hands. That's just my opinion."

"Thee thinkest, Benjamin, because one end of the skein is snarled, the best way to get it smooth is to go to work and snarl up the other end, does thee not?" asked his wife. At which small piece of feminine satire her husband laughed good-naturedly, and then as a sudden remembrance seemed to strike his mind, he turned to her and said:

"Daniel Stebbins' child is sick again, and they want to know if you haint got some more of that bark that did it so much good last spring."

"A whole bottleful. The children are off down to the creek, but if thee'll see to the baby while I am gone I'll go right over and carry them some."

This was no formidable charge, as the baby, a chubby ten-month-old, was then placidly enjoying its afternoon nap. There was nothing to hinder a quiet talk, and Mr. Hagan seemed in the mood for one. Tilting his chair back at precisely the right angle for comfort, he began,—putting in abeyance for the time a question I was about to ask, whether indeed the laws in that particular portion of the Quaker State were so imperfectly administered as to shield criminals, a painful conviction to that effect having been forced upon my mind during the preceding conversation.

"I suppose now you thought by what I said when you asked me if I was a Mason that I wan't one. But I am —or rather I was one once. Now, if I may inquire, what is the highest degree you've taken in it, so far?"

"The Master's," I answered, not feeling, of course, after what Mrs. Hagan had divulged, any surprise at the revelation.

"I didn't reckon you'd been much further," coolly pursued Mr. Hagan. "I've gone four degrees higher than that—up to the Royal Arch. Now, are you satisfied with it so far, speaking in a general kind of a way?"

For reasons that must be obvious to the discerning reader, I found it much easier to reply to Mr. Hagan than to Mark Stedman, who, it will be remembered, had once put to me a similar question. Here was a man who knew not only all the Masonic secrets I knew but presumably a good many more.

"It doesn't suit me in all respects," I answered, candidly. "I don't fancy the oaths, nor many of the ceremonies they have to go through with. But then I shouldn't think of saying there was no good in Masonry. Its teachings are on the side of morality and religion; and that is certainly a good thing as far as it goes. My grandfather belongs to it, and he is one of the best men I ever knew."

"I only put the question that I might see better how the ground lay between us," continued Mr. Hagan, with a quiet ignoring of both these arguments. "Now I'll tell you how I come to give it up. You know that when I married Mary I made myself a poor man for her sake. Not that I've ever been sorry for that, mind you; I never felt so happy in my life before as when I broke the first clod of ground about here, and thought of my slaves all free and comfortably settled on farms of their own. 'No broken hearts,' thinks I, 'to be laid to my account hereafter; no wives parted from their husbands; no babes torn out of their mother's arms and sold on the auction block.' But that's neither here nor there. It's Masonry we are talking about, and that you know is a thing Friends ain't over partial to, no more than they are to slavery. So when I married Mary I concluded not to say anything to her about my being one. While I see no great evil in it, I'm free to allow that I was anything but satisfied in my own mind. There were things about it I couldn't seem to make hinge with Scripture, no how; but I thought I'd hang on to it, saying to myself that I was a poor man and might be glad of their help sometime, seeing we are all liable to sickness and trouble as the sparks fly upward. And maybe I should have gone on deceiving Mary to this day if I hadn't fell under the power of the Spirit. I was at a campmeeting over to Bear Creek. We had some powerful preaching and it hit right and left. I thought I had religion before; I used to pray and exhort; so I was kinder pitying the poor sinners, as they fell to the ground all around me by scores, groaning and calling on the Lord for mercy, when all at once an arrow from the Almighty struck me, right between the joints of the harness, as it were. I began to shake and tremble, and almost before I knew it, I was down as flat as the most hardened reprobate there. I tell you when the Spirit gets hold of a man as he did of me then, and turns him inside out and upside down he feels like an empty vessel, as the Scripture says: there ain't much spiritual pride or anything else left in him. Folks that knew me and had heard me pray and exhort thought I was getting some deeper experience, and so they crowded round me, and some shouted 'Hallelujah,' and some prayed, and some sung 'Glory;' but all the praying and shouting and singing went over my head as idle and unmeaning as the rush of the wind in the treetops, till finally old Father Loomis came along. He wan't the smartest preacher on our circuit, folks said, but he had a kind of gift with the anxious ones, a way of seeing through 'em somehow, and putting his finger right on their trouble. And when he came to me all he did was just to kneel down and pray like this: 'O Lord, show this man wherefore thou contendest with him. Set his secret sin in the light of thy countenance.' And then he went straight off to somebody else, but that prayer just flashed the truth right through and through me. I knew I'd got to give up Masonry. And I was glad to give it up; I hated it. Why, if two doors had opened before me, and on the signboard of one was wrote, 'The Lodge,' and on the other 'The Bottomless Pit,' I'd have gone into one just as quick as into the other. The Lord had set my secret sin in the light of his countenance. I got right up on my feet, and I made confession how I had sinned by continuing a thing my conscience disallowed. And as soon as I did that the Lord restored unto me the joy of his free Spirit, and gave me great liberty in laboring with sinners; and there was a precious ingathering of souls at that meeting such as was never seen before or since in these parts."

Mr. Hagan paused an instant in his rapid narrative, and then went on:

"But our feelings ain't the thing we are to go by. It's the law and the testimony; and if we had nothing but just the Ten Commandments and the Sermon on the Mount, they'd be enough to show whether Masonry is right or wrong."

Astonishment and perplexity had taken hold of me while I listened, nor was either feeling much diminished when he handed me his well-thumbed pocket Bible open at the fifth chapter of Matthew, thirty-fifth verse. "That says, 'Swear not at all;' then are lodge oaths contrary to Scripture or not? And ain't there some things in 'em at the end that don't gibe very well with the Sixth Commandment?"

"You mean the penalties,"[16] I answered, with a vivid rememberance of my own scruples in that regard, and the soothing anodyne administered by some of the lodge brethren. "I have been told that they do not really mean anything more than merely to impress on the candidate's mind a sense of the guilt he would incur if he violates his oath."

"Ain't it breaking the Third Commandment to call God to witness words that don't mean anything? And will the Lord hold him guiltless who takes his name in vain, because he does it in a lodge, with ministers and church members round to keep him in countenance?"

I was silent, while Mr. Hagan's long fingers moved on to another passage as relentless as one of the Fates.

"You promised never to defraud a brother Mason. How about cheating folks that ain't Masons? The Golden Rule don't read much like that, if I remember right. And you know our Lord has given us some pretty plain talk on the Seventh Commandment. How did your lodge oath handle that? Didn't it say, not in just these words, but what come to the same thing: 'Break it as often as you're a mind to, and we'll wink at it; only because when you're bringing misery into happy homes, and ruin and disgrace on the innocent, that they ain't Masons' homes nor Masons' wives and daughters?' How would you like some time after you are married to sit down and tell Rachel that part of your Master Mason's oath? What do you think Christ

---

NOTE 16—"A most solemn method of confirming an oath was by *placing a drawn sword across the throat of the person to whom it was administered.*" *Pierson's Traditions*, page 35

would say to it? I don't wonder his presence ain't wanted much in the lodge. He was sharp enough on the Pharisees when they tried to pare down and clip away from the laws of God—'Ye serpents, ye generation of vipers, how can ye escape the damnation of hell?' Such a remark as that now might jar on the proceedings considerable."

I thought the same, but preserved a discreet silence; though all the while Mr. Hagan was putting to me these terrible questions, I watched with fascinated gaze that faithful hand move serenely on, marking *Mene, Mene*, against that "moral and religious" system so dear to the hearts of my grandfather, and Deacon Brown and Elder Cushing, to say nothing of a host of other worthies more or less eminent in their day and generation.

"What do you think Christ meant when he said, 'Render unto Cæsar the things that be Cæsar's'?"

I did not see very clearly the drift of this inquiry, but feeling it as a temporary truce in this severe cross-examination, I answered promptly enough, "That we ought to obey the laws of the land and be good citizens, I suppose."

"Did you think of that when you promised to warn a brother Mason of *any* approaching danger, and keep *all* his secrets, *murder and treason*" excepted?"

"I thought a good Mason was not supposed to commit criminal acts," I said, this being the best answer I could think of under the circumstances.

"Then it seems to me that when they put in them words they took a mighty deal of trouble for nothing, especially as they ain't very pleasant sounding ones," remarked Mr. Hagan, dryly.

NOTE 17.—"Treason and rebellion also, because they are altogether political offences, cannot be inquired into by the lodge, and although a Mason may be convicted of either of those acts in the courts of his country, he cannot be Masonically punished, and notwithstanding his treason or rebellion, his relation to the lodge, to use the language of the old charges, remains indefeasible."—*Mackey's Masonic Jurisprudence*, p. 510.

Again a discreet silence, in which I began to dimly perceive the beauty of at least one of my Masonic jewels. For in the lack of any answering argument, what refuge like a "silent tongue?"

"And how are you going to tell a good Mason from a bad one?" pursued Mr. Hagan, thus calling to memory the unpleasant fact that even though the lodge expelled an unworthy member, there was no Lethe process which could pour oblivion over the knowledge of its secret signs and grips and passwords, for when once imparted he would be just as free to use them as a shield from the consequences of his own criminal acts, as any member in 'good and regular standing' for legitimate purposes. But I won't be hard on you, seeing I've done a trifle worse than that myself. When I took the Royal Arch degree I promised to help a companion in any difficulty, *right or wrong*, and keep all of his secrets, without any exception. And besides, I—

"Mr. Hagan," I exclaimed, starting up, "I really can't—I mean I wish you wouldn't tell me anything that you have no right to tell. I think with your views about the order you did entirely right to leave them, but to reveal secrets that you have taken a solemn oath to keep seems to me quite a different matter."

My host answered with the same peculiar look he had worn on our first encounter, when I put to him that unlucky question regarding his Masonic connections.

"I argered that out long before you ever thought of being a Freemason, and I've seen no ground for changing my mind since. If a man takes a wicked oath, where's the Bible authority for keeping it? Is it to the glory of God that he should keep it, or break it?

But then," added Mr. Hagan, with a slight change in his voice, " a man hain't no right nuther to throw away his life. I argered that out too, and I'm mighty careful what I say before them that'll turn it to my hurt."

"Mr. Hagan," said I, startled but incredulous, "do you actually mean that if any Mason should betray the secrets of the order he would have to suffer the penalty of his oath?"

Mr. Hagan looked keenly at me from beneath his shaggy eyebrows.

"That ain't the question, whether such a thing *would* be. It has been done; and *I'm knowing to it*."

CHAPTER X.

A MASONIC MURDER—SUCCESS AND RETURN HOME.

HORROR fell upon me. The soft south wind came sighing through the cabin, the sunshine lay in great golden patches on the floor, but I felt like one on whose shuddering gaze the door of some mouldering charnel house had suddenly opened as I listened to Mr. Hagan's story, which ran as follows:

"I joined the lodge when I lived in Virginia. Now there's a difference in human nater, we all allow that; and there's a difference in lodges. Some are decent and respectable, as far as the outside of things go, and others again are as full of rowdyism and all manner of goings on that shouldn't be, as an egg is of meat. And this was the way with the one I joined. I got so disgusted after a while that I stopped going to their meetings. I hadn't much taste for profanity nor hard drinking, you see, but I kept on paying my dues, and so was considered a regular Mason in good standing. It was afterwards that this affair happened which I'm going to tell you about.

"The chaplain was Gus Peters, and though he could not read a word of two syllables without spelling it, they chose him to the office for a joke. He was a simple kind of a fellow, that got hold accidentally of some of the secrets, I never rightly knew how, so they made him take the oath and become a regular member as the best way to shut his mouth. He got into drinking ways after he'd been in the lodge a while—he'd been tolerably steady before—and that was how the trouble come. When the liquor was in him he was apt to let out the secrets, and it got to be a serious question what to do about it. Things went on so for a time, then all at once the man was missing, and he never turned up again, dead or alive. Folks settled it that he'd stepped into the water some night when he was too tipsy to go straight, and there the matter ended. As I said before. I'd pretty much stopped going to the lodge then, and I married soon afterwards and came up here to live, and what with the trouble we had, for I was sick all one summer, and the crops fell short for two seasons running, enough happened to drive the whole thing out of my head.

"Three years ago last winter, while I was on a preaching circuit, I come across an old acquaintance that was a member with me of that same lodge in Virginia. The man stuck to me like a burr, and when I found he was really sick and had no money to carry him further, I told him I'd settle the bill for a night's lodging at the tavern.

" Well, he set and shivered over the fire and talked in a queer random way for a while. Then all at once he started up and stared at me kinder wild and anxious.

"'You remember Gus Peters?' says he.

" I told him, ' Yes;' and then he said in a whisper, as though he was afraid somebody was listening at the keyhole—

"' I'll tell you, for we are both Masons and bound to keep each other's secrets. *I know what became of him!*'

"An awful suspicion shot through my mind when he said that, but I kept quiet and let him talk on.

"'You see we were chosen by lot, I and another man, to put him out of the way. We couldn't help it. *We had to do it.* Ain't we sworn to obey every summons[18] of the lodge to the length of our cable-tow? And the drunken fool was babbling out our secrets. But it wan't me that drawed the knife across his throat; I want you to know that. I helped fasten the weights to him and throw him into the creek. He'd taken the oath and knew what the penalty was, and it ain't murder I say to hold a man to his oath. Leastways its Jack Benedick, not me, that's got to answer for it. You remember Benedick, one of the dare-devil sort. He's a gentleman of the road now, and I reckon has forgot all about that little affair.'

"I let him ramble on, for I felt as though I was under a spell. I couldn't move hand nor foot. I ain't giving you all the little details of his story, but every circumstance about it fitted together like a piece of joiner's work, and I hadn't a doubt in my mind but what it was true.

"In two days he died of delirium tremens, and I see that he was decently buried."

I sat for a moment after Mr. Hagan had finished this awful recital, literally dumb with horror. Was the spirit of Cain at the heart of this "benevolent institution, and its terrible penalties not the mere lifeless formulas I had been taught to believe, but instinct with awful meaning for the betrayer of Masonic secrets?

"Benedick?" I said, questioningly, as a new idea struck me. "Isn't that the name of the head one in the gang that took my horse and nearly murdered me?"

NOTE 18.—"The Mason who disobeys a due summons subjects himself to severe penalties."—*Morris's Dictionary,* **Art.** *Disobedience.*

"He's the very same man; a Royal Arch Mason," answered Mr. Hagan coolly. "He's learned his trade thoroughly since he cut poor Gus's throat. The Stovers are all Masons, and if you don't understand how they cleared out of the settlement so easy without any hindrance from the sheriff, you've forgot the most important part of your lodge oaths, I reckon."

Over this information I pondered silently, for it certainly verified the truth of Deacon Brown's statements in a manner more convincing than agreeable. What a fine chance of "consorting on brotherly terms with robbers and marauders" I lost through undue modesty when I stopped at the Stovers' cabin!

The sudden awakening of the baby, who began to cry most vehemently, and refused to be comforted by any process with which masculine minds were conversant, stopped further revelations until Mrs. Hagan's return allowed us to continue our talk.

"Mary knows as much about Freemasonry as I do," resumed Mr. Hagan. "You may think some of the things ain't fit for a woman's ears, and I don't say they are; but to my mind no lodge oath has a right to sunder them God has joined together. And somehow you can tell things to an angel that you can't to a common woman."

Mr. Hagan uttered this profound philosophical truth with a simplicity refreshing to hear; and silence fell between us for several moments, which I spent in mentally considering how the test would apply to Rachel. Under no imaginable circumstances could I ever find it easy to tell *her* the secrets of the lodge, from which I concluded that there was considerably more woman and less saint about Rachel Stedman than Mary Hagan.

"Did you ever hear of a Captain William Morgan?" asked Mr. Hagan, finally breaking the silence. "I heard he had moved to New York State. We were boys together in Culpepper County."

"My grandfather is very well acquainted with him," I answered eagerly, little thinking how soon that name would stir the land to its very center with the greatest horror and pity and indignation. "At least I think it must be the same man you are speaking of, for I know he came from Virginia."

"I used to think he was uncommon smart," pursued Mr. Hagan; "a man the world might hear from some day. He was one that always had his thoughts, and was free to speak 'em whether other folks agreed with him or not. A frank, generous, open kind of a nature he had. Nothing underhand about William Morgan; never."

"My grandfather thinks very highly of him," I returned. "He is a very fine appearing man, I have heard him say, and one that can talk well on almost any subject. He first went to Canada, and engaged in business, but a fire reduced him to poverty, so that he has gone back to his old trade of bricklaying. He and his young wife are now living in Batavia, Genesee County."

Mr. Hagan, with his hands clasped over his knees, sat silent, his eyes fixed on one of the golden checkered patches of sunlight that wavered and danced over the cabin floor.

"Captain Morgan is a Freemason," I continued, "and unusually well posted in the secrets of the order, I have heard my grandfather say. Now, if Masonry is really contrary to the Bible, and I must admit that it seems so from your showing, how is it that two such men as they don't or can't see it in its true light? How can it be supposed that they or the members of the Masonic fraternity generally could look with anything but execration and horror on such a cold-blooded murder as you have been telling me about, planned and carried on by a few desperate villains, Masons only in name, and vile enough to use their connection with the order as a cloak for every crime?"

"I ain't a man to see visions or dream dreams," slowly answered Mr. Hagan, "*but speaking from what I know of the spirit of the order*, something as bad as that, or worse, will happen yet, and not done in a corner as that deed was. Then, and not till then, the scales will fall from their eyes. I know what I'm saying, and you mark my words."

My host did not give me much time to ponder over this startling prophecy, but after a moment of silence began on another subject by making an inquiry about the locality of my grandfather's claim. The rest of our conversation I shall not transcribe, it being decidedly too geographical in its general details to interest the average reader.

The "claim" lay about forty miles distant, and like the Good Samaritan he had already proved himself, as soon as I was able to resume my journey, Mr. Hagan lent me a horse and funds sufficient for my needs. Fortune, though she had showed an adverse face hitherto, now suddenly changed her frowns to smiles, and when I reached my destination—a tract of wilderness land near the Virginia line, where some enterprising capitalists had taken it into their heads to lay out a city whose name and precise location on the map need not be given here, being a matter of no special moment to the reader—I succeeded in negotiating such favorable terms of sale as more than realized my grandfather's most sanguine expectations; and I begun the return journey, which being perfectly free from adventure gave me time to do considerable thinking, with a light heart.

On my homeward way I stopped for a night at the Hagans'. The gentle Quakeress, whose womanly interest in my betrothed had not at all abated, gave me a couple of fine hem-stitched handkerchiefs to take to Rachel as a wedding gift, remarking in the quaint manner peculiar to her sect,—

"I have a concern on my mind for thy friend, but I do not doubt she is one of the Lord's elect, and will some day be brought into the light. But have a care that thee does not put a stumbling block in her way."

"Mrs. Hagan!" I exclaimed, feeling really hurt at the insinuation.

"Thee would never do it purposely, friend Leander, but thee might do it unthinkingly. Did Rachel wish thee to join the lodge?"

"No; she was very much opposed to it."

"Does thee imagine her opposition will grow less when thee and she are wedded?" was Mrs. Hagan's next searching inquiry.

Before this pure-souled woman, knowing that she was talking with full knowledge of all the ridiculous ceremonials of the lodge, its awful oaths and hideous penalties, I felt my cheeks glowing hot with the blush of honest shame.

"No;" I answered, after a moment's hesitation, "Rachel is not apt to change her mind when it is once made up. But I sincerely mean, after we are married, to stop attending the lodge altogether. It will be excuse enough that I don't want to leave Rachel alone evenings."

"Take heed, friend Leander, lest thy fear of man bring thee into a snare, and with thee this dear soul whose welfare should be precious to thee as thine own life. I am a woman and I have the heart of a woman. My husband never guessed it, and I have never told him, but long before he confessed to me that he had been a Mason I knew the whole truth. Does thee think I passed no miserable hours with the thought like an arrow in my heart that the one I loved and honored before all other men was deceiving me? And I would warn thee beforehand of the danger to thy mutual happiness. Thee and Rachel will make a sad mistake to begin married life at variance with each other. 'Can two walk together unless they be agreed?'"

"O, we agree to disagree, Mrs. Hagan," I answered, with an assumed lightness, " at least so far as Masonry is concerned. Rachel never really opposed my joining the lodge in so many words; but she has a tremendous power of letting me know what she thinks without saying much."

"I have warned thee," she answered, her deep, spiritual eyes not looking at me as she spoke, but with a curious far away gaze in them that awed me though I did not understand it. "I have warned thee," she repeated, in the same strangely solemn way, and said no more.

The beautiful lives of Benjamin and Mary Hagan were never wrought into a biography, but long afterwards I accidentally heard of them as keepers of a famous station on the underground railroad, ministering to the Lord they loved in the person of many a poor footsore fugitive to whom such a halting place on their weary road must have seemed like the chamber called Peace, with its windows opened toward the rising sun of liberty.

I paid for the horse and returned the money Mr. Hagan had lent me—to offer anything more I felt would be an insult to their simple-hearted kindness—and rode away the next morning, the hot tears blinding my eyes as I left them standing in their cabin door with words of farewell upon their lips.

The sun was setting when I entered Brownsville, and the first person to meet me with recognizing glance happened to be Sam Toller.

"If I ain't glad to see ye back again, Leander Severns," he said, after his first doubtful stare, for the sun was in his face, and it was not till I came directly alongside that he fully comprehended who I was.

"But they'll be a sight gladder to see ye up to the house. Been swapping horses?" he asked abruptly, as his eye fell on my raw-boned steed, which was certainly in decided contrast to the sleek and beautiful Major. "Yer gran'ther won't like that."

I had not thought it best to rouse useless anxiety by writing home any account of the adventures which had befallen me, and Sam was therefore the first person to receive the news. Certainly if its speedy publication had been an important object with me, nobody any better qualified for that purpose could have been selected.

"Wall, things did fall out with ye kinder providential, after all," grunted Sam, who was by no means of an irreligious turn of mind, and could, when he chose, make the most edifying moral reflections. It was a remarkable deliverance, and I hope ye thanked the Lord for it. Now I lay anything that the man that did so well by ye was a Mason, and I have been thinking that it might be a good thing for me to join the lodge.

"Mr. Hagan had been a Mason, it is true," I answered, cautiously, concealing with some difficulty a smile at the very idea of poor, shiftless Sam Toller, who never had money enough in his pocket to pay his entrance fee, ever being admitted. "He told me so himself; but it was because he was a Christian that he was so good to me, and not in the least because he was a Mason."

"All the same," replied Sam cheerfully, "I've kinder gathered from Elder Cushing's talk that there ain't much difference; a good Mason and a good Christian are about alike. Now what would you say if I should tell you I *had* jined 'em while you've been gone."

And to my unspeakable amazement Sam leaned over and gave me, in the most approved Masonic style, the Master Mason's grip.

"Is it possible, Sam?" I asked, as soon as I could get breath from my first bewilderment, which state of mind was nowise abated by Sam's answer,

"Hain't I got just as good a right to be a Mason as any man? If I hain't I like to know why."

And Sam, ordinarily the best-tempered fellow in the world, waxed surprisingly irate.

"I am sure I meant no offence, Sam," I answered, humbly. "It was quite natural I should be a little surprised. But now I want to know all about the folks, and how things have gone on at home while I've been away."

"Middling well," was Sam's succinct reply. "There's the Captain now, a standing at the gate as though he was looking for ye."

CHAPTER XI.

MORE TALK WITH MY GRANDFATHER.—A MODERN PAN.

IN a moment my grandfather had caught sight of me and hobbled out, his white locks waving in the wind. O the joy of that home coming! The quiet, blissful content when my mother's tears of happiness were all shed, and my story of disaster and success recounted in its every detail for the twentieth time! For, as Rachel prophesied, I had come home "quite a hero," even in Joe's eyes, who was decidedly more respectful to me that evening than he had ever been in his life before.

Rachel and I had our own little private cup of joy with which no stranger intermeddled. She listened with paling cheek, but not saying a word, when I related how the robbers struck me down and left me for dead in those dark unknown woods; but when I told the experience which followed, the strange sense of comfort and peace that stole into my heart when lying there, bruised and bleeding, I saw the constellation of the Dipper, and remembered her parting promise, she looked up with great wide eyes, in which the surprise of some wonderful, unlooked-for joy seemed suddenly kindling.

"O, I remember that night," she exclaimed. "I

was restless and couldn't sleep. A fear of something dreadful seemed to oppress me. I couldn't shake it off, but I thought a breath of fresh air might make me feel better and I got up and raised the window. As I leaned out I could see the Dipper, and I began to wonder if you were in trouble or danger that I had such a feeling. So I just put my head down on the window-sill and prayed; and then all the strange oppression seemed to slide right off of me like some heavy weight. O, Leander, do you think God really did hear my poor little foolish prayer and answer it?"

"I know he did, Rachel," I answered, solemnly and earnestly.

Two great tears rolled down Rachel's cheeks. Reaching out dumb hands of longing, her soul had at last touched the Invisible Father, and for one transcendent moment her whole being dissolved in awe-stricken bliss at the thought.

The next day, in a private aside, I asked my grandfather if he knew Sam Toller was a Mason.

"No;" he replied, nearly dropping his pipe in astonishment. "I don't believe it. There's no more harm in Sam than there is in a chip squirrel, but he's such an idle, shiftless fellow that there isn't a lodge in the State would take him in."

"He gave the Master Mason's grip last night, and gave it to me correctly too."

My grandfather looked nonplussed.

"Then of course he must at some time or other have joined the order. Worse fellows than Sam Toller have been Masons before now, but I must say I am surprised."

And my grandfather, whose good, easy, placid soul was seldom long astonished at anything, after a moment's reflection took up the Canandaigua paper which had just arrived, and would have dismissed the subject if I had been willing to let him.

"I haven't told you yet that this Methodist preacher, who, together with his wife, showed me such kindness, was a Mason," I remarked, feeling my way by slow degrees to the point I wished to reach.

"Ah!" and my grandfather looked interested. "Now, Leander, after such practical proof of its benefits, I hope you see that I was right in urging you to join the order."

"But Mr. Hagan had renounced all connection with Masonry years before. He thinks it a bad thing, contrary to the Bible. We had a long talk about it, and he made it very clear to my mind that the oaths and penalties at least, if nothing else about it, are entirely wrong."

I spoke with a little concealed trepidation which I found was wholly unnecessary. My grandfather's faith in his favorite institution was much too strong to be thus easily disturbed.

"Good men don't always feel nor think alike, Leander," was his answer, as placid as a summer breeze. "We read somewhere in the Epistles that what a man thinks to be sin, to him it is sin. I never blame any one for acting up to his conscience, even when I know he is mistaken. I've always said myself that there were things in Masonry that I couldn't understand, nor bring myself to think are really right; but my idea about them is that they are relics of a barbarous age that will fall away in time. And besides I have known a great many honest, good men to become prejudiced against Masonry by joining a lodge where there was a great deal of profanity and hard drinking going on. Why, I've known lodges myself that any decent man, if he once got into, would want to clear out of as quick as he could. By a very natural mistake they blame Masonry for the sins of its individual members, forgetting that they might just as easily condemn Christianity on the same grounds."

It dimly occurred to me that a church composed mainly of drunkards and swearers was a strange anomaly I had not yet met with; but I was anxious to know my grandfather's opinion on another point.

"If a member should divulge the secrets of the order, would he be punishable with death, according to the terms of his oath?" I asked.

My grandfather, for the first time in all our discussions of the subject, had no answer ready.

"Why, Leander," he answered at last, "in the first place there is no officer in the lodge empowered to act as executioner, and in the second place it is not supposable that any member would so perjure himself as to disclose the secrets. In my understanding of things this is one great reason why these ancient penalties, that seem so unsuited to the spirit of the age, are still kept up, for human nature is so depraved that the oath, divested of these forms, might not have sufficient restraining power over some. But why do you ask such a question?"

I concluded, as the best answer I could give, to relate Mr. Hagan's story, to which my grandfather listened, his ruddy face fairly white with horror.

"That was a fearful murder; perfectly awful. It makes my blood run cold to think of it," he said at last, after sitting for a moment in shocked silence.

"But now that story, Leander, just proves what I have been saying. In a lodge where they are half heathen it stands to reason that their acts will be heathenish. If there are men among them that care no more for murdering a man than they do for felling an ox, they'll be likely enough to do it; only such a lodge doesn't represent **Masonry** any more than the men who stabbed infants in their mother's arms on St. Bartholomew's day represents Christianity."

A reasoning so entirely satisfactory to my grandfather that, with a deep-drawn sigh for the depravity that made such deeds possible, he again took up his paper.

I was by no means entirely convinced, but added to the seeming reason and fairness of what he had said was my reverent affection, almost more than filial, for the guardian of my fatherless boyhood, the patient, loving counsellor of my maturer years. To suppose for a moment that he would advance, for mere persuasion's sake, arguments in which he did not himself thoroughly believe was to suppose an impossibility. Day and night would as soon change places as my grandfather in his stern honesty—which by the way was the only thing stern about him—seek to impose on even the credulity of a child.

Elder Cushing's influence over Mark Stedman was of an altogether different kind. At the time I did not entirely understand it, for it was a plain instance of what is not uncommonly seen in the world, the higher nature held in complete possession and control by the lower one. Mark's peculiarly unworldly spirit had yet its weak points. He was ambitious, not for money— he despised it; not for fame—he despised that too, but none the less he longed in secret to win that human recognition and sympathy of which fame is the mere outward symbol. And more than all, he was intensely curious, fond of prying into the unknown and unimagined, hopeful, ardent, unsuspicious, with all the harmlessness of a dove, but none of the wisdom of a serpent.

I was disappointed not to hear the story of his initiatory experience from his own lips, but he was now from home, having secured a tutorship somewhere in the vicinity of New York through the recommendation of Elder Cushing, who was naturally not ill-pleased with the opportunity to aid his young friend and at the same time give him practical proof of Masonic influence. Truth to tell, I had passed many disagreeable moments in reflecting on his probable state of mind when brought face to face with those terrible "obligations," and was not at all surprised to hear from a lodge acquaintance that "Mark was a great spooney, who had given them more trouble than he was worth."

"I thought we should be all night getting him through the first degree. He was just like an old bureau drawer that sticks and catches whichever way you pull it. Positively we shouldn't have got through by morning if we had stopped for all the work generally done. But we skipped a few little things, nothing very important, omitted to save time and trouble; that was all."

"Then I don't think Mark has been regularly initiated," said I, to whom this revelation of lodge tactics was rather startling.

"Oh, we asked lawyer Bacon about that. He said it was all right. Lodges very often shorten the work when lack of time or any other reason makes it necessary. And, as I said, we never should have got through, when we had to meet his objections at every step, and spend an hour trying to convince him that it would all be made right, before he would consent to go on, if we hadn't done some such way. But such milk-and-water chaps as Mark Stedman ain't of much use in the lodge. He'd better join the church and go to preaching.'

An opinion which Elder Cushing, who had played so well the part of Mr. Worldly Wiseman to Mark's spiritual needs, did not appear to share In his zeal to make proselytes for the lodge he had induced him to take the three lower degrees in one night; a very common device, let me explain, and one much resorted to when there were serious fears that the candidate's conscience would prove so inconveniently sensitive as to forbid his return to the lodge after taking the first degree, and if there afterwards remained the less easy task of pouring oil on the troubled waters of Mark's deeply disgusted soul, it was one to which the Elder was fully equal. He knew through long experience that such souls required very wily handling; that to laugh in a gentle, deprecatory fashion, and to say he was just like others, disappointed because Masonry did not reveal all its beauties at first sight; to descant on the divine grace of patience as needful in every searcher after truth, and hint at the existence of sublime and ineffable mysteries of wisdom, veiled in the lower degrees, but opening up in ever widening vistas to the eyes of the faithful ones who refuse to be deterred from exploring the inner temple by the mass of seeming rubbish encumbering its entrance, was by far the best method of proceeding under those particular circumstances.

Rachel still adhered to her general *role* of silence on the subject, and as I took prudent care not to say anything calculated to make her depart from it, her only allusion to the step taken by her brother came in the form of this very natural but inconvenient query: "I want to know, Leander, what sort of doings they can have in Masonic lodges to send a man home at two o'clock in the morning looking like death, as they did Mark. He wasn't himself for a month after."

While I could well imagine what a shock to every instinct of Mark's pure and high-minded nature the whole proceeding of initiation must have been, how could I answer Rachel's question without revealing what I had sworn "ever to conceal?"

"Why don't you try to get some information out of Mark?" I said, in a lame attempt to shirk the inquiry.

"Exactly what I should have done," answered Rachel coolly, "if he hadn't been cross as a bear. I couldn't say a word to him about it without being snapped up. Now, Mark was never cross to me in his life before, and I must say I don't understand it. An institution so 'divine' as Masonry" (and here Rachel's lips took a slight curl) "ought to send a man home at a decent hour, and better instead of worse than he went."

What could I do but have recourse to that standing argument made and provided for just such exigencies:—

"Oh, well, Rachel, Masonry is a matter women are not expected to understand."

"I know one woman," returned Rachel, with a very decided snip of her scissors, "who is capable of understanding a good many things she is not expected to."

My only answer was a laugh, but in my secret soul I wished Rachel's assertion was not quite so true.

Why couldn't she be like my mother: a gentle, docile, trusting little woman, who never troubled her head about masculine doings in general, or those of the lodge in particular, any more than she did about the aberration of the planets. I felt vaguely dissatisfied with Rachel, and vexed with myself for the feeling. Even now the hateful hiss of the serpent lying in wait to spoil the fair Eden of our mutual love was in my ears, and though an angel had stood in my path to warn me I had refused to heed the message.

Sam Toller, in his new character of Mason, flourished greatly. That very morning the non-arrival of certain domestic necessaries having thrown the whole kitchen cabinet into confusion, I found him at the store, whither I was dispatched by the despairing and indignant Miss Loker to hasten his tardy movements (Joe being, as usual, out of the way when most wanted,) holding forth to a group of loungers on the beauties of the institution.

"Nobody shall speak a word agin it in my hearing," he was saying as I came up. "It's a divinely appointed thing. That's the way Elder Cushing talks, and I'll stand by what he says aginst the hull world. Why, Masonry is older than Solomon's temple, or the pyramids, or the—" "Oh, you shut up, Sam; *you* never was a Mason," interrupted a skeptical bystander, at which Sam, catching sight of me, turned in aggrieved appeal.

"You'll do me a favor, Leander Severns, to jest tell this gentleman whether I be or not."

Actuated partly by the spirit of fun, I gave the required testimony, which appeased Sam's wounded dignity so far that after casting a glance of withering contempt on the unlucky person who was now in the awkward predicament of being proved in the wrong, he proceeded with his parable.

"She's the twin sister of Christianity, as you may say; the "—

"Christianity's grandmother, you mean," put in the irreverent Joe, who sat kicking his heels against the molasses hogshead on which he had perched himself to listen to Sam's harangue. "According to your tell she's two or three thousand years the oldest. You don't make your talk hang together, Sam."

There was a general laugh, but Sam, "vowing he wouldn't stand sarce from nobody, least of all a boy like Joe," turned in great wrath on the latter, who ran and leaped and dodged, and finally made his escape through a rear door, Sam after him in a hopeless chase, being much too stout and lumberingly built to be any match for Joe, who was nearly as fleet of foot as the Ashael of Scripture.

As I stood laughing at the absurd scene, it suddenly occurred to me how Joe's mysterious knowledge of Masonic secrets, hitherto such a baffling puzzle, could easily be accounted for. I knew the two had been much together, and that Sam should incautiously let them out to Joe was quite supposable. I was so certain that the bottom of the mystery was reached at last that I concluded to put an inquiry point blank to the latter, though I felt very doubtful about getting a satisfactory answer, for having now been at home an entire week I had ceased to be a hero in Joe's eyes. But when I approached him on the subject I was agreeably astonished to find him disposed to be frank, even confidential.

"You see, the fact is,"—and Joe, who was engaged like Pan of old in fashioning a flute, not out of a reed from **Eurotas, but** the stem of a pumpkin vine, went on notching out the **stops with** great care; "Sam don't mean to let out the secrets, and **if you** asked him he'd **say** he didn't; but when he gets **to** talking they break **out,** without his knowing it, as easy as water **runs** through a sieve. **He** don't tell the secrets right **out,** but he'll say things that anybody that's sharp can pick up **and** piece together and so find out a good **deal. And I've** been thinking for some time," added Joe, stopping **in** his work and looking serious, "that you'd better **give him** a hint to be more careful. **I'm** afraid he may get **into trouble.** But I keep mum about everything he has let out to **me.** You needn't be afraid. Only if you say anything to him, don't let him know what I've told you. **It** would only make him mad."

I promised, inwardly resolving to lose **no** time in warning Sam **to** be more mindful in future of his Masonic requirements. And Joe, having ended **his revelations,** which made me the more uneasy from their vague and indefinite character, applied his lips to the primitive wind instrument **before** mentioned, and blew a **most un-**Panlike strain."

Half an hour later, had I been gifted with clairvoyant vision, I might have seen the two, their difference of the morning happily forgotton, engaged in close conference, much interrupted by sundry chuckles on Sam's part, and perfect convulsions of smothered laughter on Joe's.

CHAPTER XII.

A FEW MASONIC PUZZLES.

RACHEL and I were married one fair Autumn day that seemed to have gathered into itself all the ripeness and glory of the summer that had fled—a day like an embodied Psalm-tune. And the world lay all before us, young, ignorant, untried souls; in the mysterious economy of divine law, twain no longer, but one flesh.

We set up housekeeping as happy as any pair of robins that ever rented an apple tree, and as full of abounding hope for the morrow. We had plenty of friends, and not an enemy that we knew of; we had youth and health, and implicit faith in one another; what else could we want more? Had the question been put to me I should have answered, "Nothing;" and Rachel, covering up the unsatisfied longings of her soul with all the little joyful cares of a newly wedded wife, would very likely have said the same.

Brownsville was a prosperous village not far from the lake-shore of northwestern New York,—a peaceable, law-abiding community, where the high-handed crimes that shock newspaper readers of to-day were utterly unheard of, and people went to bed at night without bolting their doors. Most of the inhabitants were of New England birth, and had brought with them all the thrift and forehandedness indigenous to the soil of the Pilgrims. My grandfather's family, as also the Stedman's, came from a quiet old town near Boston, which had given a Governor to the State, to say nothing of lawyers, clergymen and legislators, who had further distinguished its annals, and in whose ranks Mark Stedman might have stood, had not Destiny seemingly blocked his way by decreeing at the outset an altogether different life.

But like all noble souls he had the seeds of victory within him. The rough labor of the farm hardened muscles and sinews, and the long winter evenings passed in solitary wrestling with his books, devoloped a sturdy self-reliance worth more than all the discipline of the universities. And thus Mark Stedman had grown up as true an offshoot of Puritan thought and culture as if he had walked all his life under the shadowy elms of his New England birthplace.

Sam Toller hailed from New Hampshire, but though of genuine Yankee stock, he was, as we have seen, a a degenerate plant, so far as industry and faculty for getting ahead was concerned. But after all, Sam had plenty of faculty of a certain kind; his very laziness and shiftlessness, I am inclined to think, were nothing but their Yankee opposites turned wrong side out. And as no woman had ever been found insane enough to unite her fortune with his, he managed, in the absence of any family to support, to get along very well,—that especial Providence which is said to " watch over the lame and the lazy " not being remiss in its kindly care of Sam Toller.

· The first chance I could get to privately remind him of his Masonic oath to secrecy I took care to improve.

but it required all the tact of which I was master neither to betray Joe as my informant in this matter, nor give mortal offense to Sam himself, who was at first inclined to take in high dudgeon the charge of having even unwittingly betrayed any of the secrets.

"Wall, ye've kinder hurt my feelings, Leander," he said at last, rather more amicably. "I vow, I never thought of such a thing as lettin' out anything I hadn't orter."

"Oh, well; you never meant to, Sam," I answered, soothingly. "But the queerest thing about it is why you've never let us know before that you were a Mason."

Sam scratched his head reflectively for an instant before replying.

"Ye see there wan't no lodge in the place where I lived afore I came to Brownsville. Now you go where there ain't no lodge and stay a dozen years and ye'll a'most forget ye ever was a Mason. But come to a place like this where there's a lodge wide awake and progressin', and all yer old feelin's begin to stir. That's natur' now. And then Elder Cushing's talk when he preached the funeral sermon for yer Uncle Jerry kinder stirred 'em up more. That's natur' agin, for I thought a sight of yer Uncle Jerry."

And Sam heaved a befitting sigh.

I felt satisfied with an explanation so reasonable, and allowed him to depart without further questioning. The whole subject of Masonry was so involved with wearisome and perplexing pros and cons, that I hardly knew what to think. For on the one hand were there not general principles of virtue and morality set forth in the charges and lectures, to which Socrates himself could not have objected? truisms that were old as the fact of human existence, and just as indisputable? And on the other hand were there not many things about it that even my grandfather, with all his veneration for the institution, found it easier to excuse than defend? It was a relief to think that now Rachel and I were married, I could fulfill my resolve to Mrs. Hagan, and tacitly drop all these troublesome questions by the very easy and simple process of never appearing at a lodge meeting!

Mark was not at the wedding, but gained a brief release in the latter part of November, and took Rachel and me by surprise, walking in just as the table was set for tea.

Of course he had much to tell us,—about his school and divers matters of interest pertaining to the great world in general, whose distant pulse-beats were felt so faintly in Brownsville. In truth we were all proud of Mark. He was the scholar of the family, of whom the minister, and the school committee, and, in short, all those village dignitaries supposed to have peculiar insight into the destinies of the rising generation, had prophesied great things from his very cradle, while it had been settled at many sewing circles and Sunday noon conclaves that he would certainly make a preacher; the fact that he was " serious," in the common religious phrase of that day, seeming to form some solid basis for the general confidence. Mark's naturally sweet and humble spirit was not spoiled by the more discriminating praise of the intellectual circles in which his lot was now cast. He came home as ready to shake hands with Sam Toller as if he had not actually had the honor at some school celebration of shaking hands with Governor DeWitt Clinton himself!

Sam, by the way, still took special delight in gathering around him, at every convenient opportunity, a crowd of village loafers and small boys to whom he would hold forth by the hour together, or at least so long as their patience lasted, in a similar strain to that recorded in the previous chapter; while Joe, who usually contrived to be roosting near, would intersperse a running fire of witticisms, to the great displeasure of Sam, and the equally high delight of the audience, whose generally un-Masonic character may easily be inferred from its material as given above. And the very next day Mark and I happened to be eye-witnesses to one of these scenes.

Sam, not unlike some more distinguished Masonic orators, thought nothing of going back several thousand years in search of shining examples wherewith to glorify the craft. He was now boldly averring that Adam was not only the first man but the first Mason, at which Joe elevated his eyebrows portentously.

"Phew! what a jolly time old Father Adam must have had with only Eve to play 'cowan and eavesdropper.' And how about his Masonic apron, Sam? Oh, I forgot; he wore one of fig-leaves, didn't he? Excuse me for interrupting."

And Joe subsided once more into the character of an attentive and humble listener.

Mark was biting his lips with suppressed laughter, for he saw another listener of whom neither Sam nor Joe were aware—no less a personage than Elder Cushing himself, it being in the public room of the tavern, a most important institution in those pre-railroad times, where all the news, local and political, were discussed over mugs of flip with more or less ardor and interest, that this little scene took place. The Elder having some business with the landlord had gone into a private room to transact it, and now stepped out just in time to hear both statement and commentary.

"My friend," he said, clearing his throat and speaking to Sam with a condescending smile, "I fear you are meddling with matters too high for you. Masons can help the order best, not by talking about it but by living up to its principles. Yet the divine truths of Masonry being eternal and given to man long before they were embodied in set forms, while its symbols are old as nature herself, it follows that in a certain sense all the wise and great of past ages may be classed in the order. The precepts of Masonry," added the Elder, turning from Sam and making his remarks general, "were doubtless communicated to our first father, and thus Adam may unquestionably be called the first Mason."

And having thus cleverly rescued the whole subject from the hands of the zealous but indiscreet Sam, Elder Cushing came forward to greet Mark, whom he had not seen before since his arrival.

The low-toned conversation which followed I did not hear, but Mark himself unconsciously supplied the key to this and many subsequent talks with his minister, by abruptly inquiring on the last night of his stay:

"Leander, did you ever think you would like to take the upper degrees in Masonry?"

"Mark," said I, facing round on him, "I wouldn't go through such a tom-fool exhibition again as I did on the night I was made a Master Mason for all the wisdom of Solomon. I never in my life felt so thoroughly degraded as when I lay on the lodge floor shamming Hiram Abiff.[19] And now, Mark, as you are more learned than I, pray tell me where Masons get that story? Not

---

NOTE 19.—"We readily recognize in Hiram Abiff, one of the Grand Masters of Freemasons: the Osiris of the Egyptians, the Mithras of the Persians, the Bacchus of the Greeks, the Dionysius of the Fraternity of Artificers, and the Atys of the Phrygians, whose passion, death and resurrection were celebrated by these people respectively. For many ages and everywhere Masons have celebrated the death of Hiram Abiff."—*Pierson's Traditions*, p. 240.

in the Bible, surely; and I've looked all through the Apocrypha, and taken down Josephus on purpose to see, and not a hint of it can I find anywhere. Catch me believing that Hiram was murdered by three ruffians because he refused to give them the Master's word, and tumbled into a grave under an acacia tree, and then raised to life again by Solomon on the five points of fellowship after he had been dead fifteen days so that the flesh slipped from the bones! Sam Toller's toughest yarns wouldn't be a circumstance to swallow beside it."

"Elder Cushing admits that there is no such story in any of the ancient writers," answered Mark. "He says the true light in which to regard the legend is that of a pure myth, whose origin is lost in the obscurity of past ages; but which, as used in the lodge to-day, has a most important symbolical meaning, as typifying the struggle and final triumph of light over darkness, life over death, and good over evil in the final millennium of the world."

"Oh, well, Mark, I am not mystical and poetical like you; I am plain and practical and don't see any of these superfine meanings. But I *do* see one thing— why it hasn't disappointed[20] you as it has me."

"Oh, Leander," said Mark, eagerly, "I *was* disappointed, only the word does not begin to express what I felt. I was almost crazy, I verily believe, with chagrin and mortification, it was all so different from what I expected. I told Elder Cushing that I would never go near the lodge again, and I thoroughly meant it. But he says if I will only have patience to go on and take the ineffable degrees the things that trouble me so

---

NOTE 20.—"It is one of the most beautiful, but at the same time most abstruse doctrines of the science of Masonic symbolism, that the Mason is ever to be in the search of truth, but is never to find it. And this is intended to teach the humiliating but necessary lesson, that the knowledge of the nature of God, and of man's relation to him, which knowledge constitutes divine truth, can never be acquired in this life."—*Mackey's Ritualist*, p. 106.

will all be explained; that it is quite natural I should feel dissatisfied now, for it is just as if I had read only Leviticus and Deuteronomy and knew nothing about the rest of the Bible. He says the ineffable degrees are to the others what the gospel is to the law, interpreting their hidden meanings, and even throwing light on some of the difficult passages in Revelations and the Epistles of St. John. And he is a member of the Lodge of Perfection himself; he ought to know," added Mark, simply.

I was silent, for what was I that I should dispute what Elder Cushing said?

Now, if any reader wonders that Mark Stedman should have been willing, even on the strength of his pastor's persuasions, to search farther into Masonic mysteries in the face of continual disappointment, I can only say that on some souls they act like an intoxicating drug, and this was the case with Mark. Every bitter waking from his dream found him like the opium eater, more than ever under the spell of the enchanting delusion. Every failure to find what he sought but whetted his hope that farther on wonderful secrets awaited him, shining jewels of truth to rejoice his soul forever, hidden treasures of wisdom for time and eternity.

Oh, Mark. Mark! turning away from the green pastures and still waters of Christ's blessed salvation, what shall be said of the so-called shepherd who lured you on?

A few days afterwards I was accosted by Joe with the inquiry:

"Have you said anything to Sam yet?"

"I just spoke to him and advised him to be more careful. Why?"

"Oh, nothing; it's no affair of mine, of course," answered Joe, with the virtuous air of a person not disposed to put his fingers unwarrantably into anybody's pie but his own; "only I thought it might be a little awkward for Sam if they should ever get wind of it in the lodge. And Sam is a good fellow enough; I don't like the idea of his getting into any trouble."

The foregoing is a specimen of divers dark hints by which, without clearly asserting anything in particular, Joe had managed for some time past to keep me on pins, metaphorically speaking.

CHAPTER XIII.

MASONIC BONDAGE—SAM TOLLER'S AFFAIRS.

IN spite of much persuasion, mingled with good-humored bantering, I persisted in absenting myself entirely from the lodge, until one day I received notice of an extra meeting of special importance, at which my presence was imperatively demanded. Accordingly I said to Rachel, after supper,—

"I am going to the lodge to-night. They say it is an important meeting, and I really don't know but I ought to attend, at least now and then."

"Which one of your duties, as a man and a citizen, will suffer most if you stay away?" asked Rachel, dryly, as she stood rinsing cups and saucers at the sink.

"Don't be foolish, Rachel. You know I hardly spend an evening away from home."

"Now, Leander," and Rachel set down the cup she was wiping and spoke earnestly, "I am not one of these silly wives who are miserable if they can't have every atom of their husband's time and attention. If this was a public meeting, and the business to be transacted involved public interest, I would say, 'Go; by all means.' I should despise myself if I wanted to keep you from doing your duty."

"But supposing it *is* a duty, a solemn and bounden duty, for me to go to-night."

"I can suppose that," said Rachel, slowly; "but have I not a right to know what makes it your duty? How can we be really and truly one with secrets between us? I read somewhere that a secret between married people was like a slow poison to affection."

"Must be very slow indeed, Rachel. There's Deacon Winship and his wife, and Dr. and Mrs. Starr—devoted couples, and they've been married over a quarter of a century. Deacon Winship and Dr. Starr are both Masons, you know."

Rachel made no answer. She was setting up dishes and possibly did not hear me; but she had by no means done with the subject, for when she had just put away the last plate and hung the towel on the rack to dry, she again resumed it.

"Leander, you remember when the Freemasons laid the corner-stone of the new court-house. Well, now, in front of the procession, carrying the Bible, walked a man whom I know to be a profane swearer. Side by side with Deacon Winship I saw Colonel Perkins, a hard drinker, and people say that he breaks the seventh Commandment. I could name others in that procession, some of the hardest characters in town, but they were walking on equal footing with the rest. I never want to see *you* in such company, Leander."

Now as I happened to be a spectator of this very procession and a witness of these very same facts, I could only take refuge in the old threadbare argument:

"But, Rachel, there were good men there."

"Then am I to suppose that you would have no objection to seeing me in a procession, side by side with women of known bad character, if only there was a sufficient sprinkling of *good* women there to throw over it a mantle of general respectability?" inquired Rachel, with dry sarcasm.

"Oh, but that is a little different. Men and women are not alike, you know," I answered, in the great scarcity of original arguments making use of one that I had better have let alone—at least when arguing with Rachel.

"Why not, Leander," she asked, quickly; "when it is a plain question of morals I believe both sexes stand before their God on the same plane. Are the Ten Commandments less binding on men than women?"

"Why, of course not."

"Then don't tell me that a man, because he is a man, can touch uncleanness and not be defiled, while a woman, because she is a woman, cannot come within a stone's throw of it without risk of pollution. But to come back to the question our talk started from; what makes it your duty to go to-night?"

Should I tell Rachel that the notice I had received was actually a summons[21] which no Mason could disregard without incurring the displeasure of the secret power set over him, and risking such punishment as Masonic law might see best to inflict? That I, a freeman, with the old free Puritan blood in my veins, the blood of men that had marched to victory with Cromwell and carried their hatred of priestly and kingly tyranny over the seas; that had fought at Bunker Hill and starved at Valley Forge, was in reality no freeman at all, but a bond slave, bound hand and foot to a despotic tribunal, whose mandate I did not *dare* disobey? What remained for me but to say, with an injured air:

NOTE 21.—"A 'due summons' from the lodge or Grand Lodge is obligatory upon him; should he refuse obedience he will be disgracefully expelled from the society with public marks of ignominy that can never be erased."—*Morris's Dictionary, Art. Authority.*

"Now, Rachel; I should think you might trust me a little better than this. I don't dictate to you about your duty and you mustn't to me about mine."

Rachel "dictated" no more. But it is easy to see that such a conversation between a newly-married husband and wife can hardly tend to mutual agreement and concord. Rachel's feelings were hurt and she showed it—not by tears or any sharp retort, but by utter silence. To her brave, open nature, such shirking of plain, honest questions, was contemptible; she could neither understand nor quietly let it drop as a thing that did not concern her—all which characteristics I will pause to remark are, for very obvious reasons, extremely inconvenient in the wives of Masonic husbands.

As a result of this meeting of the lodge, (which I of course attended in obedience to the Master Mason's oath, which among its other easy and modest requirements bound me to " obey all signs and summons given, handed, sent or thrown from the hand of a brother or the body of a lawfully constituted lodge.") I might have been seen the next day in close conference with Sam Toller. Two lines of a certain patriotic ditty, very popular in its day,—

> "The British yoke and the Gallic chain,
> Was urged upon our necks in vain,"

lustily sung, guided me to the "corner lot" where he was cutting wood, and seating myself on a great hickory log, while Sam, nowise loth, did the same, I unfolded to him my errand, which was simply this:—

Joe, after all, was right in his hints. Sam's easygoing tongue had been allowed to wag too long, and though the lodge had been slow in taking cognizance of the matter, a vague rumor that he was "free with the secrets" had got about. Hence the meeting and the special summons to me, for as Sam lived at my grandfather's, having been engaged to do the general chores, it was not unreasonably presumed that I might give some information on the subject, though, as the reader has seen, I knew absolutely nothing except the few facts elicited from Joe. But many in the lodge and not a few outside held the opinion that Sam was never a regularly-made Mason, and certainly grave doubts might justly be entertained of such newly-fledged claims considered in the light of his previous reticence, which was, to say the least, marvelously out of keeping with Sam's ordinary characteristics.

But how to shut his mouth! This was the vexed question that agitated Brownsville lodge.

Finally one of the older members, considered a very Ahithophel for wise counsel, advised the brethren to adopt a course which he had known to be pursued in a very similar case by a lodge in Rhode Island. Induce Sam Toller either by persuasions or threats to take the Entered Apprentice oath. This would place him unequivocally under Masonic law and probably check further indiscretions of speech.

Interest in Sam and a desire to stand his friend now that his garrulousness seemed likely to get him into trouble with the lodge, made me willing to take upon myself the task of bringing about this desirable result. Hence the interview.

Sam, however, took the proposal very coolly.

"Wall, I dunno; I'll think about it," he said, after he had chewed a sprig of checkerberry for a moment in silence. "If I've jined once what's the use of my jining over again?"

"To tell the truth, Sam, I don't feel sure about that. Have you any objections to letting me test you?"

Sam grinned, but "had no objections," and would have passed the test very well, but unluckily gave the password for the Entered Apprentice Degree as Jachin, when it should have been Boaz, and in the Fellow Craft as Boaz, when it should have been Jachin, and also transposed the grips. While this might have been a mere lapse of memory on Sam's part, as he had always professed to have become a Mason in some very remote era of his existence, it naturally gave some color to the suspicion that he had gained his knowledge outside of the lodge-room.

"Sam," said I, severely, "this is a serious matter, and it would be better for you to tell the truth at once. If you are only playing a trick; if you have got hold of the secrets someway and are passing yourself off as a Mason when you are not, why, it is all the better for you, if you will only own up. For a *Mason* to betray the secrets of the order is considered a high crime in the lodge, and punishable by the severest penalties Masonic law can inflict."

"Wall, now, the wust thing, I take it, that the law of the land can do to a man, is to hang him by the neck till he is dead," coolly replied Sam; "maybe the Masonic law is su'thin' like that."

It was impossible to guess how much or how little Sam meant. I was silent, but shivered inwardly under the weight of an awful remembrance.

Sam was silent too for a moment and then brought his hand down on my shoulder with a resounding clap.

"I'll own up, honor bright. I never was inside a

lodge in my life. Now how d'ye suppose I ever got hold of the secrets?"

"I can't imagine, Sam."

"Wall, now," said Sam, speaking in a slow, ruminating fashion, "supposin' I was on intimate tarms, as ye may say, with a Mason that got drunk off and on. Couldn't I get 'em so? *Or*, supposin' I overheard some talk between two Masons where one was a trying to post up the other in matters pertaining to the lodge. Couldn't I get 'em easy that way?"

"Why yes, Sam; only listening is rather mean business."

"Or suppose," continued Sam, not heeding my remark, but going on complacently with his brilliant little fictions, "I was set to sweep out a room that had been used for a lodge, and I should come across some papers with the secrets all writ out on 'em jist as they were employed by the members when their memories needed a little refreshin', couldn't I pick 'em up and stow 'em away in my pocket for contemplation in leisure hours?"

"Have you got them now, Sam?" I inquired, rather skeptically.

"Haint told ye yet that I ever clapped eyes on the fust thing of that nater."

And Sam chewed checkerberry leaves with exasperating coolness.

"Now, Sam, I might as well tell you that the lodge is pretty well stirred up over this matter. You had better take my advice, and if you are prudent in future all the fuss will blow over. But really, without any fooling, how *did* you get hold of our secrets, anyway?"

"Ax me no questions, Leander Severns, and I'll tell

you no lies," answered Sam, with a curious smile. "But about jining the lodge, as ye're so kind as to be particular sot on't, why, I'll think it over."

But Sam Toller's name never adorned the roll of membership in Brownsville lodge. One or two mornings after there was no one but Joe to do the daily chores at my grandfather's, while a visit to the chamber where he slept demonstrated the fact that he had been gone all night.

CHAPTER XIV.

A DECLARATION OF INDEPENDENCE—NOT OF '76.—SAM TOLLER MISSING.

"IF I really thought any harm had come to Sam, said my grandfather," as he stirred his cup of rye coffee rather uneasily, "I couldn't rest till the neighborhood had been searched; but he was such a queer fish, it would be just like him to take himself off on the sly and let nobody know. I only wish I could be certain nothing had happened to him."

But Miss Loker, in whose good graces Sam had never stood very high, rather scoffed at my grandfather's fears. For her part she thought it was a good riddance, and as for hunting for him, they might as well hunt for last year's swallows.

"And Sam didn't drink. He couldn't have stepped off the bridge and got drowned like Homer Sprague," put in my mother.

As Sam bore the character of a kind of half tramp from whom erratic leave-takings were to be expected, his first advent in Brownsville having been on much the same sudden and unexplained order as his going, his disappearance was more of a puzzle to us than an actual anxiety. He had, in truth, one of those unsettled, roving natures, to be found more or less in all nationalities, and perhaps as often among a staid New England population as anywhere, though in the simple times of which I am writing, when the yearly rush of summer travel was a thing yet to come in with the age of steam and telegraphs, we had not earned our present reputation of being about the most restless and change-loving of any civilized people on the face of the earth.

"I'm sure its clear money in my pocket to have Sam go," said my grandfather, draining his coffee cup, though with an air that was far from being exactly satisfied. 'He had good living here and more wages by half than the work he did was worth; he's welcome to better himself if he can."

Joe alone, of all the family, proffered no remarks, but on getting up from the table he slipped three or four doughnuts into his pocket, together with a large piece of shortcake, and coolly appropriated the two boiled eggs that were left in the dish. Joe's appetite was always good, even for a growing boy, but so extensive a lunch as this made Miss Loker stop short in her task of clearing off the table and even startled my mother into saying,—

"What on earth can you need of so much luncheon, Joe?"

Here my grandfather roused up: "Let the boy have all he wants, Belinda. Nobody shall be pinched for victuals in *my* house."

And Joe left the table in triumph with his spoils.

I could not help believing in the reasonableness of the general theory; at the same time a thought of poor Gus Peters, whose blood—unavenged save by that nameless Nemesis which has tracked the footsteps of every murderer since Cain—the earth had drank in as quietly as the summer showers and made no sign, sent through me an involuntary shiver. But I kept it to myself, there being not the smallest basis for any absurd fear of a similar fate for Sam, as the few random threats uttered in the lodge meeting had been speedily silenced by the calmer counsels, which finally prevailed. I followed my grandfather into his own private room— four-windowed, freshly-sanded, with a great solemn-looking secretary in one corner and a massive silver watch ticking away on the mantle just as it had ticked in my childish ears, with its accents of awe and mystery, like a voice out of the unknown and the infinite, a prophecy without words, dimly revealing the heart's own secret of joy or sorrow, solemn or glad, as it measured off the pulse-beats of a passing life, or ticked away the happy moments before the bridal. O, my grandfather's old watch! Though it long since went the way of all mortal things, heaven keep its memory.

"The fact is," said I, for I had followed him into this, his own sacred and peculiar sanctum, for no especial reason except to tell him what could not well be revealed to the un-Masonic ears of my mother and Miss Loker; "Sam's foolish tongue has got him into trouble. He's never been a Mason, he confessed that; but somehow he's got hold of a good many of the secrets and has been pretty free with them. Joe has been hinting about it all along, but I never paid much attention to him till the other night, when I was summoned before the lodge to tell what I knew of the matter, which was precious little. But I talked to Sam and told him if he would only take the first degree and be prudent in future it would stop the fuss. He seemed quite willing to do so I thought. He can't have cleared out to get rid of joining? That *would* be a joke."

"But it may be so, after all," said my grandfather. "You see an idle, shiftless, good-for-nothing fellow like Sam can't appreciate the advantages of Masonry. Its rules and regulations seem perfect slavery to him. He don't want to be industrious, and diligent, and self-denying, and all these other things that Masonry teaches. And it's just so in religion. People don't want to join the church because they know if they do they'll have to give up a good deal they don't want to give up, and practice a good many disagreeable duties they'd rather let slide. And in my view nobody is any better for being *forced* into a good institution. And I don't hold either to filling up the lodge with members of all sorts by cajoling and persuading them in. It's bad policy. Time and again that plan has been tried in the church and always with the same result—weakness and corruption. And the lodge ranks next to the church in sacredness and importance. If a man joins either he's got to rise to the level of its claims upon him or sink below it, and if he does the last it's worse for him and worse for the institution."

And my grandfather, sublimely unconscious of any inconsistency between his views, as stated above, and the persistent "cajoling and persuading" by which Mark Stedman and I had been drawn into the lodge, proceeded to hunt for his spectacles and found them on the top of his head.

"Well, well," he said, with a placid laugh at his own absent-mindedness, "I'm growing old and forgetful. It's a good thing for your mother and me, Leander, that we've got you and Rachel settled down close beside us to keep things straight. I don't know what either of us would do without you."

For though my mother had at first wanted Rachel and I to set up housekeeping in one end of my grandfather's house, which was a large and capacious one for those days, thus thinking to keep us as near her as possible, my grandfather himself had refused his consent to any such arrangement.

"But it will seem so lonesome," faltered my mother.

"We've got Joe yet. He'll keep us from stagnating," answered my grandfather, with a twinkle of his eye. "Young folks ought to have a home of their own, if its only one room with a cup and plate between them, and the sooner they begin the better."

Accordingly Rachel and I did have " a home of our own," only divided from my grandfather's by a narrow lane; one of the cosiest, quietest nooks of peace, with trees and grass, and a bubbling brook not far off, to make it beautiful when the long summer days should come, bright with unknown hopes yet to be, crowning with glory and fragrance the end of our first year of wedded life.

"Leander," called out my mother from the kitchen door just as I was going off. "Do see if you can't find Joe. These hickory sticks are too long for the oven."

To ferret out Joe from the multiplicity of his hiding places was a serious task. But a bright thought struck me as my eye fell on Sport, curled up on the door mat. Remembering his innocent treachery on a former occasion I whistled to him to come to me.

"Sport," I said, "where's Joe? Find Joe."

The intelligent little animal pricked up his ears and looked questioningly at me, but on repeated reiterations of the command seemed to comprehend, and trotted off in the direction of the barn. But in vain I called Joe's name, while Sport smelled round in circles, a bewildered expression on his brown face, till just as I was about to give up the search he planted his forefeet on the bottom round of the ladder leading to the hayloft, and throwing his head back began to bark with all his might at a certain corner way up in the sweet, fragrant darkness.

I followed the clue, inspired by a sudden recollection of the time when Joe, wishing to enjoy the fascinating History of Henry, Earl of Westmoreland, undisturbed by any distracting calls from the outside world, had made unto himself a species of cubby-house in this identical corner, protecting it from prying eyes by walls of hay on three sides, while a knothole above gave light, and a store of nuts and apples providently laid in, satisfied the cravings of his youthful stomach; for with Joe, as with most boys of fifteen, mind and matter stood in very intimate relations.

Sure enough, a few investigating pokes in the hay revealed not only Joe, which did not surprise me in the least, but Sam Toller also; which latter discovery, it is needless to say, did surprise me exceedingly. Sam had his mouth full of doughnuts and cheese and could not conveniently reply at once to my ejaculation of astonishment, but Joe was equal to the occasion and preserved an unabashed front.

"I haint done anything I am ashamed of yet," he said, sturdily, "or hadn't just as leaves grandfather would know as not. Sam come to me yesterday and said he'd got into trouble with the Masons and had got to leave Brownsville, but he didn't know where to go, and I told him I'd fix him a place in the barn where he could stay till he decided what to do. That's the long and short of it, and if you want to be so mean as to tell of us, you can."

"Well, Joe," said I, as severely as I could considering my inclination to laugh, "mother sent me to find you and you'd better see what she wants done; if you don't, somebody else may be along that will let more out than I shall. It will be better if you will just go peaceably off and leave Sam and me to ourselves for a while.'

Joe looked at first as if he was half inclined to stay at all hazards, but thought it best, on the whole, to take the hint; and thus Sam and I were left alone, to make the best we could of the rather comical situation.

"Ye want to know what I'm here for;" began Sam, who had disposed of his doughnuts and was now free to talk. "I ain't no fool, Leander Severns, but I might ha' kept on fooling you till doomsday if I'd been a mind to risk having my throat cut across and my tongue torn out by the roots and my body drowned in Niagary river. I knowed the game wan't wuth the candle, so I jest owned up."

"I thought you had too much sense, Sam, to be frightened by such bug-a-boo stories."

"Ye needn't go to pulling the wool over my eyes," answered Sam scornfully, " telling me Masons swear to things they don't mean. I know too much for ye. I s'pose ye'd try to make me believe next, if ye could, that ye never had a rope round yer neck and a blinder over yer eyes and made to march round the lodge-room from East to West with jest yer shirt to yer back. I s'pose ye'll tell me now that ye was never knocked down by three ruffians and tumbled into a blanket and raised up again after ye'd laid in the grave fifteen days. I don't suppose such wonderful things ever happened to *you*. Oh, **no!**"

And Sam chuckled to himself in a highly provoking manner.

This was certainly pressing me hard, and with Sam, as with Mr. Hagan, there seemed to be no method of defense open but the very safe, if not remarkably original one, of silence, previously spoken of as the standing resort of distressed Masons when thus driven to the wall.

"But about jining, as ye kindly axed me to," went on Sam, who saw his advantage and had no conscience but to push it, "I can see through a ladder with any man. They think if they get me once safe in I won't dare let nothing out; but I tell ye Sam Toller runs his neck into no such noose—not if he knows it. And another thing I'll tell ye for yer information: you and the rest of the Masons have let out more'n I have by a long chalk."

A certain inspired declaration reads thus: " Verily I say unto you, there is nothing hid which shall not be revealed, nor kept secret but that it should come abroad." And of nothing on earth is this more true than of Masonry, which not infrequently, by the very pains it takes to keep its mysteries from the vulgar eye, unwittingly betrays them. The fact is, a system of organized secrecy will surely find, sooner or later, that even " the **stars** in their courses fight against Sisera;" that the whole economy of the universe in general is in some mysterious way opposed to letting one small part of the human race keep undisturbed the exclusive possession of any secret whatsoever. And Sam was shrewd enough to see that the effort to make him join the lodge was in itself a tacit admission that he had discovered the hidden things of Masonry.

"But, Sam," I finally said, "ministers and deacons, lawyers and judges, and even the Governor of our State belong to the lodge. It is considered an honor and advantage to be a Freemason and here you are running away to get rid of it.".

"Wall," answered Sam, picking his teeth contentedly with a straw, "I've noticed that it is with the Masons putty much as it is with the rest of the world, ginerally speaking. The big bugs at the top get the most of the fuss and attention and grand funerals. The little bugs have to stay at the bottom and take up with the leavings. But that ain't the principal pint of my objections. My father was one of them that fought the Red Coats at Concord. I've heerd him tell many a time how they chased the Britishers over the bridge and fired at 'em behind walls and trees. I'm a free-born American, free to think and speak what I'm a mind to. I want no Worshipful Master, nor Grand Commander, nor Grand anything else to lord it over me; and I tell ye, Leander Severns, I won't swear away my liberty in any lodge under the canopy."

And as Sam thus declared his independence there was a real dignity about the loose, shambling fellow, that inspired me with sudden respect. The *man* in Sam Toller had suddenly risen and confronted me and I stood abashed before him. What right had I to seek to fasten on another the fetters that I myself would have gladly cast off if I could? And, furthermore, it was very plain to see that the figurative and esoteric view entertained by my grandfather regarding the peculiar meaning of the lodge penalties was not shared by him. *He* believed that there was an actual punishment for the Mason who should violate his oath of secrecy, and that punishment was—*death*.

"Well, Sam," I said, finally, " I'll tell you what you'd better do. Make a clean breast of the whole thing to my grandfather. He'll find a way out if anybody can.

And accordingly, after Sam had deliberated over the plan for a while and concluded that " he'd kinder like to bid good-bye to the Captain, who was about the fairest man he ever worked for," I had the pleasure of ushering that worthy into the presence of my astonished grandfather, whose portly person fairly shook with laughter when he comprehended the situation.

" Sam, you foolish fellow!" he said, as soon as he recovered his gravity sufficiently to have the power of speech. "This is a free country. Nobody shall make a Mason of you if you don't want to be one. Still I think it might be well if you left Brownsville a while. The affair will all be forgotten in six months. And then you can come back if you don't find some better place. Where would you like to go?"

" Wall, I've thought over a number of places, but couldn't jest make up my mind," answered Sam, reflectively. " I *did* stay at Pemaquoddy one summer— hired out to Jake Brown—the meanest man. You could have put his soul into a bean pod and had room for twenty more just like his. And I lived with Mr. Greene a while that kept the brick tavern in Pembroke. I liked that well enough for a spell, but it's an *un*easy sort of a life and I got tired of it. Folks coming and going kinder keeps you on the jump all the time; don't give you any leisure at all for serious reflections. So I pulled up stakes and went away from there. Then I stayed to Squire Slack's a couple o' months. Beats me how he ever come by his name, for he was *jest* as tight as the bark to a tree. And then there's old Uncle Zebedee; lives at a place they call the Bend. I've been a calkerlatin' to go and see the old gentleman but I never could get a chance to somehow. But now my havin' to leave Brownsville seems to be kinder in the nater of a Providential opening, as ye may say."

And Sam, who was much addicted to tracing the ways of Providence as manifested in the peculiar phases and aspect of his own career, sighed profoundly,—a fashion not uncommon with good people in all ranks of life when making similar reflections.

"Uncle Zebedee," to whom his heart had taken such a sudden yearning, won the day; but there was an affecting parting between him and Joe before he turned his back on Brownsville, to which, it is needless to say, I was not an eye-witness.

A little while after Sam had made an unobserved exit by a side entrance attired in some of my grandfather's cast-off clothes and his worldly all done up in a bundle on his arm, my mother came in with the remark "that Miss Loker had seen somebody that looked just like Sam Toller close by the big hickory, only he didn't seem to be dressed exactly like him."

"It would be very easy for Miss Loker to be mistaken at such a distance, Belinda." And my honest grandfather, unused to ways of deception, coughed and hemmed and rubbed his glasses in a manner that would certainly have roused suspicion in any less innocent and unsuspecting soul than my mother.

CHAPTER XV.

THE SPRING OF 1826.—SAM TOLLER.—"COMING EVENTS CAST THEIR SHADOWS BEFORE."—"THE DEEDS OF YOUR FATHER YE WILL DO."—"HE WAS A LIAR FROM THE BEGINNING."

THE story writer is in one sense a seer. Projecting its dark shadow across his sunniest pages he sees the swift-coming tragedy of which his readers know nothing, and at no point in this history has there been a time when the remark did not hold true. I have never lost sight of it simply because I could not—that terrible event which was hastening on to make a leaf in our national records that should be an unread blank for half a century, and then, like a writing in secret ink, flash suddenly out to be (God grant it) the death warrant of the vile institution which, thinking its crime buried forever, has dared to step boldly back into its old place of power and challenge for itself an authority above all human or even divine law.

Yet the spring of 1826 has little to mark it in my memory. An era of national prosperity had begun with the eight years' Presidency of Monroe that bid fair to continue under his successor, John Quincy Adams. Florida had been added to the Union, the national debt largely liquidated, and the Erie canal built; and the social wheels of Brownsville moved smoothly on in those good old ruts of social custom so extremely hard to get out of, as most people will testify who have made the effort.

The reasons for Sam's sudden exodus had somehow leaked out in the village—I am inclined to think Joe was the bird of the air that told the matter—and caused many a sly laugh at the expense of the lodge. Now it is characteristic of evil generally that it can not bear to be laughed at. A good man or a good cause is cased in armor that no shafts of ridicule can penetrate; but not so with a system built on iniquity, or a man whose success in life is founded on wrong. When Napoleon, with a million of trained soldiery at his back, feared Madame De Stael so much as to banish her from France, it was simply because her keen wit made him ridiculous in the eyes of the French people, and nobody knew better than he that it was a dangerous thing for Napoleon to be made ridiculous. So the papacy, in Luther's day, withered under the biting satire of Reynard Reineke, for it understood perfectly well that, the popular laugh once turned against it, all was over with its claims to infallible authority. And in like manner Masonry fears nothing so much as to have the ridiculous side of her pretensions shown up.

When the lodge in Brownsville realized that it had been mocked and trifled with by "a fellow like Sam Toller," I am obliged to confess that the wrath of the brotherhood found vent in many expressions not at all compatible with their avowed principles of universal benevolence. For it was plain enough to see that Sam's whole course of conduct had been, from beginning to end, a cunningly devised plan to throw ridicule on the sublime and glorious institution of Masonry and then escape disagreeable consequences for himself by running away at the last moment.

"The scalawag has done more to hurt us here in Brownsville than a little;" remarked the same brother Mason who had called Mark a "spooney." "He never ought to have been allowed to go on so."

"I thought a man's tongue was his own," I answered, rather curtly. "How would you stop him?"

"There are ways," was the significant answer.

"What do you mean by that?" I asked, turning on the speaker rather more sharply, perhaps, for the reason that I did not like him very well; but as he is to figure hereafter in one or two important scenes it is best he should be introduced to the reader. His name was Mr. Darius Fox, and he held the responsible position of village sheriff, but as breaches of the peace were not very common in Brownsville he was obliged to vary this employment by carrying on a distillery, which in those pre-reform times reflected no discredit on anybody's personal character, especially as Mr. Fox inherited the business from his father, who was a former deacon of the church.

That gentleman gave me no explanation but to shrug his shoulders; perhaps in contempt for my greenness; at least I so interpreted the action.

"Sam Toller never did all this out of his own head. Somebody set him on, and the question is, Who? It's my opinion we shall have to look pretty near home to find out."

I was in a hurry and did not pay very much attention to these remarks of Mr. Fox's, for they did not then strike me as having any special significance, except as a view of the case hitherto unthought of, but possibly the true one.

The coach for which I was waiting came lumbering along and with a hasty " Good morning " I sprang in.

Among my fellow passengers was a man apparently about fifty, who attracted my attention, not only by a remarkably noble cast of the head and face, but by the curious contrast between his upright, military bearing, and a certain undefinable something in air and manner that usually marks the learned or literary professions.

He took a corner seat and sat for most of the way seemingly absorbed in silent reverie till the stage stopped to change horses, and his next neighbor, a chatty little man, evidently one of the class with whom a prime condition of happiness is to have somebody to talk to, began a conversation something in this wise:—

" That Erie canal is going to do wonders for the business interests of the State, I take it, but it's something I never thought to see done in my day. Why, Governor Clinton, they say, went to Jefferson when he was President and tried to talk him over to it, and says Jefferson, says he,—' Your idea is a grand one, and the thing may be put through a hundred years hence.' Shows our wise men don't know everything now."

And the speaker laughed pleasantly, as people are apt to do when Wisdom, under official robes, is caught tripping.

" Well," said the other, rousing himself up, " we live in an age of progress and improvement, and when a few years can work such wonderful changes it isn't very safe predicting what science may or may not do for us in the future."

"It seems to me that the country is middlin' prosperous. I take it that the nation has about got through its biggest trouble, now the hard times are over that come of our last war."

"I don't agree with you there," answered the other. "It is my belief that our Republic has not even begun to see the worst trouble before it. Underlying our whole social system are evils, each one enough in itself, if let alone and given time and space to grow, to sap the life of our Government. There are dangers to our political integrity, to our very existence as a nation, which, if not perceived and avoided before it is too late, will, in my opinion, work our national ruin."

"Oh, well," returned the man of cheerful views, who, like some people of the present day, was not inclined to worry himself over "evils" or "dangers" not immediately palpable to the sight, "there's always the Red Skins. They make us lots of trouble, and we may have another brush with the Britishers, but I aint much afraid of that. I guess we've had about enough fighting to last both sides one spell."

"I hope you are right," answered the man of half-clerical, half-military look, "but if foes from without are all we have to dread our country has been born to an exceptional destiny. It isn't a great many years since Aaron Burr plotted to divide the Union. Why did his plot fail? Just because he was not a leader. He did not possess the confidence of any portion of the people and his murder of Hamilton had covered him with odium and suspicion."

"Just so," assented his auditor. "Burr did not have no very great chance to do mischief after he had shown himself out so by killing Hamilton."

"But now, given different circumstances," pursued the other, "say a man that was a leader, that did have the confidence of the people, and could hatch his conspiracy under the cloak of a secret order as Burr did, who was a Royal Arch Mason, and my word for it, if he failed it would be because the hand of God worked confusion to the plot."

"Maybe you are right about it," said the man who had begun the conversation, "but then I don't believe that will ever happen. Our Union is getting too strong for traitors to try to overturn it."

"I know this much," said the other, speaking with the slow impressiveness of one whose words are weighted with a good deal of previous thinking on the subject, "I was born at the South and I see elements there that are even now tending to disunion. Should such a plot arise it will, in my view, be most likely to originate in that part of the country where there is the best chance to keep such a movement secret."

"You don't say so," said the chatty man, startled into silence for about half a minute, during which time, the work of changing horses having been completed, the stage began to move on, and several more passengers entering it, the conversation stopped, but I could not help gazing with a strange interest at that grave, noble-looking man in the corner, and thinking over what he had said about Burr's connection with Masonry. How could an institution be beneficial morally, socially or politically, that could be made a cover for secret crimes and subservient to all the vile ends of criminals and conspirators? Yet my grandfather thought it could, so did Governor Clinton, so did others whom church and state delighted to honor. And should I, in my inexperienced young manhood, presume to be wiser than they? And, besides, how could I be certain that he meant any condemnation of Masonry by his allusion to Burr's treason as being planned under its protecting wing, for how many crimes have been perpetrated under the mask of piety and in the holy names of religion and liberty?

At our next stopping place the stranger got out, and a Brownsville acquaintance who happened to be in the coach, came forward and took his vacant seat.

"That was Captain William Morgan, of Batavia," he remarked, casually. "I know him by sight. Fine looking man, isn't he?"

But the name stirred no rush of memories, thick and fast though they crowd upon me as I write it now. I was glad to have seen one whom my grandfather knew and esteemed, and felt instinctively that the character given him as a boy by his old friend, Benjamin Hagan, must be true of the man, but I never recognized in him the coming deliverer, through whose witness, sealed with his life, thousands of souls, and mine among them, were to owe their freedom from galling, bitter bondage, to a power which had made them first its dupes and then its slaves.

"I thought Captain Morgan was quite a distinguished Mason," said my companion, who happened never to have had the "cable-tow" about his neck, lowering his voice and speaking confidentially, "but some of his talk sounded to me as though he didn't think very much of it after all. You see I've had an invitation to join the lodge myself lately and I'm keeping my ears open to get all the information I can about it first. If I was certain the things Sam Toller let out were true, wild horses shouldn't get me in there, and I told Baxter Stebbins so when he asked me to join, but he says Sam knew nothing about Masonry really.

I had not yet reached the point where I could listen unstartled to such a revelation of lodge duplicity, especially as Baxter Stebbins was the very one with whose Ahithophel counsel in the matter of Sam Toller the reader is already conversant, and was silent from sheer astonishment.

"I shouldn't have thought so much of what he said," continued my companion, whose name was Luke Thatcher, a young farmer of Brownsville, a plain, honest, steady fellow, of more than common intelligence and good sense, "only Deacon Brown was standing close by and spoke in nearly the same way about it. 'Sam has contrived to get a little inkling into Masonry,' says he, ' but that is all. He knows nothing of the real secrets.'"

Now what is a young man of average conscientiousness to do when brought into a strait where he must either himself consent to a lie or tacitly charge on another, old enough to be his father, one of the most respected men in the community and an officer of the church beside, this most disagreeable accusation?

I did as the average young man probably would have done in like circumstances. I took the easiest course, helped by some shadowy recollection of the Fifth Commandment as including that honor and respect for elders which seemed hardly compatible with the other mode of meeting the case. And Luke Thatcher a few weeks after joined the lodge.

CHAPTER XVI.

AN ADHERING FREEMASON INCAPABLE OF ENTIRE LOYALTY TO HIS WIFE.—A LODGE QUARREL.—JACHIN AND BOAZ.

IN consequence of the fact that my presence had been several times required as a witness to testify in regard to the affair about Sam Toller, and partly because I saw the necessity of keeping up some show of outward interest if I wanted to retain my standing in the lodge, I was now a regular attendant on its meetings.

Rachel uttered no second remonstrance, not even when the book we were planning to read together had to be laid aside, and the subject on which we had promised ourselves a quiet chat must be deferred, while she was left to an evening of loneliness, uncheered even by the expectation that I would tell her what I had seen and heard when I came home. Between us had fallen the lodge shadow; it sat like a ghost at our hearthstone; it laid cold hands of separation on two hearts that honestly loved each other, and the current of our two lives, which should have glided on to the Eternal Sea in an indivisible unity of thought and sympathy and affection, were separating farther and farther from each other into their own individual channels of separate feeling and purpose. Not that we were either of us even dimly aware of this state of things. The bare thought would have shocked us, yet is was true nevertheless. Rachel's nature, slightly imperious, yet rich and sweet and womanly to the core, was capable of a boundless self-surrender, a royal giving up of her entire being to make the joy and blessing of another's life; but there is a divine law of equity in all true love, which, if transgressed, brings its own retribution. She had not received what she gave and she knew it, but as I said before, Rachel had a proud, steady poise of will that caused her to maintain a general silence on the subject, only flashing out at rare intervals in a manner decidedly uncomfortable. For the reader has probably observed that among people addicted to "saying what they think," there are two classes, one in a state of continual eruption, like Stromboli—nobody minds them—while with the other this operation is more like an eruption of Mt. Vesuvius—a thing to be remembered with fear and awe, and kept out of the way of as much as possible.

As the heading of this chapter may excite wonder in some innocent minds, whose idea of the lodge is a place where the utmost concord and brotherly love must necessarily prevail as a matter of course, let me hasten to remove an impression so entirely erroneous. It is a lamentable fact, but no less true, that there exists a tendency in our fallen humanity to quarrel. Editors quarrel, Congressmen quarrel; there are quarrels in high places and in low places; quarrels in the church, the parish and the family; and why, in the name of all that is reasonable, should the lodge be exempt?

Be this as it may, serious difficulty arose one evening

between Darius Fox and myself, caused by some remark of the former about " Achans in the camp," which I chose to regard as especially aimed at me. Now " the beginning of strife," according to Solomon, who, whether he ever ruled over a lodge at Jerusalem, as stated by Masonic tradition, or not, was certainly in his day a shrewd observer of men and things, " is as when one letteth out water;" and through the tiny leak of this ill-considered speech rushed a whole torrent of angry words.

" If you accuse me of being in complicity with Sam Toller you've got to prove it, that's all," I answered, defiantly. " It stands you in hand to be a little careful what you say, however."

" If the coat fits you can put it on," retorted Darius. " I won't charge you with anything. I only said that *somebody*, right here in this lodge, too, put Sam up to it, and I say so again. There is no use trying to shuffle off the truth. We've got a traitor among us."

Elder Cushing was present when this altercation took place and felt called upon by virtue of his ministerial office to say something which should calm our rising passions.

" Come, come; this won't do. This isn't brotherly love. Mutual accusation and recrimination are the last things in which good Masons should indulge. The true spirit of Masonry does not allow us to suspect evil of a brother and requires us to throw a mantle of the broadest charity even over his failings."

Respect for our minister checked the dispute for the time being, but fire was smouldering under the ashes. It should be remarked in excuse of Mr. Darius Fox, who was certainly in a most unpleasant temper, that he had just been accosted on his way to the lodge by a small boy, rejoicing in bare legs and a rimless hat, who drawled out with a provoking grimace, at the same time raising both arms to his head and then letting them drop to his side, "O Lord, my God! Is there no help for the widow's son?" Now that one of the sublimest and certainly one of the most profitable secrets of Masonry, the grand hailing sign of distress, had become the jest and by-word of profane village gamins, what zealous Mason can wonder if poor Mr. Fox felt very much like an ancient Jew when he saw the temple defiled and its glories laid waste by the hordes of heathen Babylonians?

It may also be observed that, with the desire so characteristic of human nature whenever an accident happens to lay the blame *somewhere*, a spirit of mutual chiding had taken possession of the lodge. Everybody was sure that somebody else must have been reprehensibly careless, or how could Sam have possibly obtained the secrets? Which serves to explain in some degree the reason for my being in a rather irritable frame of mind as well as Mr. Fox, and inclined to see occasion for offence in a remark that I might have passed over in silence at any other time.

"I've heard of such a thing as stealing the lodge keys," suggested a member, Mr. Silas Pratt by name, who seldom spoke, but when he did had generally something to say. "If any outsider should get a chance at that 'ere book that's kept here—what's its name?—Jachin and Boaz, they might find out the secrets fast enough."

I had noticed that when initiating candidates reference was frequently made to a certain volume, which I supposed contained merely the charges and lectures, but I had taken no nearer view of it than as I had seen it in the hands of some officer of the lodge on the above-mentioned occasions, and not being in the least a "bright Mason" myself,. was quite ignorant of the fact that many of the members who astonished me by their glib speech and ready memories were assiduous students of its pages.

In spite of the assertion so frequently heard at the present day, that "Masonry cannot be revealed," it is an undeniable fact that there existed in many lodges, as well as in the secret keeping of many individual members of the fraternity, an old book first published in England in 1762, called Jachin and Boaz, which at the time it was published was a complete revelation and exposure of the first three degrees. But to prevent the downfall of the entire system which any discerning mind will at once perceive would have been the result had no protective measures been taken, the lodge reversed the grips and passwords of the Entered Apprentice and Fellow Craft degrees. Otherwise the book remained for all practical intents and purposes a complete guide to the mighty and august mysteries of Masonry, and, as such, proved very useful to the craft, who were not above taking advantage, as far as possible, even of so untoward a circumstance as the illicit publication of their boasted secrets.

But what of the author of Jachin and Boaz? He was, of course, a Mason; but the most that has come down to us regarding him across the shadowy gulf of the last century concerns the manner of his death. He was found one morning in the streets of London, a corpse, his throat cut from ear to ear; and whatever his motives in publishing the secrets of Masonry—whether for gain, or notoriety, or the purest and holiest motives that ever throbbed in a patriotic bosom—published they were. And under the knife of his Masonic murderers in great, populous London, the soul of a man who had broken no law of his country took its flight to Him who has said, "Vengeance is mine." But how? Did he face his terrible doom like a martyr and a hero, doubly a martyr and a hero that he had not the incitement of crowds of spectators to bear up the sinking flesh; that if he yielded up his life nobly for truth and right the world would never know it? Questions that cannot be answered for eternity keeps the secret, and to those dim, silent shores whither the murderers sent their victim, they themselves long since passed away to receive their just reward, while the system which made them its tools proudly boasted of its benevolence and charity, and with the blood of the innocent crimsoning her skirts, called herself the handmaid of Christ's pure and holy religion.

It must not be supposed, however, that all this was told me in the lodge. By no manner of means. I was given to understand that Jachin and Boaz was a very rare book (as indeed it was, the fraternity having been pretty successful in preventing its publication in this country), and that its author, for purposes of speculation disappeared from the public view and had it given out that he was murdered by Masons in order to give his book a more rapid sale—a statement honestly believed by many members of the lodge, for it does not follow that because a man is joined to a system which is, in itself, a gigantic fraud upon humanity, he must be himself a conscious and deliberate liar. Masonry, like the fabled enchantress, mixes a draught for her victims, which may not indeed change them into beasts, but has a strange power of so darkening the moral consciousness that they lose that most God-like attribute of the human mind, the power to discern between truth and falsehood. Such an one, maddened by the cup of her sorceries, will call evil good and good evil, until, in the awful words of the Hebrew prophet, "He cannot deliver his soul nor say, Is there not a lie in my right hand?"

Owing to Elder Cushing's interference there was no further interchange of sharp words between Darius Fox and myself, but their memory rankled unpleasantly, for I knew the lodge regarded me as in a certain sense mixed up in the affair, and it was a disagreeable question how far he voiced the opinions of the rest. Mr. Pratt's suggestion that some one might have stolen the keys was followed by various other attempts to solve the mystery, equally sagacious; but no light, either from the East or any other quarter, dawned on the vexed subject. Finally, after a rather heated discussion, the lodge adjourned from "labor" to "refreshment," and in the general unstopping of bottles and clinking of glasses good fellowship was in some measure restored. "Confusion to the foes of Masonry," which was the toast given by Elder Cushing, was duly applauded and drank; others followed of much the same tenor, ending off by a general drinking to the health of all good and faithful brother Masons. For though the lodge in Brownsville was no more convivially inclined than most others, there were always certain members who, in drinking all these various healths, generally contrived to so seriously damage their own as to need assistance home.

Could it be that Sam had in some way got possession of Jachin and Boaz? Remembering his curious reversal of the grips and passwords, together with the fact that throughout the affair there seemed to be a good mutual understanding between him and Joe, I resolved to make one more effort to probe the secret to the bottom.

Which was easier said than done, Masons not being the only people in the world who know how to keep secrets. But Joe himself opened the way for such a conversation by innocently inquiring as soon as he saw me next morning—

"Say, Leander, what was the row in the lodge last night?"

I had never before considered Joe a wizard, but I certainly stared at him for an instant as if some such idea was in my head, quite forgetting that in going home from the lodge Deacon Brown had kept me company as far as my grandfather's; I suppose for the purpose of giving me a little paternal advice, and the wind had been just right to waft his parting words, "Keep your temper, keep your temper, Leander; there's nothing to be gained by losing that, you know," into the open window of the chamber where Joe slept, who, being blessed with a pair of sharp ears, had heard it and drawn his own deductions.

"For pity's sake, Joe!" said I, fairly thrown off my guard, "how did you know anything about it?" Joe grew suddenly thirsty and went to the water-pail for a drink.

"I didn't know but there might be some fuss brewing about what Sam let out," he answered, turning round with a preternaturally grave face, though I had my own reasons for suspecting that the dipper a moment before had mirrored one vastly different. "Sam was a goose to get scared and clear out as he did. The Masons couldn't do anything to him as long as he'd never been one himself, and I told him so. But he was bound not to join the lodge anyhow, and he was afraid they might work it so as to get him in. He said he'd heard of such things; and then if they shouldn't believe him that he'd never been a Mason, some of them might cut his throat for telling the secrets. I told him it was perfectly ridiculous to talk of any such awful thing as that ever being done in Brownsville."

And Joe whistled a stave of "Hail Columbia."

"Joe," said I, thinking it about time to push the question, "when you and Sam were so much together I know that he must have told you who put him in possession of the secrets."

"What if he did," said the undisturbed Joe. "Supposing I promised him that I would not tell. You don't want me to break my promise, do you?"

"Not in ordinary circumstances, of course, but if some member of the lodge was accused of it and your testimony could clear him it would be your duty to tell."

For once I had touched the right chord in Joe's bosom. Under all his wildness and mischief there was honor and conscience, and I could see in a moment that my shaft had struck home.

"Well, I vow; that's plaguey mean, Leander, if they have done any such thing. Was that what the fuss was about?"

"How do you know that we had any fuss?" I asked again.

"O, I'm acquainted with an old woman that's a witch. She showed me how to make myself invisible and lent me her broomstick;" coolly fibbed Joe, the spirit of fun again getting the upper hand. And then he added, with a sudden change of tone: "They have not been accusing *you*, have they, Leander?"

"Not exactly, only Darius Fox"—

Joe started.

"If I don't shut *his* mouth! Darius Fox. That's good. Never you fear, Leander, I'll make him whist as a mouse."

And Joe chuckled to himself like a young Machiavelian.

CHAPTER XVII.

LUKE THATCHER.—RUMORS.—MASONRY IN ITS RELIGIOUS
ASPECTS.

ON a warm evening in the latter part of July, Luke Thatcher happened along, and leaning over the fence in the approved fashion of rural communities, began a general chat with me about the weather and the crops—one of those quiet bucolic discourses in which the heart of your true farmer delights, for Luke Thatcher was in every fiber of his being a true son and lover of the soil. Nobody in all Brownsville raised finer cattle or gathered in a heavier harvest than he, for even in those days, when there was no such thing as an agricultural college thought of, and treatises were few and costly, there were thinking farmers; and Luke Thatcher, out of a very ordinary common-school education, had brought what some fail to bring from the universities—habits of observation and study, together with a keen, inquiring mind, that liked to know something of the philosophy underlying nature's wonderful operations. He could talk intelligently about the various minerals that go to make up the soil, and tell how a preponderance of one or a scarcity of the other could best be remedied; he knew the fine points in cattle and was something of a veterinarian, whose services were in frequent demand among his neighbor's live stock, his own, by judicious care and feeding seldom being on the diseased list.

It could hardly be supposed that such a man would find in the foolish ceremonials of the lodge anything especially pleasing to his mental or moral sense, and in silent disgust Luke had quitted the institution like many others, feeling that his manhood had been disgraced and degraded; that he had been duped and lied to; yet, through motives of mingled fear and shame, willing to remain silent rather than confess that in surrendering his neck to the cable-tow he had put himself under a secret power which exacts of its slaves, silence—anywhere and everywhere, SILENCE. No matter how much they despise it in their hearts, no matter if heaven-eyed Truth herself stands before them and commands them to testify; no matter if Justice falls in the street and Liberty dies on the very threshold of her birthplace, a Mason must be silent—and it is the very least the hoodwinked, cable-towed system of darkness demands of him.

"I heard some news to day," said Luke, just as he turned to go. "I came across an old acquaintance from Batavia, and what do you suppose he told me? That Captain Morgan was going to publish all the secrets of Freemasonry up to the Royal Arch degree."

"Did he tell it on good authority?" I asked, astonished, but at the same time utterly incredulous.

"Of course I don't know just how the story started," answered Luke, "but I know it is something more than mere rumor. The one that told me was a Mason, and he said they had just had a meeting of the lodge in Batavia to consider what could be done about it."

"Well, what do they intend to do?" I asked.

"Suppress the book if they can; but I don't see how, unless"—

Luke stopped abruptly, and whatever the thought that was in his mind it remained unuttered.

Of course I went to my grandfather with the news, but he was one of that easy, good-natured class of human beings who, in relation to evil tidings, have a happy faculty of skepticism.

"I don't believe it, Leander. He may have some enemy that has set the story to going. Perhaps he is getting up some book for the use of the fraternity; but Captain Morgan is the last man that would go to work to expose the secrets of the order. I am certain of that."

"But they seem to believe it there in Batavia," I suggested.

My grandfather smoked his pipe for a moment without replying, a look of trouble on his round, cheerful face; but it cleared up as he finally said—

"Lies most generally start in a man's own neighborhood just as toadstools grow round an old house. I made it a rule years ago, and it is a good rule, Leander—I wish everybody would follow it—not to mind evil reports. Ten to one they will turn out to be false, and even if they are true it's bad stock to invest in. I remember when I was a young man courting your grandmother, somebody told her an awful lie about me—that I had two strings to my bow and was courting another girl besides her. Well, your grandmother—there ain't many women now-a-days as handsome as she was, though Rachel has a look like her, tall, with color in her cheeks like a rose and black eyes that would flash if anything was said that didn't suit her—just turned round to the one that told it (it was Jack Stebbins—he liked her and wanted to cut me out, so there was some excuse for him after all, poor fellow), and says she, 'I don't believe a word you say;' and marched out of the room like a queen. I've often thought what an effect it might have had on me if your grandmother had believed Jack Stebbins. But the next time I saw her she told me the whole, and put it right to me if it was true. And then for the first time we saw straight into each other's hearts. I never felt sure before that she really cared for me, there were so many others that wanted her that had more money and could make more show in the world than I did. But she gave me her promise that very night, just fifty years ago, Leander."

And my grandfather's eyes grew dreamy, as he leaned back in his chair, having ended his story and moral lecture together. Memories of the past, like a sweet-scented wind, were breathing through his soul, and the gentle smile on his aged lips told that for the moment he had forgotten the joys and sorrows of half a century and was a young lover once more, happy in the greatest earthly gift God can bestow upon man—the heart of a true woman.

I knew now why my grandfather had always been so fond of Rachel, why he laughed at and seemed to enjoy her little imperious speeches, why his eyes often followed her about with such a look of pensive pleasure. She reminded him of his own buried love, over whose head the daisies had blossomed for many a long summer since he laid her to rest in that quiet New England churchyard, and thought his heart was broken. But while her name grew dim under the gathering moss, time did its blessed work of healing, and though my grandfather's sorrow for the lost partner of his youth had been so deep as to forbid him ever taking to himself another, he could speak of her with a smile, and when he read in his large-print Bible of the City which hath no need of sun or moon, because the Lamb is the light thereof; he could stifle every pang of mortal regret, thinking of a white-robed angel-form that, free from all stain of earthly infirmity, waited for him with love's sweet patience on the other side.

I would not break in on my grandfather's reverie with any words, and in a moment or two silently quitted the room.

Rachel had proved herself a careful housewife, a prudent manager, a loving helpmeet,—one in whom the heart of her husband might safely trust. She made the door-yard gay with marigolds and pinks and prince's feather; she coaxed morning-glory vines to clamber about the windows; she cooked to perfection all the honest, homely dishes that in those days were the common bill of fare, even of the most well-to-do; she spun and wove, and that pearl of good managers, "the virtuous woman," herself could not have excelled her in this particular line of household industry. But all the while that her busy hands moved so lightly and deftly from one task to another, any one of keen spiritual insight might have seen in her dark eyes the look of a soul not at peace, but covering up its inward unrest with the thought that "it was no use to tell."

But one Sunday Rachel, who, had been sitting for a while with her Bible open on her lap, suddenly closed it, and hiding her face on my shoulder burst into tears.

"O, Leander! how I wish I was a Christian," she sobbed. "I have always wished so, but lately more than ever."

"O, well;" said I, in my mingled perplexity and desire to comfort her, saying the first thing that came uppermost, "if we pray, and read the Bible, and try to do as near right as we can, it seems to me that is all that is required of us. Even a Christian cannot do anything more."

"I used to think so myself," answered Rachel, "but I have done all these things and no good has come of them that I can see. No, I don't mean just that. It isn't a right way of expressing myself. These ought to be done, but there must be something left undone; there must be some truth that I don't understand which needs to be understood and brought into some relation to my daily life before I can feel satisfied. And now, Leander, I am going to ask you a question and I want you to answer me truly."

Thus adjured I promised to do so to the best of my ability, not without some misgivings, however, due to the fact that Rachel's "questions" were often of a rather startling, not to say embarrassing, nature.

"It is just this, Leander. Ever since I can remember I have heard Masonry called a 'religious institution.' Now I don't care a pin's worth for your secrets, but even the Jews would let the dogs under the table eat of the children's crumbs, and if there is one single divine truth taught in the lodge that would help me, I am willing to take up with the merest crumb of it.'

I could not suspect Rachel of concealed sarcasm,— not with those unshed tears still trembling on her eyelashes, but I think Elder Cushing himself might have felt somewhat embarassed by such a peculiar claim on his Masonic charity. If I kept my promise and "answered Rachel truly," I must either say that Masonry was less benevolently inclined than even Judaism in its worst estate, or confess that it had in reality no divine truths to impart; not a whole or even a half loaf to its own children, much less the crumb for profane cowans outside.

"Masonry is a moral institution," I said, at last. "It doesn't profess to make men Christians."

"But it is certainly religious,"²² contested Rachel. "It has chaplains and high priests, and of course prayers and an altar, and some kind of a ritual. That all follows as naturally as B follows A. And whoever heard of an institution that was just "moral" and nothing else, doing what Masonry does, and claiming for itself what Masonry claims? This is all I judge by, and it is enough. Haven't I been to Masonic funerals and haven't I heard Masonic ministers preach and pray? If they told the truth it is a great religious system; and if it is anything less than that, all their preaching and praying was just a lie from beginning to end. Haven't I heard them call it time and again a divine institution? Don't they claim that it is founded on the Bible? that its teachings are the very essence of Christianity, the sum total of truth and virtue? that it actually contains in itself everything needed to make man perfect in this life and insure him an entrance into the Grand Lodge above? Of course John and Paul must have been mistaken when they called Heaven a city instead of a Grand Lodge," added Rachel, who was, I am afraid, growing a trifle sarcastic, "or it may

---

NOTE 22.—"The Speculative Mason is engaged in the construction of a spiritual temple in his heart, pure and spotless, fit for the dwelling place of Him who is the author of purity."—*Mackey's Ritualist*, p. 39.

be only an error of the translators. I have a great mind to ask Elder Cushing's opinion on that point the next time I see him."

"Perhaps it *would* be a good idea, Rachel," I said meekly.

Did the conversation draw us nearer together in that close, enduring bond which reaches into eternity, of two souls united in one high purpose, to know and serve their Maker? Did it not rather drive us apart? Rachel had spoken the truth, though as yet not conscious of the whole truth, about Masonry. It was a religion. But while Rome honored her Vestal virgins, and the old Goths their fair-haired Valas; while the grand, all-embracing faith of the blessed Redeemer, sweeping away such superstitious reverence, had raised woman wherever it found her, to the broadest social and mental equality with man, Masonry classes the whole sex indiscriminately with "fools and atheists," and then has the audacity to flaunt before the eyes of the world as the "essence of Christianity."

Meanwhile a cloud was gathering that was yet to cover the land, and the low mutterings of the distant thunder began to be very audible, even in Brownsville.

CHAPTER XVIII.

THE GATHERING STORM.

MY grandfather said but little after it ceased to be rumor and became report that Captain Morgan of Batavia was writing out the secrets of Masonry with intent to publish them to the outside world, and feeling rather curious to learn what shape his thoughts were taking I asked him one day if he really believed the book would ever be published.

"I don't know, Leander. I don't know," he answered, with a dubious shake of his gray head. "I am sorry Captain Morgan has been so unwise as to undertake such a thing. It will only hurt him, and being a family man he ought to consider his wife and children. And of course it will hurt Masonry to begin with, but I have been thinking it over, and it is my opinion that in the end it will only be an advantage to it."

"How so?" I asked, somewhat surprised at this sanguine view of the case.

"Why, don't you see, Leander," said my grandfather, laying down both pipe and newspaper in his earnestness. "Masonry will have to be altered if this thing goes on. I don't mean in any of it's essentials, for of course it cannot change in spirit or principle; but I have been thinking there could be no better chance to reform the institution in a few points—to drop for instance some of its forms and ceremonies that are only a needless offence to young candidates, and substitute others in their stead more in agreement with the progressive spirit of the age; in short, to have less of the law and more of the gospel in it. And if this should be the result of Morgan's publishing the secrets, I, for one, don't care in the least how soon it is done."

And over this agreeable outcome of the whole affair my grandfather waxed decidedly cheerful and turned to his pipe and paper with a very untroubled air; pausing, however, almost as soon as he began to read, with his finger on a certain paragraph, to which he called my attention. It ran as follows:—

NOTICE AND CAUTION.

If a man calling himself WILLIAM MORGAN should intrude himself on the community they should be on their guard—particularly the MASONIC FRATERNITY. Morgan was in this village in May last, and his conduct while here and elsewhere calls forth this notice. Any information in relation to Morgan can be obtained by calling at the MASONIC HALL in this village. *Brethren and companions* are particularly **requested** *to observe, mark and govern* themselves accordingly.

☞ Morgan is considered **a swindler and a** dangerous man.

☞ There are people in this village who would be happy to see this Captain Morgan.

"*Canandaigua, August 9, 1826.*"

"May last," I repeated. "That was the time I saw Captain Morgan in the stage coach. Don't you remember my speaking about it?"

But my grandfather did not answer. He generally read anything important over twice, and was now engaged in giving the notice a second careful perusal.

"Leander," he said, finally, pushing back his glasses with one hand while the finger of the other continued to point at the italicized words, "what did they do in the lodge last night? I haven't thought to ask you before, but I suppose Elder Cushing and the rest of the committee made their report."

"Well, not a report, exactly; Elder Cushing said it was a matter to be settled in the chapters, but not ripe yet for discussion in the lodge. He had no authority to say anything more than this, that Morgan's book should and would be suppressed."

My grandfather looked thoughtful but said no more, and after a moment of silence resumed his reading.

In those days a newspaper was not the lightly esteemed article which it is now, and all my grandfather's were carefully saved for Rachel and I to read, and after we had done with them they were passed to somebody else, and so on *ad infinitum*. Thus it happened that Rachel's eye fell on the same notice, and her wonder and curiosity were at once aroused.

"Leander," she said, "I don't understand it. What has Captain Morgan been doing so bad that he must be pointed out to the public as "a swindler and a dangerous man?" And what do these words mean: "observe, mark and govern themselves accordingly?"

"Only violating his Masonic oath," I replied, thinking it best to answer the easiest question first. "So I suppose this is intended to warn the fraternity against him."

"Then why don't they use good common English?" said Rachel. "What is the use of all this beating about the bush? Or is it intended that it should only be understood by Masons?"

Now I knew well enough what had made my grandfather so suddenly thoughtful. I knew that under that form of words lurked a sinister meaning, detected by Rachel's quick and pure perceptions, as one feels the slimy, creeping presence of a serpent. For the report of what was doing in Batavia had spread like wild-fire through the whole Masonic camp, and created an excitement not at all to be wondered at when it is considered that on the keeping of its secrets inviolate hinged the whole question whether Masonry should continue to be what it had been in the past, "the power behind the throne," swaying the decisions of bench, and senate, and council chamber; or whether, its silly secrets and impious ceremonies fully unvailed, it should go down like a mill-stone before the popular scorn, in the graphic words of Scripture, "a hissing and a reproach." Brownsville lodge even forgot Sam Toller in this more immediate and absorbing subject of interest. It held several meetings in which there was much free and hearty abuse of the worthless miscreant and perjured villain, Captain Morgan, and many stout assertions made that Masonry not only never had been revealed, but never could, would or should be. And considering how often this sentiment was repeated the general excitement among Masons of every class and condition over a thing that could not possibly happen was certainly a curious phenomenon.

Still the ordinary social life of Brownsville remained undisturbed. There was the same sound of village gossip, the same small tragedies and comedies that go to make up the sum of daily living. Every Sunday standing in the sacred desk, Elder Cushing preached and prayed precisely as he had preached and prayed so many Sundays before, and how should anybody suspect that he, a minister of the Gospel of peace and good will to men, was all the while cherishing murder in his heart? Still less, that the same remark could just as pertinently be made of many of his brother ministers whose devotion and piety no one thought of impugning. And, furthermore, would it not have been a strange and startling thing to tell in the ears of any lover of law and order that not in Brownsville only, but scattered through the whole county and State were sheriffs, justices of the peace and ex-legislators, either committed personally to the same course of action or giving it their tacit approval? Yet it was true, nevertheless, though many an honest Mason would have been full as slow to believe it as the most skeptical outsider. For, like most other systems of evil that have cursed poor, weak human kind since the Fall, Masonry understands perfectly well that the fanaticism or even the depravity of its members are not more valuable aids in carrying out a plan of concealed iniquity than the honest stupidity of good men; men who would not themselves injure a fellow being, and are therefore slow to suspect it of others; men who have practically deserted its counsels and can deny with all the assured confidence of ignorance that "these things are so."

"There is something about this piece that I don't like," continued Rachel, decidedly; "it is too much like stabbing a man in the dark to call him a 'swindler' and 'dangerous' to the community, and not tell what he has done. But of course it is wrong for Captain Morgan to break his oath."

Rachel sat for a moment with her eyes fixed on the floor and had only just resumed her reading when Joe brought in a letter from Mark. He wrote that we must not expect him home this vacation as he could not well afford to spend either the money or the time. He was now making rapid progress in the classics and the higher mathematics and felt that the few weeks of exemption from school duties must be improved to the utmost, especially as he had a prospect of advancement to a higher position next quarter. The letter contained, as usual, much love to all at home, and many inquiries after sundry four-footed friends about the farm, and ended with a grateful mention of Elder Cushing.

"Dear boy!" was Rachel's only comment, though she looked disappointed.

"Well, Rachel," said I, folding up the letter, "you must acknowledge that Elder Cushing has done a good thing for Mark in getting him this situation, and you see how deeply Mark seems to feel his obligation to him. He might have been plodding along in the old ruts to day if the Elder hadn't happened to take such an interest in him, and now there is no saying what he may get to be—Judge, or Senator, or perhaps President —who knows?"

Rachel smiled, but it was a very thoughtful little smile. Then she turned suddenly round to me.

"Leander," she said, "I want to tell you a short story. There was once a beggar who was heir to a throne, only he didn't know anything about it. And one day a man came across him who was a royal embassador from his father's court, specially commissioned to find the missing heir. But what did the man do? He was very kind to him; he took pains to procure him a good situation with a fair prospect for rising in life; but all the while, though he knew he was the king's long lost son, *he never told him of it!* Now do you understand my parable?"

"Not very well. What has all this to do with Mark and Elder Cushing?"

"A great deal, as you will see after I have explained it to you. Mark is a Christian, I firmly believe, and Elder Cushing knows, or ought to know it. Why hasn't he ever told him? Why hasn't he been at least half as anxious to prove him an heir of Christ as to make him a Mason? I tell you, Leander, if he had been, even though he had never got him this situation, Mark would have a thousand times more reason to feel grateful to Elder Cushing than he has now."

And having had her say, Rachel dropped the subject till some other time when the spirit should again move her.

No one in the lodge denounced more severely the doings of that "vile, perjured wretch" in Batavia, than Darius Fox, who, by the way, had been very civil to me since our little disagreement previously mentioned, and had even apologized after a fashion for his offensive words in the lodge meeting. As for me I was very willing to let bygones be bygones, and only quietly wondered at his change of manner, though not without a hidden inkling that Joe might have explained the mystery had he felt so disposed.

"It won't do to mind all a fellow says, especially when he gets worked up, and the time has come now for all true Masons to hang together; if we don't, our secrets will get to be nothing but a by-word from one end of the country to the other. The publishing of that book must be stopped. There are no two ways about it. If we can't do better we'll send Morgan to travel East one of these days—consign him to a kind of honorable exile, you know."

And Darius chuckled over his little joke, the point of which I failed to see very clearly, but not liking to show my stupidity, let it pass.

Mr. Fox was a Royal Arch Mason, and so had the right, not possessed by ordinary members of the lodge who had taken but three degrees, to know what was doing in the chapter. Deacon Brown was another thus privileged, and expressed himself quite as decidedly in regard to the matter as did Mr. Fox, though in a little different fashion, as befitted his age and ecclesiastical standing.

"This is the time for every good Mason to rally to the support of the most moral, humane, and, next to the church itself, the divinest institution on earth. To be indifferent or careless in such a crisis is to provoke the wrath of heaven. 'Curse ye Meroz, curse ye bitterly the inhabitants thereof, because they came not up to the help of the Lord against the mighty.'"

It struck me that the worthy Deacon was a little out in his quotation; that it was a rather violent stretch of the imagination to say the least, to class that open-browed, clear-eyed, brave-souled man who sat writing in his little room in Batavia, among the "mighty," however apposite the term might be when applied to a vast secret power that numbered its adherents by tens of thousands all over the land, and boasted itself invincible. But the Deacon seemed quite oblivious of having made this little slip, and it was not for me to enlighten him.

Thus matters went on in Brownsville lodge, the air charged with a kind of brooding electricity, like the subterraneous lightning which foreruns the earthquake. But though there was plenty of talk like the above which made me vaguely **uneasy,** it was mostly of that enigmatical sort which may mean much or little, according as one chooses to interpret it. To my understanding it only expressed a determination, more or less decided, to suppress, if possible, the publication of the book, and I was sufficiently ashamed of my own share in Masonic fooleries to feel quite willing to see this done. But the idea of violence, of actual *murder!* —who, as I said before, could possibly suspect such things of his neighbors and fellow townsmen—worthy, respectable men for the most part, who went to church regularly and voted at every town meeting, and demeaned themselves like Christian citizens of a free Republic! *I* **did not** and could not believe it, especially after my grandfather's easy way of viewing the subject, and I put it to the reader if he could, in a similar situation, have thought otherwise.

So the days wore on—those August days of Anno Domini 1826.

"We are going to gather in a splendid crop this year, but I've worked hard enough to do it," I said to my grandfather with a little pardonable pride, as we stood looking at the acres of waving grain ripe for the sickle.

"That's right, Leander; the hand of the diligent maketh rich," answered my grandfather, approvingly. "But now I think of it, I wish when you take your flour to market you would contrive to stop at Batavia coming back and see Jedediah Mills for me. A man at my age ought to have no loose ends to his affairs, and there's a little matter of business between us I would like to have settled up."

I readily promised, little thinking that in so doing I was about to become a spectator, and in some sense an actor, in scenes so strange and startling that to the reader of to-day they seem more like romance than a part of sober, veritable history.

CHAPTER XIX.

A NIGHT IN BATAVIA.

MR. SAMUEL D. GREENE kept the Park Tavern in Batavia, at which I put up late one Saturday night. He had moved there from Pembroke a few years before, and it was in the latter place that Sam Toller had spent a brief period in his employ, with a result already known to the reader.

A still, quiet man, not yet forty, was mine host of the Park Tavern, born of a line of godly ancestors in the quiet old town of Leicester, in Massachusetts; a gentleman and a scholar, who had received his education at a famous New England University, and while fitted by his superior breeding and culture for a higher position was by no means disqualified thereby for the homely practicalities of his present manner of life, as evinced by the fact that his house was widely known as one of the best places of entertainment in the country. Furthermore, he was a Christian man who believed in prayer, and tried to square his every action by the Bible; a patriotic and public-spirited citizen, moreover, to whom his townsmen naturally looked when there was any responsible office to fill, and, at the time I write, general guardian of the young and prosperous village of Batavia, being chief of its board of trustees. Such was the man whose name was forever to be linked with Morgan's— a man who could not be coaxed, nor bought, nor frightened; who could take his stand on the Rock of Ages, grandly defiant of the malice and persecution that was to follow him, not for a month or a year, but for over half a century—perhaps a more searching test of loyalty to truth than many a martyr's brief hour of agony at the stake.

But it must not be supposed that I knew all this about Mr. Greene, when, finding that Jedediah Mills had moved to Tonawanda, a few miles off, I put up at the Park Tavern for that night and the following Sunday, travel on the Lord's day, except in the plainest cases of necessity and mercy being a thing my grandfather never countenanced; nor had sneers at the "Puritan Sabbath" at that time so far let down the bars of public opinion as to make it either respectable or common. To know that my host, calm and quiet as he outwardly appeared, was in reality passing through one of those ordeals that "try men's souls" of what stuff they are made; that he was playing a most difficult and dangerous part with full knowledge of the risk he was running, would have surprised me very much, but it would doubtless have surprised Mr. Greene's neighbors more.

For I had made my visit to Batavia in troublous times. Men stood talking in excited groups on the street corners, and the general air of the place was more that of a village standing in the way of some invading army and hourly expecting to be pillaged, than a quiet American township whose peace no war nor rumor of war was ever likely to disturb.

But a key to this state of affairs had been furnished me by a rather singular encounter which took place when I was coming down on the canal. I had just stepped off the boat at one of the landings when a man came up and clapped me on the shoulder with the words—

"We've got to play 'possum for a while. There's some traitor in the camp. Blast him! Miller has got warning and is on his defence."

But as soon as I turned round and confronted the speaker, naturally startled at this style of address, the quick change in the man's face showed him to be aware of his mistake and not a little disconcerted thereat.

"Beg pardon," said he, "but I was expecting to meet an acquaintance here, and you were dressed so much like him, and are just about his build, that I could have sworn it was he as you stood there with your back to me. You are a Mason, perhaps?"

This was spoken in a low interrogatory, the stranger scanning my face meanwhile with a pair of snake-like eyes. He was dressed in light clothes, outwardly like a gentleman, and to the unobserving might have readily passed for such, but under a critical view there was much in his whole air and appearance that was at variance with this idea.

"Yes, I am a Mason," I answered, with a quick noting of the look of relief that overspread the stranger's sinister visage. He had made a mistake, but by no means so bad a one as he feared.

"Ah, going to Batavia?"

"Yes; but may I ask why you make these inquiries?"

I said, for I did not entirely like the stranger's cross-examination, and the possible meaning of that speech to his supposed friend just then flashed across my mind, for I knew that a certain Colonel Miller of Batavia was associated with Captain Morgan as his publisher, and in the general Masonic zeal to suppress the book, though by no means fully aware of the deadly form that their hatred towards Morgan was taking, I knew there were men in the fraternity ready enough to use violence if they could be assured of safety to themselves.

"I merely ask these questions to see if you, as a Mason, are prepared to govern yourself accordingly," answered the stranger, with a cautious glance around to see if any one was within hearing distance. "You are going on to Batavia. Well and good; only remember that whatever a Mason knows, he must know nothing where the interests of Masonry are concerned, for his oath is above every other possible obligation."

In his anxiety not to be overheard, the stranger had hissed rather than spoken these last words in my ear, and now walked rapidly off, probably thinking it best to let this small lump of Masonic leaven do its work unhindered. It certainly raised considerable fermentation in my mind, for I could not doubt there was some Masonic conspiracy against Morgan and Miller on foot, and the stranger who had so mysteriously addressed me was one of the chief ones in the plot. Now to be mistaken for a fellow-conspirator was unpleasant enough, but to be told that I must be blind and deaf to everything I saw and heard "where the interests of Masonry were concerned," or else violate my obligations as a Mason, was more unpleasant still, because it was the truth.

But the whole mystery stood revealed when I reached Batavia, for it was as I have said, the theme on every street corner. To protect his life and property from midnight violence by a Masonic mob, Colonel Miller, in this land of equal rights and general respect for law, had been obliged to set an armed guard over his printing office, the plot against him having been revealed—nobody knew how—by some unknown member of the fraternity so poorly instructed in his Masonic obligations as actually to put his duty to God and his neighbor first.

From one source and another, from Masons, and those who were not Masons, I had gained a tolerably correct knowledge of the state of affairs in Batavia before I entered the bar-room of the Park Tavern, where the one exciting topic of the hour was being discussed by several new arrivals like myself, after the free and candid fashion peculiar to American citizens in public places.

"I say now, Masonry is a good thing;" spoke up one of the said "new arrivals." "There's ins and outs in trade, and a whisper in the ear from one of the knowing ones that can tell you just when and where to sell, I've found as good as hard dollars many a time when I've been to market with flour and grain. And I say that to reveal the secrets as Morgan and Miller are doing is a vile, dastardly thing, for it is like taking money right out of the pockets of the farmers and working men who pay their lodge dues and have a right to enjoy the benefits of Masonry without hindrance from any one. That's my view." And the speaker, an individual of a genus very common everywhere, who was not so much consciously selfish as he was morally obtuse, blew his nose with the air of one who has made a point not easily carried.

"That's right, 'always speak well of the bridge that carries you safe over,' my old grandmother used to say," put in a jocular looking man who stood ordering a drink at the bar, and now walked forward and joined the group.

"I believe in free and equal rights for everybody," said another and younger man. I never could see any reason, for my part, why Masons should be privileged before other folks."

"You ain't one, that's plain enough," put in the jocular man. "I have noticed that it generally takes a Mason to see the beauty of that kind of thing. You'd better join 'em and you'll find the grapes are a mighty sight sweeter. Fact now."

And with a grin that spread from ear to ear he went up to the bar to take the tumbler of punch that he had ordered, while the other retorted with some spirit:

"I won't just yet, anyhow. Pretty business, I say, here in free America, if a man can't write and print what he's a mind to without the risk of having his life taken and his house burnt over his head!"

"Now such talk as that is all bosh," answered the first speaker, decidedly; "there has been no attack made on Miller yet, and there won't be. The man that got up such a story was a fool, to my way of thinking, and the people that believe him are more fools yet."

But at this point the waiter came to show me to my room and I lost the rest of the conversation.

No midnight alarm disturbed my rest, and the Sunday dawned as fair and peaceful as any Sunday morning in Brownsville. During the day I took a stroll through the village, feeling a curiosity to see the building where a work that had raised so much commotion and passionate excitement was going on. It was in the second story of a building separated from another by a narrow alley (a private family occupying the lower part), while from the corresponding office on the other side hung the sign of the Batavia *Advocate*, of which Miller was publisher.

Suddenly I saw, or thought I saw, lurking in the shadow of one of the stairways that lead up to these rooms from the outside, the figure of a man, but when I turned again, thinking to be certain, it had disappeared; but something in that momentary glimpse recalled to my recollection the stranger who had so mysteriously accosted me when leaving the canal boat. Was it he? And if so what was he there for? Mischief, undoubtedly. But the day had so far passed in perfect quiet, and many in Batavia were quite ready to think themselves fooled, and feel ashamed of their alarm, as people are always apt to when they have reason to think it groundless. Even Colonel Miller had decided after having guarded his office two nights to pass this without any particular precautions for defence.

As for me I retired to rest at an early hour so as to be ready to rise betimes on the morrow, go to Tonawanda, and thence homeward.

But I could not sleep. I was sure I had seen that man lurking by Miller's office. If I shut my eyes his face was before me, his hissing whisper in my ear. The incident which in the daytime I had tried to assure myself was nothing, came back to me in the solemn night hours instinct with fearful possibilities. What should I do? Rouse the whole house with my story and get laughed at for my pains? This clearly would not do. I sat up in bed for a moment and thought it over.

My resolution was soon taken. I dressed myself all but my boots, which I took in my hand, so as to make no noise in the passage-ways or in descending the stairs, and found as I had hoped a window easily raised on the lower floor, out of which I swung myself, and was soon hastening in the direction of Miller's printing office. I could at least give warning if I saw any indications of an attack, but beyond this I had no clearly formed resolve what to do when I got there. Circumstances, however, with their general kind inclination to act as guides in difficult cases decided the matter for me. For when I was within a few rods of the office, I saw a bright flame leap suddenly up, dying down with a sizzle, as if somebody had dashed water on it.

I quickened my walk to a run and joined the chase with two others after the flying incendiary. But it was a hopeless pursuit for he had the start at the outset and the imminent danger of being caught seemed to lend him wings. Panting and breathless the pursuers gave up the chase one by one and came back. One of the two, puffing and blowing and uttering most extraordinary ejaculations was — Sam Toller! But when I turned and laid my hand on his shoulder, in the excitement of the moment I came near being mistaken for an enemy.

"Hands off! Help!" shouted Sam, with a strength

of lungs that brought his companion instantly to the rescue, prepared to give me rough treatment under the impression that I was an accomplice of the villain they had been pursuing.

"Why, Sam. Don't you know *me*—Leander Severns?" I said; at which the man who had collared me let go his grip, and the astonished Sam nearly shook my hand off in the vehemence of his surprise and gladness.

"Know ye? Ruther guess I do. But how in the name o' creation should I think of seein' you here, this time o' night?" And I imagined a slight shade of suspicion in Sam's voice.

"But I wasn't thinking of seeing you either, Sam," I answered, coolly.

"Wall, I guess we're about even. How's the Captain and the rest of the folks?"

"Nicely, Sam. And how has life gone with you since you left Brownsville?"

"Ups and downs," answered Sam, philosophically. "That's what I take it life is to most folks. I've got a job at teamin' now. That kinder suits me, not havin' to buckle down to one place. We were calkerlatin' to load with flour early in the morning and start for the canal. And we'd just camped down in our wagons to go to sleep when we see the fire. It all happened providential like. Ye see there's a providence to a'most everything that does happen, if folks would only stop to think about it," added Sam, who had lost none of his old gift at moralizing.

The wood-work had been thoroughly saturated with inflammable material, while a quantity of combustible stuff, all ready to ignite as soon as the match should be applied, showed that the incendiary understood his business, for the fire had been set directly under the stairway, and nothing but the timely appearance of the two teamsters had prevented a serious conflagration. Some of the village people, roused by the alarm, now gathered about, while Sam and I indulged ourselves in a brief aside.

"I might ha' known you were too much a chip of the old block to go in for any sich rascally doings," said the former, when I detailed to him my experience with the suspicious looking stranger; "but I tell ye, Leander Severns"—and Sam, leaning up against his team spoke low but with mysterious earnestness—"if I ain't no Mason I've got a kind of open sesame, as ye may say, among them that are. And only the other day I fell in with a chap that axed for a ride on my team; I found out he was a Mason and gave him the grip and that loosened his tongue to talk about what Captain Morgan is doing. And that ain't the fust time nuther I've talked with Masons about it. And I tell ye I don't like this style of talk; it's the roundabout kind that goes all about the bush to say one word; and that word, to speak it out plain, is jist *murder!*"

I was silent, for I too had heard plenty of such "round-about" talk among Masons and by this time had begun to surmise what it meant. Sam continued:

"I wouldn't give a four-penny for Colonel Miller's chance, nor Captain Morgan's nuther, if this thing goes on. Tain't in human nater to be all the time like a treed coon, and when they're off their guard, why then"—and Sam ended his sentence with a significant gesture, for it was nothing less than to lift his hand

and draw it obliquely across his throat—the penal sign of the Entered Apprentice.

"Nonsense, Sam," I answered; but, I must confess, rather faintly. "The law of the land is against murder, I believe; and, mad as the Masons are against Morgan and Miller, I don't think they would take their lives and run the risk of hanging."

"Wall, I hinted as much to that Mason I told ye about, that axed me for a ride on my team, but softly like, ye know; I didn't want to mad him—and lawful sus! you'd a thought to hear him talk that we were all governed by their Grand Lodge and Grand Chapters, and what not. 'What are yer sheriffs?' sez he. 'Who are yer jurors, and yer lawyers, and yer judges on the bench? Who are yer army officers? Who are yer constables and yer justices of the peace? Who's yer Governor? and hain't he got the pardonin' power, I want to know?' I knew it was jest so, and I laid my hand on my mouth. I hadn't another word to say, but I tell ye it jest stuck in my crop. Tain't a right state of things no how. Wall, I guess I'll camp down agin. I'm real glad to have come across ye, anyway. Jest give my compliments to the lodge, will ye? Tell 'em I ain't quite ready to jine 'em yet till I see how this little affair is coming out."

And Sam again disposed of himself comfortably with his team, the excitement having in some measure subsided, while I pursued my way back to the tavern feeling very wide awake indeed. So this was Masonry! a mighty secret power that laid its plans in the dark and carried them out in defiance of every law both of God and man. But as yet my eyes were only half opened. I considered the whole thing as the work of low-bred scoundrels, but at the same time I could not help suspecting that men to whom it would be scarcely truth or charity to apply such a term, winked at the lawless proceedings, if they did nothing more.

Of course the affair was duly discussed the next morning at the Park Tavern over an abundant breakfast, mine host moving quietly about, attentive as usual to the wants of every guest, but having very little to say himself except when obliged to reply to some direct remark. I began to watch this quiet, grave-faced man with a new interest, having learned accidentally from one of my fellow-lodgers that he was a third degree Mason like myself. What did he think of the institution? I wondered. That it was of direct heavenly origin and this attempt at arson a mere incidental freak on the part of some misguided member?—a view of the case which was being held forth with much ardor by a gentleman of ministerial dress and countenance, who took pains to inform his audience that "he was both a Royal Arch Mason and a Baptist clergyman; that he would as soon think of speaking against Christianity as against Masonry, and considered those that did no better than infidels."

"Ain't there something in the Bible," put in the jocular man previously mentioned, "about 'a strong ass crouching between two burdens?' One religion, I take it, is all human nater can stand under, and I don't blame any poor fellow unless he is an ass outright, for turning infidel when he has to shoulder two." And doubling up his flapjack, the buttered side in, and cutting it across with mathematical precision, he proceeded to dispose of it in just four scientifically proportioned mouthfuls, while the other, not quite certain whether there might not be a personal reference intended by this allusion to the animal with the short name and long ears, looked as if he did not know whether it was best for his dignity to let it pass in silence or attempt a reply, and before he could make up his mind a sudden diversion stopped the conversation and converted the whole tableful into listeners to a startling piece of news—Captain Morgan had been kidnapped! Having rather imprudently left his boarding place, which was somewhat out of the village, a little before sunrise, he had been roughly seized, thrust into a carriage and driven rapidly off in the direction of Canandaigua—all to recover a shirt and cravat which he was alleged to have stolen when in that village the preceding May. So cunningly had the whole plot been laid that even those most in sympathy with Morgan could see nothing in it but a legal process that must take its course, however much it might be regretted that such a thing should happen at this particular juncture.

"It's all in the way of law, and that won't be interfered with, you know," said one. "It's just the affair of last August over again."

"But that was rather different," interposed another. "Who's to go bail for him in Canandaigua, fifty miles away? Here in Batavia he was among friends."

"And his poor wife and children," said another.

"That's too bad, of course," replied the one who had first spoken, "but men with wives and children are arrested for debt every day. I don't see how it can be helped."

In all the excited exclamation and questioning I noticed that Mr. Greene bore but little part, yet to this day I remember the expression of his face on reception of the tidings—neither startled nor disturbed, but outwardly calm—as a hero is calm, who, called upon to act in a crisis such as comes to few, stands prepared, fearless of consequences, to do his duty, cost what it may.

"You see it is all legal, perfectly legal," pronounced the Masonic clergyman. "Unfortunate circumstances usually do attend cases of this nature. That is always to be expected. We must not allow our feelings, which of course are right in themselves, to blind our judgment or make us wish to interfere with the law."

"Yes; I see, I see," said the man who had spoken of Morgan's wife and children, and who perhaps was thinking of his own.

And to this conviction all minds seemed to finally settle down. It was a pity, of course, but the majestic progress of the law must not be obstructed.

Meanwhile, to Morgan's young wife, with her two infant children, this was but the beginning of long, weary days of waiting and watching for a step that came not—that would never come again. God pity her!

CHAPTER XX.

AN EXCITING SCENE.

AFTER leaving the Park Tavern (which I was to visit under circumstances less memorable, perhaps, but with much clearer knowledge of many things, the character of my host included, than I then possessed) my intention was to transact my business as speedily as possible and resume my journey homeward without delay. But Mr. Jedediah Mills had gone to a neighboring village on some errand which would keep him till the middle of the afternoon, and, under the circumstances, though inwardly chaffing at the unexpected delay, I was glad to accept good Mrs. Mills' invitation to dinner.

Is the reader so fortunate as to hold in his remembrance the picture of a well-appointed farm-house kitchen of the olden times? Does he remember the huge oven, out of which came the smoking brown bread, the pumpkin pies, the Indian pudding, baked to that perfection of comely toothsomeness which no modern " range " can ever hope to rival? Does he remember the whole-hearted hospitality that welcomed. him, that heaped his plate with every goodly viand,

and made him "feel at home" in the truest meaning of the phrase? If so, he can imagine the style of entertainment without more description, and I will proceed at once to introduce him to the family.

Mr. Jedediah Mills was a prosperous farmer owning a large farm in Tonawanda, which he tilled with his own hands and those of his two stalwart sons. In person he was tall, with keen eyes, a short, stubbed beard, thickly sprinkled with gray, and that peculiar development of head which is apt to mark an excess of the combative quality. Mrs. Mills, fresh-faced and motherly, assisted by her daughter, Hannah, with occasional seasons of "hired help," brewed and baked, pickled and preserved, and made butter and cheese; and with all these multitudinous occupations found time to read and sew, to make broth for an invalid, or tidy up a neighbor's sick-room—all with the most perfect unconsciousness that they were doing anything in the least remarkable.

Hannah was just like her name, if the reader remembers the meaning of the old Hebrew derivative, "kind, gracious." She had none of Rachel's bright bloom and quick, imperious ways; she was not fair and spiritual like Mary Hagan, but was womanly and capable and something else besides. The soul that looked out of her honest gray eyes was that essentially *motherly* soul, which is the same in the maiden and the matron of four-score; one that as the years went on would "abound more and more" in good works and practical sense; cheerful, helpful, courageous ready to advise, whether it concerned some question of domestic economy, such as the best way to take out mildew, or how to cut a garment from a yard less of material than is usually required, or some perplexing matter of duty or conscience that a ripe experience and a loving heart can solve better than all the philosophers and theologians in the world. Anybody who has carefully studied the lives of reformers, will doubtless have noted the fact that their wives, either through some instinct of natural selection, or the kindly orderings of Providence, are apt to be women of this peculiar calibre—a remark whose connection with my story the reader does not probably see at the present moment. But I have a reason for giving him so special and particular an introduction to Hannah Mills, which will appear in due time.

"So they've actually took Captain Morgan off to Canandaigua;" began Mr. Mills, as soon as the "business" for which I had come was over and leisure allowed for other topics. "And on such a silly, trumped up charge. And then to think of their trying to set fire to Miller's printing office last night. Well, it *does* beat all what the world is coming to." And Mr. Mills looked decidedly sober as he felt it to be a very serious question indeed.

I asked him if he was much acquainted with Colonel Miller.

"I've known him these years; knew him when he was carrying on the publishing business in Saratoga, and I'll tell you how he happens to be so against the Masons, though he has taken one degree, just as I was fool enough to do myself. It was about twenty years ago that he joined the lodge in Albany. He was going to bring out a new edition of an old book, I forget the name of it, that tells all about the secrets"—

"Jachin and Boaz?" I suggested.

"O, yes—Jachin and Boaz—that *was* the name, come to think of it. So the Masons went to work to stop him by telling him Masonry was altered. Well, he joined and took the Entered Apprentice degree, and he found that all the difference was just a change in the grip or the password. Of course it maddened him to be so lied to," graphically concluded Mr. Mills, "and the Colonel has been dead set against Masonry from that day to this."

I had come to the conclusion that my entertainer, though a Mason of one degree, was not over friendly to the order, and now ventured to ask how long it was since he joined the lodge.

"Well, let me see. I guess it ain't far from thirty years, for I remember it was just before our twins died —Isaiah and Jeremiah. I was just through with a spell of typhus and was sitting by the fire feeling real discouraged about making ends meet, when my wife's brother came in. He'd talked to me about joining the Masons before, but I never took up with the idea at all till now I began to think it over, and I concluded if it really was as he said, the best thing I could do for my family to become a Mason, why, I was ready to do it. So I sent in my application right off and joined that very week. But, as I was saying, I had just been down to death's door with typhus fever, and I suppose I was a trifle weakly. Anyhow, after they had put me through the usual tomfoolery and went to take off the hoodwink I fainted dead away, so it was a good while before they could bring me to. And I haint been nigh the lodge since. My wife—she's at me now sometimes to know what made me have that fainting fit, but I've never let on. And its the first and only secret I ever kept from

Mehitabel. I wish I had never bound my conscience in any such way, but an oath is an oath. Maybe when Morgan's book is printed she'll have a chance to find out."

And Mr. Mills laughed as if he considered it in the light of a joke. But I had little heart to join in his merriment, feeling that if Rachel once knew those horribly silly secrets I could never look her in the face again. So I took occasion to suggest that possibly the volume in question might never be published at all.

"Maybe not," assented my host, "for I believe they got hold of most of Morgan's papers when they arrested him last August. It's going to be serious business—serious business, *I'm* afraid."

And Mr. Mills sat for a moment seemingly absorbed in studying the texture of his pantaloons. I finally broke the silence by making some inquiry about the time for meeting the next stage.

"Now you ain't going to stir away from here to-night," answered the good man decidedly "I won't hear of it. I've got to go to Savin's Bend to-morrow. That's only a little this side of Brownsville, and I can take you along just as well as not."

I could do nothing but yield to such kindly despotism and about noon the next day we entered Batavia, that village lying in our route.

"I did calculate to make an earlier start," said Mr. Mills, as we set out, "but something has been happening all the morning, till I begun to think I never should get started. The minute I opened my eyes I remembered there was a weak place in the harness that ought to have been seen to before, and the boys were busy, so I had to see to getting it mended myself; and

Merrill—well, he's a good workman, but awful slow about taking hold of a job. Well, now, it is a queer thing, but I've often noticed it—if matters begin to go wrong with me before breakfast, accidents are pretty sure to keep happening all day, just like a row of bricks —you topple one over and the rest all go. But a bad beginning makes a prosperous ending, they say. We shall be in Savin's Bend by sundown, and you can take the coach from there to Brownsville."

And thus cheerfully conversing we arrived, as before stated, in Batavia, to find a new source of excitement agitating the village people. Colonel Miller had received warning from the same unknown source that, at the ringing of the noon bell, the Masons had planned to rally in a body and attack his printing office, and though in his first alarm he had prepared to have some handbills struck off containing an appeal for help from his fellow citizens in the crisis, he had been dissuaded from distributing them by the advice of his friends, who put no faith in the report.

"What do *you* think about it, Mr. Mills?" I ventured to ask, when our informant, who averred that the very idea of such a daring outrage in open day was utter nonsense, had passed on. Mr Mills' answer was rather startling. It was merely to point with his whip down the street and utter the single ejaculation—

"There!"

A crowd of forty or fifty men beseiged Miller's printing office, armed with clubs cut from hoop-poles. I saw two men, one of whom I supposed to be Miller, the other I did not know, dragged into the street and carried off by the mob, and then I turned to Mr. Mills:

"What does this mean?" I asked. "Where are they taking those men to?"

"It is a lawful arrest on some charge or other," said a bystander, who, like us, was watching the proceedings. "Jesse French, the constable, is there, so there must be something legal about it."

Mr. Mills uttered something which sounded very much like an imprecation, either on the law or its representative in the person of Mr. Jesse French, and giving his horse a sharp touch with the whip, drove on, the mob having left with their prisoners.

"You and I are Masons," he said, grimly; and volumes could not have spoken more of the inward rebellion that was raging in his soul. To be sure there was a difference between us—the difference being a man who is only bound with one pair of fetters, and a man who is bound with three; but when the one pair is riveted and clinched beyond mortal power to break, what matters it, except for the added burden, whether the number be one or fifty?

We were but a little way out of the village when the horse began to limp. The law that accidents, like disasters, follow each other, which many people besides Mr. Mills have discovered in the course of their daily living, still continued to govern events, for the horse had loosened a shoe, and there was nothing to be done but to stop at the nearest blacksmith's. We were about to start on again, when up the road came a cavalcade of men, some in wagons, some on horseback—all seemingly animated by one common object, which was, as we soon learned, the rescue of Colonel Miller from the hands of the Masonic mob, who, under color of law, were bearing him off the same dark way that Morgan had gone the day before.

Fire flashed from the old man's eyes. He turned to me—

"Hang it all! I don't care if I am a Mason! I won't stand and see a man like Colonel Miller kidnapped in open daylight without lifting a finger to help him. But then," he added, hesitatingly, "seeing that you are a third-degree Mason, I don't know as I ought to do anything that will get you into trouble. And I suppose you are in a hurry to get home besides."

"Never mind me, Mr. Mills," I answered, for his spirit was contagious, "I am too far from Brownsville to be recognized. And they seem to be going the same way we are. We may as well join them." And so we two Masons, in company with the rescuing party, swept on up to Stafford, meeting the others where they had halted at a stone building, the upper part of which was occupied by a Masonic lodge into which Colonel Miller had been taken for safe keeping, the other prisoner, Captain Davids, having been released. A lawyer by the name of Talbot had accompanied the party from Batavia, and now demanded entrance into the lodge-room, which demand was refused. But the party pushed their way, Mr. Talbot leading, into the room, where a curious scene was transpiring. There stood Colonel Miller, a helpless prisoner, while one of his captors stood over him brandishing a naked sword over his head and uttering loud threats in which we heard the name of Morgan mingled as the door burst open.

"This is no court of justice," said Mr. Talbot, in a firm, clear voice, stepping up and taking hold of

Colonel Miller's arm. "You must go on to Le Roy where the warrant was issued." And as the men of the hoop-poles, having laid so much stress on legal forms when they arrested their prisoner, could not well make resistance now their own weapons were turned against them. A way was cleared; Colonel Miller, closely guarded, was ordered into a wagon, and we naturally supposed that nothing now remained but to proceed directly to Le Roy.

But the opposing party were fertile in shifts and expedients. They were not in the smallest hurry to go on to Le Roy, knowing very well that the case would drop through as soon as they appeared before a magistrate. Colonel Miller was ordered out of the wagon, then ordered in again, then ordered out, in the most capricious manner, all apparently to consume time, while Mr. Talbot, in stern and angry tones, was demanding of the constable why he did not do his duty and carry the prisoner on to Le Roy.

"Easy enough to see why. They hain't got no case against him," whispered Mr. Mills, excitedly. "I'm afraid I've come about as nigh swearing these ten minutes past as a Christian man could and not do it."

And, apparently relieved by the confession, Mr. Mills leaned forward in his wagon to watch this extraordinary scene. But I was too much attracted by a face that I saw and recognized among the crowd of Masons, and which I was certain recognized me, to pay much attention to his remark. It was Darius Fox. How did he happen to be here, thirty miles from Brownsville, engaged in this evil work? But I did not mention my discovery to Mr. Mills, and after a while the whole noisy and excited assemblage moved on towards Le Roy with many stops by the way, till finally the party having Colonel Miller in charge halted at a tavern for supper, and after a brief consultation with Mr. Talbot we saw the former leave the wagon as if released and start off in the direction of Batavia. But there was a rush made headed by the constable French, and he was once more a prisoner. This, however, gave occasion for repeating the demand with greater urgency to take him before a magistrate. It was at last acceded to, and before Judge Barton occurred the strangest scene of all. The constable Jesse French, so active in arresting him, oddly disappeared, while neither plaintiff nor witnesses came forward to support the charge against Colonel Miller, who was accordingly set at liberty. But in a few moments after he had left the justice-room there was a hallooing and shouting down the street. Jesse French and his posse had reappeared and were trying to arrest him again.

There was a rush of Colonel Miller's friends to the rescue. And I have here to record a most extraordinary feat of arms on the part of Mr. Jedediah Mills who could by no means sit quietly in his wagon, but jumped nimbly out, forgetting his three-score years, and joined in the melee with as much ardor as if he had also quite forgotten the pressure of the cable-tow—which perhaps he had.

Three times there was a rush and a rescue. The third time right and might prevailed, and Colonel Miller was put into a stage and driven rapidly homeward.

Mr. Mills jumped into the wagon and wiped his heated brow.

"This is about the hardest afternoon's work I ever

did. I'd rather break up new land all day. Well, I'm going on to Savin's Bend. I've been promising old Aunt Dorcas Smith a visit this some time. And she is given to entertaining strangers. She'll take you in over night and be glad to."

But I chose instead to take the night coach to Brownsville, and reached home just as the glow of dawn was flushing the eastern sky.

CHAPTER XXI.

THE MYSTERIOUS CARRIAGE.

RACHEL was by nature and habit an early riser, and as I came up to the house in the gray dusk of morning, she herself stood in the open doorway breathing in the sweet, fresh air; and then, suddenly turning her head, she saw me coming up the walk, and uttered a quick cry of pleasure.

"I really began to feel worried for fear something had happened to you, Leander," she said. "We were expecting you home sooner."

And I, not caring to enter into a detailed account of the strange scenes of yesterday, only laughed as I returned her kiss of welcome at what I called "her foolish fears," and told her that I had been unexpectedly detained.

At that instant a low rumble of approaching wheels made us both turn our eyes to the street, and we saw a common hack carriage drive by, the curtains closely drawn and the horses looking weary and jaded as if from a night of hard travel—this latter circumstance being the principal thing that attracted our attention to the vehicle, although Rachel remarked as she leaned forward to catch a last glimpse as it was disappearing around a curve of the road—

"Strange that people want to travel such a beautiful morning as this with all the curtains down."

For it was one of those delicious mornings that sometimes comes in September, cool and dewy and fresh as any in early June, though it promised to be hot farther on in the day when the sun should reach its meridian. Still there was nothing in the appearance of the closed carriage unusual enough to excite more than a passing comment. And then Rachel hurried in to see to the breakfast while I took a general view of matters and things about the farm, and thought over yesterday's events in Batavia, finding a constant and ever recurring source of uneasiness in the fact that Darius Fox was there and saw me in the party of Miller's friends. It was easy enough to say that "I didn't care, and it was none of his business anyhow," when I knew perfectly well that I did care, and how easily he could make it his business if so disposed.

"Now do tell me what detained you so," said Rachel, as soon as we were seated at the breakfast table. "Not bad luck, I hope."

And considering that she would probably hear sooner or later what was going on in Batavia, I related the whole story, to which she listened in wondering silence, only giving her head an emphatic nod of approval when I told her of my own share in the events of the day.

"You were on the right side, Leander—just where I always want to see you."

"But it might get me into trouble," I said, cautiously (I had concluded not to say anything to her about my seeing Darius Fox, the valiant, armed with his hoop-pole, in the company of Masonic rioters), "if it should be known by the lodge that I was one of the party that rescued Colonel Miller."

"Why?" asked Rachel, quickly. "Of course what Masons were engaged in the affair must have been of the baser sort. They can't hurt you any."

O, my innocent Rachel! But it was not easy to undeceive her when I was not more than half undeceived myself, and still considered the outrages on Morgan and Miller as the work of misguided individuals, rather than what it really was—only the deliberate carrying out of the principles of the institution. For though I had seen enough of Masonry by this time to fear its power to vex and annoy, of the iron hand that could smite in secret, and, most horrible thing of all, so enslave the souls and consciences of men as to make even ministers and deacons consenting to the bloody deed, I knew nothing as yet.

"I don't like the way things are going on, Leander," was my grandfather's comment. "These lawless proceedings only dishonor Masonry. No good institution needs to be defended by violence and fraud. As I was telling Elder Cushing only the other day, if Masonry is of God, neither Morgan nor Miller can overthrow it. And if it isn't"—my grandfather came to a pause, and there was such a look on his face as that old Roman might have worn when he delivered up his erring and yet darling son to the axe of the executioner—"if it isn't, then it is of the devil, and the sooner it is thrown back on his hands the better."

And having uttered this startling sentiment my grandfather closed his lips and said no more.

Neither Rachel nor I thought again of the strange carriage we had seen in the morning till it was referred to by Miss Loker.

"It must have been the same one Miss Lawton was telling about seeing. She was standing at her chamber window and saw it drive up and stop a little way from Deacon Brown's on the back road—a yellow carriage with gray horses. And she see the driver get off and go somewhere after a couple of fresh horses, and when he came back with them they looked just like the deacon's new span. And that ain't all. My brother's wife's cousin, Nathan Leach, that keeps the toll-gate up at Platt's Corner, says he knew the driver, one of the foremost men of the place, and a man that wouldn't be likely to turn stage driver without there was some very particular occasion for it. And the queer part of it was, he handed Nahum the toll without saying a word and then walked off quick to where the carriage was standing two or three rods away. And he didn't answer even when Nahum said, 'How d'ye do?' You see it was in the night, and the carriage drove up kinder softly and mysterious with the curtains all down, and no more sound of anybody inside than if it had been a hearse. Why, it gave him a real ghostly feeling, Nahum says. And he hollered out loud enough to wake himself if he was dreaming, 'What's the matter?' 'Nothing,' says the man, never stopping or turning his head; and then he mounted the box and the carriage drove off just as it had come."

But my grandfather only uttered an energetic "Pooh!" when Miss Loker had ended her uncanny recital.

"Maybe Nahum was fast asleep. I wouldn't wonder. Now I remember that when I was Captain of the Martha Ann, the crew were frightened half to death one night by something they thought was a ghost in the forecastle. Well, it did look just like a woman in white, with her hair floating about her face, and turned out to be nothing after all but a mischievous trick of one of the midshipmen."

"But there was certainly something very queer about it—the carriage, I mean," persisted my mother, who did not feel quite satisfied at so easy a disposition of the subject.

"Well," answered Miss Loker, who was not addicted to smoothing down hard facts either in Scriptures or human life, " Nahum says, if it had been a stranger instead of a man so well known to him, as a church member and a town officer beside, he wouldn't have had a doubt but what he was on some evil errand. And says I, ' Nahum, you'd better take your Bible and read about David, before you warrant a church member for not committing murder and adultery, if the Spirit leaves him to himself. It's only by the grace of God that we stand a minute without falling into sin, even the best of us!' says I."

"That is very true," answered my grandfather, seriously.

And there ensued a period of silence such as usually follows the utterance of one of those great, mysterious, awful truths that hedge in our finite weakness with the eternal strength.

Through town and village and hamlet all that day and night the closed and silent carriage drove—horses and drivers supplied as if by magic so as to cause scarcely more than a moment's detention in the whole route of one hundred and twenty miles. And within sat a man, gagged and bound, who knew that every step of the way was leading him to death—not on the scaffold where friend and foe alike might witness his last heroic stand for truth, but a death in secret, bitter with prolonged suspense and agonizing uncertainty, and all that could add poignancy to the martyr's doom.

Who shall say what thoughts filled the bosom of that pale, silent man, as the faces of wife and children rose before him on that strange journey! Were there moments of weakness when he half regretted the awful sacrifice?—moments when flesh and spirit failed him, when the tempter whispered, "You have thrown away your life and what have you accomplished?"

Doubtless there were, for William Morgan was human like the rest of us, but surely the noblest of earth's martyrs and heroes never rose more grandly triumphant over mortal weakness than the man who could say to his foes with a cruel death staring him in the face, "*I have fought for my country, and as a soldier I would die for her.*"

* * * * * * *

The scene changes. Betrayed under the mask of friendship, taken from the jail where, however illegal and unjust his imprisonment, he was at least under the protecting arm of law, he is whirled farther and farther away from wife and child and friend, till finally a gloomy prison house rises to view over which floats the stars and stripes, as if in bitter mockery of him who, because he has dared, with a patriot's noble scorn of consequences, to expose the dark, secret power which is plotting against his country's free institutions, is thrust into its gloomiest hold never again to see the light of day—for when he is taken out it is a moonless starless night, fit shroud for the tragedy which follows, as the river closes dark and chill over the hapless victim, and the murderers chosen by lot for the horrid deed of blood row back swiftly and silently to the shore, and, disbanding, go their separate ways. William Morgan's wife is a widow, her children fatherless.

Verily Thou art a God that hidest Thyself, or else would the wicked triumph, and law and justice be foiled at every turn, while over the martyr's name and memory, Falsehood, that familiar spirit of the lodge, is busy erasing, defiling, destroying—till at last a generation rises to whom Morgan's story is an idle tale, a mere myth of the past? The deadly wound of the Beast has healed, and again his worshipers ask boastingly and tauntingly, "Who is like unto the Beast? who is able to make war with him?"

But there is One who in righteousness doth judge and make war, and ranged under his banner I see a small but faithful host, who, counting not their lives dear unto them have gone forth to attack the monster in his stronghold. He chafes and rages, but the archers wound him sore. The fiat has gone forth against him.

* * * * * * *

I look again. In Batavia's quiet cemetery where the martyr has slept for over fifty years in his nameless and unhonored grave, I see a monument rise to his memory. It is crowned with his statue, and I look once more on the grave, noble, thoughtful face seen so long ago in the Canandaigua stage coach. It is the free-will offering of men, women and children. The hard-earned pennies of the poor and the dollars of the rich have gone side by side to help build it, and the dark system of falsehood trembles to its foundation, for like the trump of doom in its ears is the witness William Morgan bears once more through those lips of stone.

Thank God that I live to see the day!

But let me wake from these dreamings, remembering that it is not in 1882, but in 1826, that the scenes of my story are now laid.

Contrary to my fears no notice was taken by the lodge of my share in the rescue of Colonel Miller—a reticence on the part of Darius Fox at which I silently marvelled, little thinking that my mischievous brother Joe was all the time holding over his head a wholesome fear of that particular mode of punishment threatened by Scripture on the crafty who lay in wait for their fellow men—"He shall be taken in his own snare."

The fact was he had once been a suiter for Rachel's hand, and when he found that she would have none of him, some coolness of feeling towards his successful rival might be naturally expected to spring up, while on my part, dislike to a certain arrogance of manner had widened the breach, though we still preserved an outward semblance of cordiality.

Elder Cushing reported in the lodge "that effectual measures had been taken to suppress Morgan's book, and though he was not at liberty to state, there and then, precisely what those measures were, all good and faithful Masons might rest assured that no further alarm need be apprehended of any publication of Masonic secrets to the world, and he trusted that all true brothers and companions would join him in a fitting tribute of praise to the great Architect of the universe who had been pleased to bring confusion on the adversaries of their ancient and glorious order."

Though I saw nods and winks pass between particular members of the lodge, the awful meaning couched under those smooth-sounding words was as yet a sealed book to me; but when the hour for "refreshment" arrived there was an unloosening of tongues, and a very curious style of talk succeeded the Elder's speech.

"I say," said one, "there's big game in Niagara River for anybody that wants to go fishing there."

A laugh chorused this statement, while another inquired—

"What sort? Bass or sturgeon?"

"Well, it is an awkward sort of fish to handle, and not very common, so they say," answered Darius, coolly draining his tumbler. "I understand there are parties out already with their nets and lines, but if they ever haul it to shore they'll be good fellows."

I had listened to the talk at first with a mere feeling of wonder as to what all the chaffing could be about, till the thought flashed over me with a suddenness that made me turn sick and giddy: *They were talking about Morgan!*

"What do you mean?" I asked of one of the speakers as carelessly as I could.

"Our young brother seeks for more light;" answered Darius, with a slight sneer.

"A most laudable desire, but at present he must be content to learn the truth in riddles," said Elder Cushing, who, though not one of the group, stood where he could overhear the talk, and had once or twice joined in the laughter. And what wonder that the dark suspicion melted suddenly away under the genial influence of the Elder's benign smile!

I was going home from the lodge when I heard quick steps behind, and turning round saw, to my astonishment, for it was a bright moonlight night, Mark Stedman.

"How did you happen not to send us word you were coming?" I asked, the first salutations over. "But Rachel will be pleased enough to see you."

"You know I am fond of surprises," was the rather evasive answer. "They don't know anything about it there at home. I am coming to see you and Rachel first."

I ushered him into the great comfortable kitchen. Rachel was not in the room, but a candle was burning on the table, and as its light fell on Mark's face I saw that it looked worn and haggard.

CHAPTER XXII.

MARK RELATES HIS MASONIC EXPERIENCES.

RACHEL, hearing our footsteps, came hurriedly in from another room, but stopped short with an exclamation of glad surpaise as soon as she saw who I had with me.

"O, Mark! How does this happen? Did you work so hard all the holidays that you have to come home in term time to be nursed up, you poor, foolish boy?"

"I have come home for good, Rachel," answered Mark, quietly. "I have lost my situation; but Masonic influence gained it for me in the first place, and I have nothing to complain of if I lose it by the same means."

Rachel and I sat down in astonished silence by Mark's side and waited for him to explain. But instead of doing so he turned to me with the startling inquiry—

"Leander, do you know what the Masons have done with Captain Morgan?"

"No."

"Do you have your suspicions?"

"Yes."

"Well, I know where he is."

Now, in Brownsville, as well as through all the region generally, the sudden disappearance of Captain Morgan had become the one exciting subject of talk. It was known that on arriving in Canandaigua no case was found against him, and the magistrate had ordered his discharge, when he was again arrested on an alleged claim of two dollars and thrown into jail, from which he had been taken on the night of September 12th, and carried off amid his struggles to escape and cries of "murder," in the manner described in the last chapter. In un-Masonic circles there was a general hope and belief, shared by not a few in the lodge, who, like myself, were not admitted into its secret counsels, either from a suspected lack of Masonic zeal, or because they had not advanced far enough in Masonic mysteries, that he was kept concealed somewhere in Canada, and when no further danger was to be apprehended from the publication of his book, would be set at liberty—rumors of this kind being very rife, though if their origin had been carefully traced out, a paragraph from some newspaper in the interests of the lodge would have been found to be in most cases their starting point. For this reason Mark's words aroused more curiosity than surprise.

"I was told the other day that Morgan's place of imprisonment was discovered, but I hardly credit the report."

"Leander, his prison is one whose doors will only open at the sound of the last trumpet; Captain Morgan lies at the bottom of Niagara River."

Rachel uttered a low cry of horror. I was silent—struck dumb with the reflection of Elder Cushing's speech and the coarse, horrible jesting which had succeeded it. Every allusion made by Darius Fox and the group of which he was the center, most of them Royal Arch Masons like himself, grew clear as daylight. They were talking about the **murder** of Captain Morgan. Elder Cushing **knew** it and that benign smile and smooth speech **was** intended to blind me as well **as** some others in the lodge to a truth it was thought best not to have us learn too suddenly.

"How do you **know** Captain Morgan has been murdered?" I inquired at last.

"From the best authorities possible—Masons themselves. Full five weeks before he was kidnapped in Canandaigua, **I heard** the subject discussed at a meeting of the Chapter, in **a** way that left no doubt **on** my mind what the fraternity intended. A minister of the Gospel, **a** Royal Arch Mason, gave **me** my first information that Captain Morgan was writing out **the** secrets of Masonry. He said that Morgan had forfeited his life by the act, and he himself would be willing to be one of a number to put him **out of the** way, for he believed God regarded the Masonic institution with so much complacency that he would never allow **his** murderers—**his executioners** was the **word** he used—to **suffer for** the deed. I understood from a reliable source that Morgan and Miller were both apprised of this danger and prepared for defence or I should have sent them warning."

"But how does **it happen**"—

"That I know **so** much more about this horrible business than you?" said Mark, anticipating my unuttered question. "You are only a Master Mason; you have promised to keep every secret of a brother Mason, murder and treason excepted. But I am a Royal Arch

Mason;[23] I have promised to keep all a companion's secrets, murder and treason *not* excepted. Furthermore, I am what they call a high Mason; as high as Elder Cushing himself. I took the Ineffable Degrees in the city of New York. I am a Knight Templar; I have drank of wine from a human skull, and over the horrible draught I have invoked in awful terms a double damnation on my soul if I violate the least of my Masonic obligations. You and Rachel look horrified. I don't wonder; but I speak the words of truth and soberness when I affirm that this is actually what I and every other Knight Templar has done. It is called 'the sealed libation'[24] because it seals all other obligations the candidate has taken or will take. Henceforth he is bound by double penalties—a horrible death and perdition on his soul, both invoked by his own lips. What wonder that the secret[25] of Morgan's murder can pass safely and silently from one Knight Templar to another without the smallest fear of disclosure!"

"But if this is so, Mark, how dare you"—and again I stopped, while Mark completed the unfinished inquiry:

"How dare I reveal all this, you mean? But it is a very small part of what I intend to reveal to the world should God spare my life. I am Masonry's slave no longer; I am Christ's freeman. And if the foul institution whose hands are red to-day with the blood of Morgan should require my life also, may He give me strength not to shrink from the sacrifice!"

"But O, Mark! my brother, be careful!" cried Rachel, turning pale, while I put in a word or two of caution. "Don't go to throwing away your young life, Mark.

NOTE 23.—"None that deserve the name can ever forget the *ties* of a Royal Arch Mason."—*Pierson's Traditions*, p. 339.

NOTE 24.—"Libations are still used in some of the higher degrees of Masonry."—*Mackey's Lexicon*, Art. Libation.

NOTE 25.—"One of the most notable features of Freemasonry—one, certainly, which attracts, more than anything else, the attention of the profane world—is that vail of mystery—that awful secrecy, behind which it moves and acts. From the earliest periods this has invariably been a distinctive characteristic of the institution; and to-day, as of old, the first obligation of a Mason—his supreme duty—is that of silence and secrecy."—*Sickel's Ahiman Rezon*, p. 61.

You can bear testimony in a quiet way, and do just as much good, perhaps more than by testifying publicly."

But when once the martyr spirit is fully roused in man or woman, words of merely worldly prudence will go as far towards quenching it as water poured on Greek fire.

"Ah, Rachel and Leander, you both love me, but you must forgive me if I have already taken counsel of a higher wisdom than yours. Why should I continue to deny the Lord that bought me? If I have let fear and shame govern me in the past, must they hold a base dominion over me all my life? Never!"

"But Mark"—

"He that loveth his life shall lose it. He that hateth his life in this world shall keep it unto life eternal;" answered Mark. solemnly. "I have learned not to fear them which kill the body. And if you want to know where, it was in an encampment of Knight Templars, when I saw the sword of every Sir Knight in the room drawn to charge upon me, a poor, shivering, helpless wretch, because I refused either to drink wine from a human skull or take the blasphemous oath required of me, and was told by the Most Eminent—'Pilgrim, you here see the swords of your companions drawn to defend you in the discharge of every duty we require of you. They are also drawn to avenge any violation of the rules of our order. We expect you to proceed!' For one instant I thought I would submit to anything, even death itself first. And then a clergyman, who was an acquaintance of mine, and had accompanied me—all the rest were utter strangers —stepped forward and told me that he and the rest of the Sir Knights had taken the oath and drank of the fifth libation; that it was all perfectly proper, and would be qualified to my satisfaction. Fear accomplished the rest. I drank the cup of a double curse, but better I had died a martyr's death on the points of those naked swords than have done it! Satan desired to have me that he might sift me as wheat; but now that I am converted shall I not strengthen my brethren, bound in these terrible meshes—longing to escape, yet seeing no way of deliverance? Shall I not by revealing all I know of this monstrous system save other poor souls from being fooled and betrayed as I have been?"

I looked at Mark in a wonder which was due to the fact that while his Masonic obligations to secrecy seemed to rest on him with the lightness of a feather's weight, I felt them as binding as ever on me, and did not understand how he, with his more delicate moral sense could dispose of them so easily. Mark must have understood the look, for he continued—

"Not a single one of those unholy vows has the least binding force on my conscience. Once they bound my whole soul and mind and will as with fetters of adamant, but now the law of the spirit of liberty in Christ Jesus hath made me free from the law of sin and death. Those vows were made to Satan and not to God. Shall I by continuing to regard them acknowledge his authority over me? Shall I have secret fellowship with the unfruitful works of darkness because too cowardly to come out boldly on the Lord's side and expose them? Shall I give the god of the lodge even a silent worship?—for it has a god, and lately I have found out his name. Not Jehovah, maker and preserver of men; not Jesus Christ, our ever blessed Redeemer.

His name is Baal, the sun-god of ancient Moab and idolatrous Israel. And in every lodge all over the land are practiced rites borrowed from the old pagan mysteries;[26] the same that Ezekiel described in his vision: 'Behold at the door of the temple of the Lord, between the porch and the altar were five and twenty men with their backs toward the temple of the Lord and their faces toward the east.' You and I, Leander, did exactly what those old idolatrous Jews did when we were conducted round the lodge three times with our faces towards the east. We, too, were worshiping the sun,[27] or, call it by another name, Baal."

"But how did you find out all this, Mark?" said I, in mingled astonishment and perplexity, greater, if possible, than when I sat in Benjamin Hagan's cabin and listened to the honest backwoods preacher as he weighed the boasted morality of the lodge in the scales of the Ten Commandments and found it—wanting.

"The murder of Morgan was the first thing that opened my eyes, and this little book," added Mark, at the same time drawing a small volume from his coat pocket, which he handed to me, "has, under God, been the instrument of converting me forever from the worship of this false, unclean, red-handed deity of the lodge."

I turned it over. It was entitled: "An inquiry into the Origin and Nature of Speculative Freemasonry, by Elder John G. Stearns." Mark continued—

"Quite as much for the crime of introducing this book to the notice of some of my Masonic acquaintances, as for my outspoken abhorrence of Captain

---

NOTE 26.- "In the rite of circumambulation we find another ceremony borrowed from the Ancient Freemasonry that was practiced in the mysteries. * * * In making this procession great care was taken to move in imitation of the course of the sun."—*Pierson's Traditions*, pp. 32-33.

NOTE 27.—"The Worshipful Master himself is a representative of the sun."—*Morris's Dictionary*, Art. Sun.

Morgan's murder, a hint was soon dropped me by the Faculty—all high Masons—that my resignation would be acceptable. Of course I resigned at once, though I let them know at the same time that I understood perfectly well the reason of my dismissal. Now you and Rachel know the whole story. I have come home a humbler, wiser, and I trust better man than when I went away. I believe the Lord has a work waiting for me. Till he shows me when and how to take it up I shall go back and fill my old place on the farm. And now, Leander, I have a question to ask. Are you content to remain longer with the institution that has taken the life of Morgan?"

"No; and may heaven bear witness that I leave it henceforth forever," I answered, solemnly. And then Rachel, who had sat silent hitherto, gazing in blank bewilderment from one to the other, as what woman would not on discovering that her nearest male relatives have been secretly practicing heathenism, turned to me with the quick tears of a sudden joy in her eyes—

"Now you are mine, Leander, all mine! Nothing to come between us more. Thank God!"

I clasped her hand silently, and it was like a second sealing of our marriage vows.

"Leander," said Mark, as we were parting for the night, "I know your grandfather is a zealous Mason. What does he say about this affair of Morgan's?"

"Very little; but I think you will find it hard to convince him that Morgan is not alive and safe somewhere in Canada," I answered. For the fact was, my grandfather, though hitherto the most easy and good natured of beings, had developed of late such a strange testiness in regard to this one particular subject, that

I hardly knew what to think of him. He refused to listen to the least hint of any suspicion on my part that Morgan might have possibly fallen a victim to Masonic vengeance. "Don't talk nonsense to me, Leander," was his invariable way of disposing of the subject, and after a few attempts I finally shut my mouth and talked no more of the objectionable "nonsense."

The next morning we went over to see him. There had been a sharp frost during the night and my grandfather, who suffered much with rheumatism, and felt keenly the sudden oncoming of cold weather, we found seated in the kitchen—which no one *au-fait* in the domestic economy of those primitive days will need to be informed was, in ordinary cases, the family sitting room—enjoying the warmth of the bright fire blazing in the huge fire-place. He shook hands heartily with Mark, and the latter after replying to sundry surprised exclamations and inquiries from my mother and Miss Loker, took a seat beside him and quietly told the awful tidings.

But contrary to all my expectation there was no impatient outburst of disbelief on my grandfather's part. He sat for a moment not speaking a word, his head bowed and his eyes fixed on the floor.

"I can bring proof, if that is necessary," said Mark, who felt as I did, at a loss to interpret his silence.

"Proof! I want no proof." And my grandfather rose up, tall, straight as in the days of his youth; and taking off the glistening Masonic badge that he had worn for so many years, he walked up to the fire blazing on the hearth and deliberately flung it into the flames, while my mother and Miss Loker looked on, amazed.

"I want no proof," he repeated. "It is all there—in the Entered Apprentice oath. Fool that I was never to see it before!"

And tottering back to his chair, the excitement over, my grandfather bowed his gray head and wept.

CHAPTER XXIII.

AN EVENING IN THE LODGE.

THOUGH Captain Morgan's fate was by no means definitely settled in the popular mind, the suspicion grew stronger day by day that he had been foully dealt with; and the low-muttered ground-swell of that coming whirlwind of indignation which was to lay low every lodge and Chapter in the land, had already begun to make itself heard in the ears of the startled fraternity. As a result, a special meeting of Brownsville lodge was soon called—about a week after Mark's unexpected home-coming. To this meeting the latter announced decidedly his determination to go.

"For pity's sake, Mark! What for?" I asked in surprise. "I should think you might have had enough of their confounded foolery by this time. I don't care if they summon me fifty times over; I am not going."

"Nor would I, Leander, were it not that I feel called of the Lord to bear my testimony against the abominable wickedness of Captain Morgan's abduction and murder. It is like a fire shut up in my bones night and day. And what better place than right here in

Brownsville lodge, among friends and acquaintances, to stand up and testify?"

Now this "testifying" spirit in Mark had already begun to make me uneasy, with the fear of what might follow if allowed to have its way unchecked by a little prudent advice, which I accordingly proceeded to administer.

"O, come, Mark; it won't do the least bit of good. You'll only stir up a hornet's nest about your ears. And as to their being old friends and neighbors in Brownsville lodge, you know precious little of human nature if you think it will make any difference with their reception of what you have to say. They will only be ten times more bitter and abusive on that very account."

All of which was hard matter-of-fact truth, but it failed to move Mark an iota. The Lord had given him a message to speak in the ears of the lodge that would probably make them tingle; that would alienate some and anger others; but of all such merely human considerations he felt that sublime carelessness which belongs to intense conviction. For wonderfully had Mark advanced in spiritual life since his soul burst the lodge fetters, and soared at one glad, exultant bound, into the full liberty of a child of God.

"Let them abuse me if they will!" he answered, his eyes kindling. "I shall go and bear my testimony. I know there are some in the lodge who will hear me."

"Now, Mark." said I, "I'll tell you just the way this matter stands. Brownsville lodge has its disaffected members who believe that Morgan has been foully murdered, and detest the crime; who feel just as I have felt many a night when I have been to the meetings of the lodge, glad from the very bottom of my heart to have seen the whole abominable thing blown sky high the next day. But the mischief is, there won't be a soul of them there to-night. They are ashamed of their connection with Masonry, but are afraid to come into open collision with it. And the consequence is all such ones will stay at home just as I was intending to do, and only the part that are bound to stand by the institution through thick and thin will be there to hear you."

But none of these things moved Mark. He rose with quiet determination and proceeded to put on his coat and hat, saying as he did so—

"Anyhow I'm going. It is the only way I can free my mind and conscience. Silent withdrawal from the lodge is not enough. There must be a testifying; and whether they will hear or whether they will forbear is none of my concern."

"Well, old boy," said I, as his finger was on the last button, "it's no use talking, I see, so I may as well make up my mind to go along with you. I'm no hand to make speeches myself, but I should be sorry to lose your's. And if I am not mistaken you'll need a friend to back you up and see that you have fair play before you get through. But I must tell Rachel that I am going." Accordingly I stepped to the door of the buttery where she was busied in some household avocation, and said—

"Rachel, you told me once that you could imagine circumstances that might make it my duty to go to the lodge. Now nothing will satisfy Mark's conscience unless he goes and 'testifies,' as he calls it. Shall I go with him or stay at home? What do you say?"

Rachel covered up the batter she had been setting to rise over night, and was silent for an instant. Then with a look which I told her afterwards was quite Deborah-like, she answered—

"Leander, I never wanted you to go to the lodge before, but I say now, to you and Mark both, fear God rather than man. Go, and do your duty."

And thus strengthened for the fight as only the strong, brave words of a true woman can strengthen a man, Mark and I went forth to find the brethren assembled ready for business as soon as the usual preliminaries should be gone through with. Which preliminaries, for the enlightenment of the un-Masonic reader, I will state consisted in calling up the lodge by three distinct knocks of the Master's gavel, and a series of catechetical questions and answers between the latter and the two principal officers of the lodge in which might have been learned several instructive facts —for instance, that "his obligation makes a Mason;" "that the Junior Warden stands in the south like the sun at high meridian, the beauty and glory of the day;" "that the Senior Warden stands in the west like that same luminary at its close;" "and as the sun rises in the east to open and adorn the day, so presides the Worshipful Master in the east to open and adorn his lodge"—allusions which Mark had said were clear proofs that Masonry was identical with ancient sun worship[28] practiced among the natives of antiquity under the name of the mysteries of Baal among the Jews and Canaanites, of Osiris among the Egyptians, and Eleusis among the Greeks. [See note 19.] Then came a prayer to the unknown god of the lodge, the Great Architect of the Universe; at which some bowed their heads decorously,

---

NOTE 28.—"The identity of the Masonic Institution with the Ancient Mysteries is obvious from the striking coincidencies found to exist between them. The latter were a secret religious worship, and the depository of religion, science and art."—*Pierson's Traditions*, p. 13.

while others assumed all those curious varieties of attitudes congenial to the undevotional mind—Mark himself sitting like a statue, his **arms** grimly folded, his eyes looking straight before him, and on his face such an expression of silent scorn and contempt as Elijah's might **have had** when listening to the prayers of Baal's prophets. **And** the lodge was declared open for the regular dispatch of business.

First in order came the reading of the minutes of the last meeting by the Secretary, which as it of course included Elder Cushing's report, naturally brought up **the** business of the present hour—what should be said **and d**one in relation to the widespread excitement about Captain Morgan's fate?

Deacon Brown was the first **one** who took the floor, **and his** views, **as** stated to the lodge, amounted in substance to this: "Let it alone and it would die down of **itself.** Our ancient institution had always been subject to the malice and hate of ill-wishers who did all they could **to impose** on the ignorant and bring the craft into disrepute. In his opinion the wisest policy for all Freemasons at this critical juncture was to preserve a discreet silence, remembering that a silent tongue was always and everywhere the chief jewel of **faithful Masons**."

Another old and respected member of the lodge then **rose:** "He was sorry to differ, even slightly, with the Deacon, but would like to express his view of the **case.** Morgan had forfeited his life by attempting to expose **the** secrets of Masonry, **but** whether or not the penalty **of his** violated oath had actually been visited upon him, there was one unanswerable answer **for** those who would charge his death upon the lodge. *Where was the proof?*"

Mark was on his feet in an instant, and a flattering hush of attention succeeded. For the lodge was inclined to take some pride in Mark Stedman as a rising young man of talent and worth, and a high Mason besides; and as his change of opinion had not yet become known, young and old prepared to give respectful heed to whatever he might say.

"I have proof, positive proof," he began, speaking with calm, deliberate utterance, "that Captain Morgan of Batavia was murdered somewhere about the 19th or 20th of September, by being drowned in Niagara River. This proof I am prepared to furnish to any brother in the lodge who may not feel satisfied in his own mind that so great a crime has actually been committed. But for the majority of the members now present I believe that no such proof is necessary. Lodges and Chapters through this entire section of country, in conjunction with the Grand Lodge and Grand Chapter of the State, have planned and plotted—not as distinct bodies, but in groups lyingly termed committees, in reality conspirators—the murder of Morgan and Miller. Miller has escaped, but the blood of Morgan is on the heads of the entire Masonic fraternity; and he who seeks to cover up this unholy work instead of exposing and denouncing it, but lays up vengeance for himself against the great day of final doom."

Up to this point Mark had been listened to in perfect silence, but it was a stupified silence. He had taken the lodge completely by surprise—the more so as his calm, slow utterance had at first acted as a partial disguise to the scathing denunciation contained in his words. But as his meaning fairly broke on the startled assembly, looks of contempt and anger took the place of satisfied complacency, and murmurs which broke at last into audible hissing, filled the hall. Mark had roused the lodge dragon. My prediction made before starting had been fulfilled with disagreeable exactness. What a comfort the mere sight of Luke Thatcher's honest face would have been in that sea of scornful, contemptuous looks!

Elder Cushing and one or two other members tried to quiet the disturbance, and so far succeeded that when Mark again rose to speak in response to a call half in earnest, half derision, for his proofs of Morgan's murder, there was quite a profound silence.

"If I should bring forward my whole array of evidence, beginning with the first intimations that I received of the conspiracy against the life of Morgan last August, and the numerous conversations held with Masons on the subject who both acknowledged and justified his murder, I should trespass on the time of the lodge. My proof is nearer home. Sheriff Fox"—and Mark leaned forward with a look that was swordlike in its keenness—"you, a minister of the law whose business it is to punish the guilty and shield the innocent, you have helped forward this work of blood. Deacon Brown, you have done the same. And must it be said that against you, Elder Cushing, I have the same damning charge to bring? God knows that as my pastor I have loved and revered you; that I have been sincerely grateful for all your many kindnesses to me, but though every word I speak is like an arrow in my heart, God's truth must be uttered without respect of persons. On the night of the 14th of September there was held in Lewiston an installation of the Royal

Arch Chapter. That meeting decided Morgan's fate. You were present and consenting to his death."

There was something in Mark's face and voice that seemed for an instant to awe the lodge. Even Darius Fox was content with silently looking his rage and defiance, while Deacon Brown, a kindly, well-meaning old man till his fanatical devotion to Masonry made him a murderer, fairly cowered in his seat. Elder Cushing flushed almost purple, but he rose to reply.

"Some allowance must be made for the rashness and presumption of youth. Brother Stedman in thus venturing to accuse his elders and superiors in the lodge shows his ignorance of the very first principle of Masonic law: unquestioning obedience and the swift execution of its penalties when violated. Masonry has its system of laws and the right to punish their infringement as much as the State or the Church. And what crime more detestable than treason? To what government under heaven can you point, however humane or enlightened, which does not punish it with death? Morgan was a traitor to his Masonic vows, and if he has died the death of a traitor, if his throat has been cut from ear to ear, his tongue torn out by the roots and his body buried beneath the rough sands of the sea where the tide ebbs and flows twice in twenty-four hours, he could not complain of not having justice done him."

"Amen. Amen. So mote it be;" was the response all through the room to the Elder's speech. Mark took in the scene with eyes in which a deeper fire was slowly kindling, and when he once more rose to speak his voice was low and solemn as with a prophetic burden of approaching doom.

'Because ye have said, we have made a covenant with death and with hell are we at agreement; when the overflowing scourge shall pass through it shall not come nigh unto us, for we have made lies our refuge and under falsehood have we hid ourselves. Therefore thus saith the Lord: Your covenant with death shall be disannulled, and your agreement with hell shall not stand; when the overflowing scourge shall pass through then ye shall be trodden down by it.' From this unholy institution whose authority is based on deception and terror, whose morality is a lie, whose laws are murderous, whose oaths are high-handed blasphemy, I withdraw forever. God shall yet judge her, and if there be among you, as I would fain believe, some who do abhor and detest this great crime which has been committed, I call upon all such to stand up and unite their testimony with mine against it, that they be not partakers in her doom."

I had sat in silence fairly appalled at Mark's daring till now, but true courage is always contagious, and amid the storm of hissings, hootings, cries of "traitor," and threats to send him after Morgan, which interrupted his speech, with one thought of Rachel I rose and stood beside him. But no one else stirred in the lodge. It was an awful moment. Neighbors, friends, with whom we had held pleasant social intercourse all our lives, glaring upon us with looks of scorn and hate, abusive epithets hurled at us from lips that heretofore had never anything but kindly greetings! At this moment I can shut my eyes and see it all, then open them shuddering as if from a dream of hell. But Mark stood unmoved, brave as a lion; and when a slight lull in the clamor allowed his words to be heard he again spoke:

"Threaten us if you will; carry out those threats if you dare; but remember that there may be consequences you will not care to face. I have spoken freely against the principles of this institution. I believe it to be anti-Christian and a dangerous foe to our republican government. For holding and expressing these opinions you murdered Morgan; but I shall not be deterred by his fate from holding and expressing them too. Freedom of opinion, the liberty of the press and the right of free speech I will never surrender to the bidding of any earthly power. They are rights given to me of God, purchased by the blood of my fathers; I inhaled them with my first breath—I will only lose them with my last. Remove my objections to Masonry if you can, when these very threats you utter against me to-night prove their truth as no mere assertion of mine can possibly do. But till then, as I said before, I withdraw from all connection with the institution, and disavow every obligation taken in blindness and terror. I bow no longer at an altar defiled with human blood; I own no High Priest save him who has passed into the heavens; and no Worshipful Master but Jesus Christ my Lord."

Mark had said his say; the lodge had not. For two or three hours the stream of invective and abuse continued to flow, and then the meeting broke up after certainly one of the stormiest and most exciting sessions Brownsville lodge had ever known.

CHAPTER XXIV.

FREEMASONRY'S MASK REMOVED.—SILENT ANTI-MASONS.
—THE CIRCUIT PREACHER.—RACHEL FINDS
"PEACE."—HE GIVETH HIS
BELOVED SLEEP.

IN spite of the lateness of the hour Rachel was sitting up waiting for us, and as soon as she heard our footsteps, flew to open the door and light us in, the candle which she carried revealing mingled anxiety and relief in her countenance. Mark noticed it.

"We have been in a den of lions, Rachel." he said, "but we have come back safe. God has shut their mouths; we have received no harm."

"Shut their mouths for the present," said I, rather skeptically; "but I tell you, Mark, if you keep on the rig you are running now there is no saying what the consequences may be. The fact is public opinion in this matter of Morgan is beginning to press so hard on the lodge that it is just like a wounded wild bull—ready to plunge its horns into everybody rash enough to stand in its way. What they have done to one man they will do to another, if they dare. That's all the question there is about it."

"I don't think my life is in any present peril," answered Mark; "nor do I intend to rashly endanger it. Half the battle is in taking a bold stand at the outset. They can expel me, 'derange my worldly interests,' 'point me out as an unworthy vagabond, and transfer my character after me wherever I go.' This I expect. But I have counted the cost. You see it is an easy thing for me to do who have only myself to count it with. But it is different with you, Leander. You, who stood up with me like a rock to-night against all the fury and abuse of the lodge, must count it over with another dearer than yourself. What do you say, Rachel?"

"That the cost shall never be made more through any selfish shrinking on my part," answered Rachel, with glowing cheek and sparkling eye. "Do you think that I will not help Leander bear all the persecution and reproach that may come upon him—loss of property, anything—if I can only have my husband back again, none of these terrible lodge secrets between us? O, Mark!" and Rachel's voice choked and her eyes overflowed.

I wonder how many Mason's wives have thought the same in the solitude of their lonely vigils, bitter of soul against the institution that robs them of the true wife's most precious treasure—the entire confidence of her husband!

To my grandfather it seemed as if the murder of Morgan, revealing as by a lightning flash the hellish spirit of the institution, to which, like many another honest Mason he had rendered a blind fealty only next to that he gave his God, was like a blow at his own vitals. He lost much of his old loquacity and cheerfulness, and as the cold weather set in he grew feebler, but he said little—only once when he asked my forgiveness—my dear, blessed old grandfather—for having persuaded me into the lodge.

"I never thought I was advising you for your harm, Leander," he said, pathetically; "but you see I became a Mason when I was a young man, just before I sailed on my first long voyage. And the way it happened, Dr. Damon stopped at our house one day when mother was fixing me off. He was a great man in our part— Dr. Damon was. So mother bustled round and set out the decanter and sugar and hot water; and he stirred and sipped while she was telling how bad she felt to have me go off to the ends of the earth on a three years' voyage. I remember just how the Doctor looked. He was a handsome old gentleman with silver knee buckles and a great flowing wig, and just as stately and polite in his way of speaking, especially to women, as if he had been brought up at Court. 'Madam,' said he, 'your son ought to become a Freemason. I may say that I have heard of numerous well attested cases where inability to give the Masonic sign has cost a man his life. But I would not wish to be understood as referring entirely to its advantages in times of peril. Admirably as you have trained your son he needs the moral safeguard which joining such an institution will throw about him, and I trust, my dear Madam, that you will use all your maternal influence to induce him to take this step before he sails.' Well, mother—poor dear soul—believed what Dr. Damon said. Why shouldn't she? And so after he had gone she pondered it over for a while, and then she said to me, 'Well, David, my son, perhaps you *had* better do as the Doctor says. It is because sailors are subject to such dreadful temptations that I worry about you so. There is nothing in the world that I want so much as to see you a Christian, for then no matter what happened to you, if you were shipwrecked or taken by pirates, I should know you were all right for the other world. Next to that I want to see you possessed of principles so strong that they will resist all temptation. A young man can have these and not be a Christian, but he can't have them and be far from the kingdom. So if becoming a Mason will help you to be more steady and moral and upright, why I want you to join them.' That was enough for me. I thought a good deal of my mother. Well, when I came to join, it was all as different as could be from what I expected. The oaths and penalties shocked me, but the charges and lectures all had such a good moral and religious sound to them that they helped to quiet my mind a good deal, and I never let mother know that I wasn't perfectly satisfied with it. When I came back from my first voyage she was dead. I only stayed at home a few weeks and then I was off again. It was on my second voyage that I experienced religion—you've heard me tell about it, Leander. It was one awful night when a typhoon had struck our ship, and every man of us seemed booked for destruction. I kept thinking of mother, and how unfit I was to join her in the other world. I could see her just as she used to look going about her work and singing, 'When I survey the wondrous cross.' Why in all that awful noise of wind and water, and the crash of falling masts and parting timbers, I could seem to hear her voice, and it was just like an angel's telling me to repent of my sins and flee to Christ for refuge. Masonry didn't help me much then. It was Christ alone that I wanted. Well, of course between my voyages there wasn't much time to attend the lodge, and when I give up the sea and settled down to a landsman's life I had got out of the way of going at all. But I reverenced the institution. I thought it must be good and according to the Bible, or else ministers and deacons wouldn't uphold and support it. My objections to the ceremonies and obligations I reasoned away—you know how, Leander—till I really saw nothing in them inconsistent with my Christian profession. I thought it was a divine institution that could neither do nor teach anything wrong, till the murder of Morgan opened my eyes. Mark Stedman told me no news. I was already convinced in my own mind that Morgan had been killed, but I fought against the conviction; I wasn't willing to acknowledge it till Deacon Brown, in private conversation with me, justified his murder—only the day before Mark came home. Then I knew that the whole system was of him who was a murderer from the beginning. God deliver me from the stain of blood-guiltiness in this matter."

My grandfather leaned back exhausted in his chair, and I realized with sudden pain how pale and feeble he had grown.

Now one word with that large and respectable class of readers who "can't believe that Masonry is such a very bad thing after all when so many good men belong to it." It is true there are good men in the Masonic order. Remembering my grandfather's spotless life, his spirit of universal kindliness to all created things, his humble conscientious performance of every known duty, God forbid that I should deny it. But if we once admit the sophism that a system must be good because good men support it, where will it land us? Shall I tell you where, dear, intelligent Christian reader? Into the days when so many good people believed religiously in hanging witches, and if pressed hard for a reason for the faith that was in them could have given chapter and verse in support of their sanguinary creed with refreshing promptitude; into the days when good Christian judges believed that the prison, the scourge and the pillory were means of grace for enlightening the blind consciences of heretic Quakers; into the days when so many good people, North and South, upheld the system of human slavery, and wished reformers would stop all this disagreeable agitation, all this unpleasant talk about " coining the heart's blood of the oppressed—it was so much better to let disagreeable subjects alone!" O my Christian brother, O my Christian sister, shame not the thinking mind and noble heart God has given you by any such fallacious reasoning! Accept like honest men and women this one square issue. Either Masonry is right or it is wrong. Either it is a false religion or the true one—a worship of God or a worship of devils. Is indifference to it compatible with loyalty to Christ? Can you be truly his yet care not whether he reigns over the world or anti-Christ? There are good men in the lodge—poor, hoodwinked, cable-towed victims—Sampson-like shorn of their strength, and made to grind in the prison-house of a secret, oath-bound organization. But these good men would come out of it by scores and by hundreds, walking open-eyed and unfettered in the full strength of their Christian manhood, if you bore your faithful testimony against it; if you refuse to fellowship Masonry in your churches or tolerate Masonic pastors in your pulpits.

Which reminds me that I have another word to say to a certain class of Christian ministers "who never were Masons, and don't believe in secret societies."

"My dear sir, I am glad to know that you have such decided views of the evils of secretism. Of course you sometimes preach on this subject from the pulpit?"

"O, no. In fact it wouldn't do. I have two or three Masons in my church and quite a sprinkling of Oddfellows and other secret society men, and I should only stir up a rumpus and perhaps split the church. Besides I am set to preach the gospel, not Masonry or Anti-masonry."

"But Christ preached against the corrupt doctrines of the Scribes and Pharisees. St. Paul preached against idolatry, Luther against the sale of indulgences. Didn't Christ and Paul and Luther preach the gospel? And you yourself, if I am not greatly mistaken, have been known to allude more than once in your pulpit discourses to the sin of intemperance."

"Ah, well, that is a safe subject. It can't stir up strife nor hurt my influence as a public discussion of Masonry would be sure to do. A pastor must be careful not to give unnecessary offence, and so hurt the cause of Christ. I trust you understand me."

"My dear sir, I understand you perfectly. A certain old Hebrew prophet and reformer who was never afraid of hurting his influence by denouncing popular sins, has well described what the cowardly, time-serving pastor, too fearful of his bread and butter interests to wage any warfare against those same unpopular sins does *not* do. 'Ye have not gone up into the gaps, neither made up the hedge for the house of Israel to stand in the battle in the day of the Lord.' Shame on such hireling shepherds 'who daub the walls of Zion with untempered mortar!' It may be more tolerable in the day of Judgment for men like Elder Cushing, who, blinded by their fanatical zeal for the lodge, committed the sin of Cain, than for you who acknowledge Masonry to be an evil yet will not lift up your voice when you see the sword coming."

Mark Stedman, since his renunciation of the lodge, had gone contentedly back to the most common drudgery of the farm, but that strange peace and joy which he had so vainly sought in the puerile traditions of men overflowed his soul like a river when all the windows of heaven are opened, and bank and dyke are powerless to keep in the swelling waters. And it was no surprise to us when a proposal came to him to preach. Mark after thinking and praying over it for one whole day as he chopped the wood and fed the cattle, chose his life work—to be a poor circuit preacher not always knowing where his daily bread should come from; and only sure of two things: poverty and the contempt of the world, on all whose honors and preferments he was now turning his back.

But poor Rachel seemed to profit but little from the spiritual help Mark was so eager to proffer her. There sometimes are souls that in their vain struggles after spiritual light and liberty are like birds that fly into a room and beat blindly against the windows when all the while the door stands open. The kindest endeavors to help them find their way out only adds to their bewilderment.

I have already mentioned that a peculiar attachment

existed between my grandfather and Rachel. One day she was sitting by his side. His great print Bible lay open on his knee, but he was not reading. With spectacles pushed back he was gazing fondly on the tiny two-month's-old who represented his name and line in the fourth generation, but whose advent I have hitherto neglected to chronicle.

"I don't know, Rachel, as you ought to have given him my name," he said, finally. "David is so old-fashioned. You might have found one prettier."

"I don't care for that," answered Rachel, promptly. "I want my boy to bear the name of a good man and grow up like him. And I always fancied David. There is something so strong and brave in the sound. Who knows what Goliath my boy may have to fight when he grows up."

"That is true," said my grandfather, gently.

"And I want to train him right," continued Rachel. "I am afraid I shall make mistakes. If I was only a Christian I should know how."

"But, Rachel, why ain't you one?" asked my grandfather. "There is Mark, now; I never saw anything like the boy. It almost seems as if he had seen the Lord face to face just to hear him get up and pray."

"Mark is so different from me. He could always understand and enjoy things in books that I never could. And it is just so in religion. When he talks to me I feel as though he was standing on a ladder of sunbeams and calling to me to come up. I see no earthly way of getting to the top. Now Leander and I would understand each other better I think, but there is another thing. When Leander went to the lodge that seemed to shut us off from talking about religion to each other. It seemed as if he was seeking salvation one way and I another. So the wall kept growing higher. I've seen the same thing in other women. They go to the prayer-meeting and their husbands go to the lodge. How can they sit down together and talk of their spiritual interests? But I don't want to blame Leander; he never meant to make it any harder for me. And if I had been the right sort of woman I never should have let such a little thing hinder me. But it must be I am not one of the elect. If I was I should have been a Christian before this."

And poor Rachel, who felt that Mark's call to the ministry was only another proof that the same inscrutable will, which had made him a chosen vessel of grace, had only doomed her to be an heir of destruction, sighed as if the end of the matter was reached.

"Rachel," answered my grandfather, seriously, "I am a poor, unprofitable servant, not fit to teach the way of life to anybody; but my Bible tells me that the blood of Jesus Christ cleanseth from all sin, and I believe what it says. Now the way I feel about Mark is that the Lord is separating him to a special work, and that is why he is filling him so full of grace beforehand. He'll need it all before he gets through. But the free gift is for you and me just as much as for Mark. God makes his sun and rain to come down as freely on a blade of grass as on the tallest oak. And so I take this gift—this unspeakable gift, just as I take my daily bread, without asking any questions whether I'm elected or not. I do as David did. I take the cup of salvation and call on the name of the Lord. O it's just wonderful, this free gift to poor sinners like you and me, Rachel!"

Rachel had listened with a new light dawning in her eyes which finally spread all over her face like the sun new risen.

"I'll try your way." she said, slowly. "Somehow it seems common sense. I can understand it."

And then she put on her shawl and bonnet, kissed my grandfather and tripped home. But that night she sang snatches of hymns over her baby's cradle; she sang when she was getting tea and moulding biscuit; and the light did not leave her face. It never has left it, it never will; for it was the peace which passeth all understanding.

In the hours of the early morning between two and three there came a knock at our door. It was Joe.

"Come over, quick, Leander." he said, "*Grandfather is dying!*"

Quickly as Rachel and I obeyed the summons Joe's words were all too true. The shadowing presence of the dark angel had gone before us and filled all the hushed silent room as we entered it.

He lay breathing heavily, but smiled on us both, though it was on Rachel that his eyes slowly filming over with the mist of death, rested with the tenderest, longest gaze.

His lips moved as she knelt weeping by the bedside, and we just caught the low accents—Huldah. It was the name borne by the beloved wife of his youth, and in that hour of near reunion, with the shores of time fading away, and all the eternal realities of the unseen world ready to burst on his vision, he blended the sight of one with the memory of the other.

Joe had gone for the doctor. But his face when he came inspired us with no hope. He asked a few questions, then took a seat in silence as powerless as any of us in the dread presence of death.

The sun was rising when my grandfather passed away. He had been lying very quiet. Then all at once a strange rapt look came into his face. Who did he see, in that last solemn moment when the veil was rending which hid all that wonder of gold and jasper and emerald, of white-robed multitudes and harping choirs from his view?

"Who shall separate us? Who shall separate us?" he whispered. And then a few deep breaths, and my grandfather was where in truth nothing should or could separate him from his Lord and Savior. No lodge with its man-made traditions, its false worship, its anti-Christian rites, to come between and make his love wax cold. As a bird from the snare of the fowler he had escaped—into the free, immortal air of heaven.

* * * * * * *

"Leander," said Mark, as we stood looking sadly down on the dear, familiar face settled to its last long sleep, "I can't help feeling glad that he is now out of the reach of slander and persecution. The lodge would no more have spared his gray hairs, after he had renounced it than it will spare us. But we are young and strong for the conflict, while he was old and feeble, and it would have broken his heart."

I could not speak for tears, but I knew that Mark was right. My grandfather had been taken from the warfare that was even then beginning; a slow, insidious, wearing warfare—that would only end when we laid our armor down forever.

CHAPTER XXV.

MOVING.—THE MASONIC "OBLIGATION" REMOVED.—THE WARFARE BEGINS.

HOW we missed him! how hard it was to keep on missing him every day!—but over our loss, as over every other void that death makes, flowed the cold, remorseless tide of plans and purposes for the morrow. Miss Loker had received a pressing call from a lately widowed brother to come and keep his house for him; and my mother, in her invalid state of health, was only too glad to resign all her household cares into Rachel's hands, while I took my grandfather's place as head of the family. So Rachel and I prepared to move from the little home he had built and furnished for us with such loving care scarcely more than a year before, thinking, doubtless, as we ourselves believed and hoped, that with his hale, hearty frame, a long, green old age might yet lay before him.

"He took such pleasure in planning it for us," said Rachel, tearfully. "Even that end window he had put in just because I happened to say that I always wanted a kitchen to have the morning sun. How I wish Joe might live here some day."

"Joe isn't one of the stay-at-home sort. By the time he is twenty-one he'll be striking out for himself in Kentucky or Illinois."

"Then Mark, perhaps, if he should ever get married—and I suppose he will some time."

But any thought of marriage seemed at present far from Mark's head, which I privately considered was a lucky thing, for while I cherished the most profound respect for his talents and learning, I had an equally small regard for Mark's abilities in any such practical line of effort as the supporting of a family. And I only smiled at Rachel's last suggestion.

So in that immutable order of things which has ever been and ever will be while the human generations come and go, new hopes blossomed where the old had perished, and one morning when the snow lay thick and white over my grandfather's grave I took his place and conducted with faltering voice the family worship.

Rachel had told me the whole of that last conversation with my grandfather, keeping nothing back. The gentle Quakeress had uttered no false warning. Unwittingly I had put a stumbling block in the way of Rachel's salvation. Instead of joining her in her search after Him who is not far from any one of us I had tried to satisfy my conscience with the Christless prayers and rites of the lodge. But now we were indeed and in truth one—fellow pilgrims together through a troublous world, and heirs of the same blessed hope: a far more eternal and exceeding weight of glory when we both should pass to an immortal reunion beyond the veil.

But I was not yet entirely free from the lodge fetters. Like Mr. Jedediah Mills, I considered that "an oath was an oath" under all circumstances, and any violation thereof a crime "to be punished by the judges." It was Rachel, who, with her clearer understanding of Scripture truth, gave the blow that finally knocked apart those shackling obligations too fully and completely for any earthly power ever to clench again.

"Leander," she said suddenly to me one day, "I thought at first it was a dreadful thing for Captain Morgan to break his oath. But I have begun to think differently. Now listen while I read this verse in Leviticus, fifth chapter, fourth verse: 'If a soul swear, pronouncing with his lips to do evil or to do good, whatsoever it be that a man shall pronounce with an oath, and it be hid from him, when he knoweth of it, then he shall be guilty in one of these. Then it goes on to tell how he must bring a trespass offering for his sin. Now if there was any provision made under the old dispensation for rash and foolish oaths there must be under the new. Masons don't know what they are swearing to when they take these obligations, or in ninety-nine cases out of one hundred they wouldn't take them at all. It is hid from them."

"But, Rachel," I said, doubtfully. "are you sure that is what the verse means?"

"Well, if you don't believe me, come and read Bagster's explanation of it: 'This relates to rash oaths or vows which a man was afterwards unable, or which it would have been sinful to perform.' I hope you don't doubt Bagster. There now," continued Rachel, triumphantly; "what can be clearer? Shall a Christian keep a wicked oath that wouldn't have been binding even on a Jew?"

I did not reply at once, for I was reading the verses

that followed. How graciously that old Levitical law stooped to the necessities of the poorest. "He shall bring his trespass offering unto the Lord, a lamb or a kid of the goats * * * or if he be not able to bring a lamb then he shall bring for his trespass which he hath committed two turtle doves or two young pigeons * * * but if he be not able to bring two turtle doves or two young pigeons, then he that hath sinned shall bring for his offering the tenth part of an ephah of fine flour." Should the blood of God's eternal Son be of less efficacy to purge my conscience from the guilt of these rash, blasphemous Masonic vows? To this day I feel the thrill of recovered freedom that tingled through every vein when I read that old Jewish law, and realized that once more I was a *man,* no longer a cowering, shivering, faltering slave, bound with the self-forged manacles of a lodge oath.

Just then Mark Stedman came in. There are some natures that the first bugle note of any great moral conflict seem to rouse instantly to action. Like the war horse of Scripture, pawing in the valleys and rejoicing in his strength, they smell the battle afar off and say, ha! ha! to the sound of the trumpet. And Mark Stedman belonged to this class of minds, predestinated by their very constitution to fill the ranks of the world's martyr's and reformers.

"I have been subpœnaed to appear at the next sitting of the county court to tell what I know about the murder of Morgan," he said, as he stood warming his hands at the fire. "I shall start early to-morrow morning. It really looks now as if the courts were going to take up the matter vigorously; and if so they can't help finding bills of indictment against some of the leading actors in this outrageous business."

"But what is the use of indicting if they don't convict? I wouldn't snap my finger for any chance of conviction with a Masonic jury to sit on the case. And what else can you expect but a packed jury when the sheriff who summons it is a Mason? Depend upon it the Masonic institution will shield Morgan's murderers to the uttermost. I am not enough of a prophet to say what the final outcome will be, but I am sure that law will be evaded and justice hampered in every conceivable way to clear the guilty parties."

"I know that," answered Mark, "but I believe in the final triumph of right."

"So do I—when there comes that grand general settling up in the other world," I returned. "By the way I saw a newspaper paragraph the other day which convinced me that the father of lies was busy at his usual occupation. It reported that Captain Morgan had been seen by a lately returned sailor in the streets of Smyrna, disguised as a Turk."

"As though anybody would be fool enough to believe such a silly falsehood!" said Mark, indignantly.

"There'll be plenty to believe it. Falsehood is the chief engine of the lodge. But here comes Joe with a letter—for you, Mark."

Mark tore open the epistle, gave a brief glance at the contents and then handed it to me with a smile on his grave, resolute young face.

"You see the fight has begun, Leander."

It was a wretched scrawl—for the writer had evidently tried to disguise his hand—threatening Mark in scurrilous and abusive terms and ending thus: "I know four Royal Arch Masons who stand ready to despatch you as a traitor against the most heavenly and beneficent institution on earth. ONE OF THE FOUR."

"Quite an interesting communication, isn't it?" said Mark, coolly; "but not the first I have received of like nature."

"Mark, you must go armed. You ought to carry pistols."

"No, Leander. I have thought it over, but the servant of the Lord must not strive. Shall I rely on an arm of flesh when Jehovah himself has promised to be my shield? Besides, men who will take the time and pains to write anonymous threats are usually too cowardly to dare do anything more. Nothing troubles me about these letters but the postage on them. It is rather too bad to have to pay for the privilege of receiving personal abuse."

"Mark," said I, finally, "You are not going to start on this journey, short as it is, alone. I shall tell Rachel that I really want to hear the proceedings of the court, which is the truth. And having none of your conscientious scruples about the use of carnal weapons, I mean to go armed to the teeth. If anybody meddles with us it won't be for their health."

Mark demurred, but my mind was made up. I took Joe into confidence, however, for since our grandfather's death there had been a wonderful change in the lad. The maturity and steadiness of manhood was fast replacing his boyish thoughtlessness and mischief, and I knew I could trust him not only to keep the alarm I felt from Rachel, but to manage matters during my brief absence. So that everything was in readiness for my early departure with Mark the next morning, when just as the candle was beginning to burn low in the socket, and the great kitchen clock stood on the stroke of nine, there was a rap at the door. As I opened it, to my inexpressible surprise the light fell full on the familiar features of Sam Toller.

"Why, Sam!" I exclaimed. "Come right in. How do you happen to be in Brownsville?"

"Wall, I'm on kinder pressin' business," said Sam, as with weary, foot-sore tread he followed me into the kitchen. "I've walked a'most from Rochester to let ye know about it. The Masons have laid a plan to kidnap Mark Stedman on his way to court so as to stop his giving testimony."

"How did you find out about it, Sam?" I asked, after a moment's silence.

"Wall, ye see the way of it was I overheard accidentally enough of their talk to make me suspicion that they were up to some mischief. So I jest steps up to 'em and gives 'em the sign, and sez I, 'I'm yer man, ready to do anything ye set me to; ready to shed my last drop of blood in defence of the glorious institution of Masonry!' And after I had made 'em think by talking in that way awhile they could make a tool of me easy, I found out what they were up to. Their plans are all cut and dried. There's a lonesome part of the road, jest the other side of Savin's Bend where he'll have to walk a piece if he goes by stage, and they calkerlate to waylay him there. They'll all have masks on, so it can never be known who they be. Wall, I spoke up and sez, 'Gentlemen, I can help ye in this ere business. I know Mark Stedman and he knows me; and I can make him play into yer hands as easy as a woodchuck walks into a trap.' So they kinder debated over it awhile, and then the leader sez to me, 'The d——d villain's mouth has got to be stopped. We'll pay you fair for the job if you undertake it!' So we struck a bargain, and then the whole party of us went to the tavern to get a drink, and while they were treating each other, I contrived it to slip off by saying I had got to see to the horses. So here I be. Now what's to be done about it."

"Sam, you're a good fellow, worth your weight in gold," said I, shaking his hand with a fervor of gratitude, as I realized how narrow had been Mark's escape. "But I don't want Rachel to know anything about this at present. And Mark need not be told of it till morning. Then we can take counsel together. Do you think any of the Brownsville lodge are in the plot?"

"I don't want to name names when I ain't sartin," answered Sam, cautiously. "Them that's got the job on hand don't belong in Brownsville. But I tell ye, Leander, Masonry is as full of long arms as that devil-fish Tim Kendall was telling about seeing when he was off on his cruise. They keep swaying about ready to clutch ye, and once get a hold they never let go. The only way to do when they grapple a man is to chop off its arms and leave a part of the critter sticking to the flesh."

Rachel just then entered with that smile on her face which only mothers wear when they come from bending over the rosy leep of their first born. Our little David was growing finely, a bright, healthy babe, and we were as proud of all his little budding infantile accomplishments as most young parents who see in their eldest darling something they will never see in any child later born, for it is the first blossoming of their young hopes—as Scripture puts it, "the beginning of strength."

She started at seeing Sam quietly domiciled in his favorite corner, but it had been a family prophecy that "we should see Sam Toller back some day when we least expected it,' and after a few surprised inquiries she hastened to set out a substantial supper of cold meat, brown bread and cheese; nor did she hesitate to cut a generous triangle of mince pie, to all of which Sam did justice in a way that would have appalled the dyspeptic generation of the present day.

But Sam seemed to miss something. His eye kept wandering to the empty arm-chair. There it stood in its old corner, just as my grandfather left it the night the death angel summoned him. Even his Bible lay on the stand with his spectacles beside, for Rachel. with that strange clinging of soul to the poor mute things its beloved will never again need, would not have them put away. Then he said hesitatingly—

"The Captain—he's well I hope."

But when we told him with voices broken by tears that the kindly smile had vanished forever, and the eyes that never glanced sternly save at some story of wrong and oppression would beam on us no more—that the Captain had reached a port beyond storm and shipwreck—even the Eternal City of our God, with its pearly gates, its golden streets, its never ceasing fruitage—Sam Toller lifted up his voice and wept aloud.

CHAPTER XXVI

THE FALL OF 1826.—OUR JOURNEY.—FREEMASONRY VS. JUSTICE.

I WILL now drop the thread of my narrative to give a brief statement of the general situation a few months after the murder of Morgan, lest some reader finding history so silent on the events of those thrilling times should accuse me of a tendency to romance. Hitherto Masonry had held her own unchallenged by church or state, but now she was undergoing a metamorphosis similar to that of the fair maiden in the witch story who suddenly turned into a loathsome, wriggling serpent. But her power was nowise abated. Though she could no longer captivate good men by her harlot beauty she could intimidate and appall. Under her basilisk eye the press quailed and was silent, or sounded false notes to baffle public inquiry, and even the majestic Muse of History succumbed to the same withering spell, and expunged alike from the ponderous tome of the student and the text-book of the school-boy all record of those exciting years with their far-reaching political effects, their strange thwarting of justice, their vivid lights and shadows of personal experience; for it is a fact that many a Mason who chose to obey the voice of conscience rather than the mandates of the lodge, trembled under a fear of its secret vengeance, and rumor told of more than one who dared not stir out at nightfall for dread of the assassin's knife at his throat.

For as these things were talked over in store and tavern, and round the kitchen fire, and the conviction gathered force that Morgan had met his death at the hands of Masonic executioners, ugly tales began to start up. Men remembered Smith, of Vermont, who undertook to republish Jachin and Boaz in this country and was believed to have shared the fate of its original author, as well as Murdock of Rensselaerville, New York, who likewise rendered himself obnoxious to the lodge by an attempt to betray the secrets and was found mysteriously murdered soon after. It was therefore no wonder that my fears had been seriously excited for Mark's safety before they were so disagreeably confirmed by Sam Toller's tidings of the plot against him; no wonder that I passed a sleepless night thinking of his peril, and vainly trying to answer Sam's inquiry: "What is to be done about it?" But a strong, brave soul that has cast out of its calculations every factor of self-interest, fully resolved to follow truth wherever she may lead, even to martyrdom if so be, has a wonderfully direct way of settling all such difficulties.

"My duty is plain, Leander," was Mark's answer, when I communicated to him his danger the next morning. "I must tell what I know, but I shall certainly give good heed to Sam's warning. I shall take one of the farm horses, and by making a detour from the direct road both in going and coming foil, as I trust, all their plans. But I must go alone. Nobody shall be involved in any risk that I may run."

But my resolution was unshaken to accompany Mark. I could not let my chosen friend from boyhood, Rachel's brother and mine, take the perilous trip alone. And we accordingly set out under circumstances that recalled with curious vividness to my mind the memory of another journey—a vision of dim, silent woods, with the same unseen foe lurking in my track—the same that betrayed me at the Stover's cabin, that struck me down without warning and left me for dead under the covering veil of solitude and night.

"I never thought it was going to turn out such a lucky thing for you, Mark, when I taught Sam the grips and signs," said Joe, slyly, as we were about to ride off. For he alone of all the family had been told the latter's real errand to Brownsville.

"So *you* initiated Sam Toller," said Mark, with a quiet smile. "I have always rather suspected that was the way of it. But don't you ever intend to let us into your secret."

"Well, that depends" answered Joe, coolly, "on how a certain individual, who shall be nameless at present, minds his ps and qs."

And with one glance backward at Rachel as she stood smiling her farewells in the open door-way, and a furtive look at my pistols to see that they were in order I rode on after Mark. And thus like two palladins of old, with this notable exception that they met their giants and fire-breathing dragons in fair, open fight, while our enemy was a snake lurking in ambush, whose deadly presence could only be known when we felt its fangs, we set forth for Ontario court house.

"It is my belief that the lodge in Brownsville has something to do with this plot against you, Mark," said I, during one of the brief intervals when we allowed our horses to indulge in a walk.

"Very likely," was Mark's quiet reply. "And a lodge fifty miles away may feel just as much interest to suppress my testimony. Masonry is not only a complete despotism, but it is a perfectly organized system, and under it men are like figures on a checker-board, with neither will nor volition of their own except as the lodge may choose to handle them. Nothing shows so much the terrible power of the institution as the fact that men who had never seen each other's faces or heard each others names, who were separated by long distances and could not possibly have held any personal communication with each other acted in perfect concert in this matter of the murder of Morgan."

"I wonder who that man could have been who mistook me for one of his fellow plotters when I was coming down on the canal boat last fall. I shall always think he was the one who made the attempt to burn Miller's printing office that Sunday night when I was stopping at the Park Tavern."

"You are right, Leander," said Mark. "That man lurking in the shadow of the stairway was Richard Howard, a Knight Templar, one of the chief conspirators against Morgan, and one that drew the lot to murder him. He was then acting in concert with Daniel Johns, the spy from Canada, who wormed himself into the confidence of Morgan and Miller, and by absconding with the Chapter degrees a few nights before his abduction, made, as the fraternity then supposed, a fatal break in the publishing of the work. But I understand that Morgan kept duplicate copies of the three first degrees, which were taken from him under cover of a civil process in August last, and that they are now in the hands of Colonel Miller all ready for issue from the press. If these things are so Blue Lodge Masonry will soon be published to the world."

"Mark," said I, solemnly, "I believe this cursed institution killed my grandfather. That long, inward struggle wore his life away. I am glad Colonel Miller is brave and patriotic enough to go on and publish, and may it prove a final death-blow to the lodge."

"The end is not yet, Leander," said Mark, significantly. "The institution whose secret plottings made the streets of Paris run red with blood in 1789, whose subtle schemings undermined the power of the Puritan party in England, and placed Charles II. on the throne, will not down without a fierce struggle. And it will be a struggle between light and darkness; between the liberty our fathers crossed the seas to win and old world despotisms; between Christ and anti-Christ. I think I see it dimly shadowed forth in Revelation where John says—'And I saw the beast and the kings of the earth and their armies gathered together to make war against him that sat on the horse and against his army.' It may not come in this generation. Other issues may rise and stave it off for awhile, but come some time it surely will."

"But what do you think the beast represents? Papal Rome?"

"Papal Rome, you remember, is the woman who sits on the beast. How can the two be identical? To my mind the beast rising out of the sea is the old Roman Empire, savage, cruel, despotic, so that 'the image of the beast' must refer to some organization of modern times which reproduces its spirit and character. And what is more like it than Freemasonry, with her aim at universal empire, her despotic government and savage laws, her Baal worship, her hatred and contempt of Christ's name. No parallel could be plainer."

I always liked to hear Mark talk even when I did not understand him, or was disposed to think him mystical. For his mind had that rare balance of faculties—on the one side the logical and on the other the poetical—which seems necessary to the full enjoyment and understanding of that strange book of Revelation. In pondering over its wondrous imagery, its panorama of ceaseless conflict with the dragon forces of evil, Mark felt his own earnest, intense nature kindle into a new zeal and fervor, while for the outward poverty and bareness of his life the Apocalyptic splendors of the New Jerusalem, with its glorified inhabitants, its endless chants of victory, its perfect freedom from all that can vex and annoy, was the same that it has been to God's sorely tried ones in all ages, a glorious "recompence of reward."

It was expected that bills of indictment would be found at this sitting of the court against some of the chief actors in the terrible tragedy, as a number of witnesses were to be examined, some of whom were supposed to have important testimony, and thus a more than ordinary interest had been excited. But several curious circumstances attended the sitting of this court of law.

"They may question and cross question till they're gray; they won't get the truth out of witnesses that are bound not to tell," remarked one of those obligingly communicative individuals who are as ready to dispense information as a spring to send forth its waters. "Now that last chap that was on the witness stand, he knew all about their taking off Morgan, and he perjured himself when he swore he didn't. In my opinion there's been an agreement beforehand among a good many of the witnesses not to know anything worth telling. Things look suspicious when a man comes into court and swears to tell the truth, the whole truth and nothing but the truth, and has his counsel all the while by his side to advise him when to answer and when not."

"That's a fact," pronounced another in the group, for this conversation took place during an adjournment of the court, when tongues wagged in busy and not over favorable comment on these palpable obstructions thus laid in the way of justice.

"Well, now," went on the first speaker, "my brother was witness once in a trial for murder, and he's told me that he see Masonic signs pass betwen the prisoner and his counsel and members of the jury. And the upshot of the matter was the man was never convicted —hain't been to this day—though nobody had the least doubt of his guilt. Talk of Morgan's being alive! They'd better tell that to the marines. If Morgan is alive why don't they produce him and stop all this fuss?"

"That's hitting the nail on the head square," assented another with an approving nod. "But some of the come-outers are going to testify this afternoon. Them are the ones I want to hear, especially that young Stedman. They say he's going to be a hard witness agin 'em."

And a hard witness Mark Stedman proved himself, but no harder than one or two others, among whom was Mr Samuel D. Greene, our old friend of the Park Tavern. His part in the dark and terrible drama was now fully revealed, for the unknown divulger of Masonry's murderous plottings, the man who nobly dared to stand in the breach and warn its defenseless victims of their danger, who would have saved Morgan if the public apathy had not refused to believe such things possible, and who did save Miller by finally rousing a band of citizens to start in pursuit of his abductors, was one with that grave, silent inn-keeper, who had moved so quietly about among his guests during those memorable days in Batavia.

I remember how he looked standing there in the old court room in the prime of his manhood, his strong, squarely built frame telling of generations of sturdy yeoman ancestry, as well as I remember him half a century later when the waves of Masonic hate in every conceivable shape and form had dashed over him and left him—grand, heroic old man that he was, unmoved at his post and penning such words as these—

"I am an old man and I shall soon be gone, but I leave it as my last injunction to my countrymen that they watch this institution with a jealous eye. It is an enemy to their liberties. It has no thought of the general good. It is not founded and worked upon any such idea. It is built upon the principle of tyranny in all ages—*the good of the few at the expense of the many.*"

As he unfolded the whole history, the secret plans of the lodge and his own efforts to baffle them; as in clear, unvarnished language his scathing testimony branded names before unimpeached for respectability with the murderer's stigma, a shiver went through the court room. Men looked in each other's eyes questioning if it were possible that under all our free institutions lay a quaking Vesuvius ready to overwhelm and destroy the right purchased so dearly for every American citizen to "life, liberty and the pursuit of happiness."

Mark's testimony, in spite of the efforts made by the counsel on the other side to shake it, was full, clear and convincing. Legal cunning, with all its artifices, was no match for simple truth. And when, as the last weapon in a closing fight he sneeringly asked if all the information Mark had been detailing was communicated to him Masonically, the venomed point of the inquiry —which was plainly to prejudice the minds of the jury by holding him up as a foresworn witness revealing secrets he had been solemnly pledged to keep—was so palpably evident that it met with a prompt over-ruling from the court as irrelevant to the case. But he was a wily lawyer; as people said of him, a "deep fellow," and as after developments showed had been given an immense fee by the lodge to clear Morgan's murderers. And in his closing address to the jury he made free use of those weapons of falsehood and innuendo so popular with the institution which had chosen him to defend her from the serious charges of kidnapping and murder.

He cautioned them not to be influenced by the excitement then prevailing—an excitement he assured them "got up by ambitious demagogues to serve their own political ends." Language that received its proper rebuke from the Judge in his address from the bench. In grave and dignified words he portrayed the aggravated nature of the outrage committed, and then alluded to the spirit of indignation which it had excited in the breast of every patriotic citizen "as a blessed spirit which he hoped would not subside but be accompanied by a ceaseless vigilance and untiring activity until every actor in the conspiracy had been hunted from his hiding place and received the punishment due to his crime."

Well, it is all over now. Judge, jury and counsel have gone to their final reward. That same Judge, afterwards Governor of New York, sullied his bright record, and from the Governor's chair bowed to the Masonic power which he had battled with from the bench. As for the lawyer who, Judas-like, betrayed the truth for gold, an avenging Nemesis followed in his track. God hath requited him.

"I believe things are in train now for a speedy ferreting out of Morgan's murderers," said Mark, hopefully, as we turned our heads homeward. If so terrible a crime goes unpunished after so many of its details have been laid bare and so great an excitement has been created it will be something new in the annals of justice.

Could we have foreseen that four long years would drag away while case after case was tried before Masonic grand juries which failed to convict on the clearest evidence; that witnesses would be secreted, bribed, threatened; that even the Chief Executive of the State would be corrupted, and confidential communications exposed to the gaze of the lodge, thus thwarting every design to arrest the murderers; that in short the shield of a vast, secret, irresponsible power would always interpose at the most critical moment between them and the sword of justice; and furthermore, could we have known as lodge after lodge surrendered its charter, and the whole dark system seemed to be in its last death throes, it was only feigning to die, that the popular attention turned to another question it might recuperate its strength, and under a hundred protean disguises secretly and silently seize the places of public trust, muzzle press and pulpit, and cause even the watchmen of Zion to be dumb dogs—what should we have thought? what should we have said?

But it was well that we did not foresee the future; that, as we rode homeward, urging our horses to a swifter gallop as the shadows of night fell darkling around us, we believed that the end was near, or our hearts might have sunk within us at the seeming hopeless nature of such a struggle with such a foe.

Mark Stedman had escaped for this time the trap laid for his feet, and the only resource for his baffled enemies of the lodge was to plan some other and subtler scheme—if they dared.

But would they dare? We shall see.

CHAPTER XXVII.

THE SWORD OF DAMOCLES.

AMONG my private papers is one yellow, time-stained document which reads as follows:

November 30th, 1826.

BROWNSVILLE LODGE, NO. ——.

Brother Leander Severns:—Whereas sundry charges have been preferred against you of un-Masonic conduct in falsely accusing brother members, aiding and abetting the enemies of the order, and otherwise deporting yourself to the general injury of the fraternity, you are hereby summoned to appear at the next regular meeting of Brownsville lodge to answer said charges, and show good and sufficient reason why you should not be expelled for the same. By order of the lodge.

BAXTER STEBBINS, *Secretary.*

I put the summons in my pocket to show to Rachel. It may as well be stated in passing that I had just received a certain wifely reproof, which on looking the matter over seriously with the golden rule for a measure and guide—which same old-fashioned rule by the way is just as admirably adapted to married people as any one else—I came to the conclusion was deserved.

"Leander," she said, laying down her sewing and walking up to me with the flush on her cheek decidedly deepening, "I thought there were to be no secrets between us any more. Do you think I would have said a word to keep you back from sharing Mark's danger? Don't you know yet what kind of a woman you have married?"

"A woman as fair as her namesake and brave as Deborah, and"—but here Rachel put her hand over my mouth and stopped me.

"Don't be silly, Leander. I don't want compliments. I want you to promise when you or Mark are in any danger again not to keep it from me."

"I thought it would save you from worrying, Rachel."

"If that isn't just like a man!" replied Rachel, the laughter coming back into her eyes. "Don't you think this mystery about Sam Toller's coming worried me any? As soon as I saw your face I felt it all through me that he wasn't here for nothing. You see we women shut up at home grow to have a kind of sixth sense, and it isn't quite so easy keeping things from us as you men seem to imagine. Now don't you ever do so again, Leander." And with a little imperative shake of her finger Rachel went back to her sewing. But her words bore fruit as was evidenced by my showing her the lodge summons and asking her advice what to do about it.

"Do nothing, of course. Pretty business to suppose they have any control over you, a free man under a free government!" And Rachel's eyes glowed with an indignant fire.

"Well, shall I burn it up?"

"Yes. No; give it to me."

And as Rachel dropped it into her work-box I think there was a subtle sense of triumph in the action. And who can blame her if she did take a certain fine revenge on the institution that had wronged and insulted her womanhood just as it wrongs and insults womanhood everywhere, by consigning its most dreaded weapon to ignominious imprisonment among needle-books, hooks and eyes, and skeins of sewing cotton!

Though not so shining a mark for Masonic obloquy and persecution as though I had been a Mason of higher degree, I did not escape a series of petty insults and vexations from members of the craft, which is not to be wondered at when it is considered that Masonry solemnly swears its devotees to " take vengeance on all traitors." And as this lovely creed had no stronger supporter in Brownsville than Darius Fox, it followed naturally that he should be chief among my persecutors. Like many another man of small moral caliber he loved the lodge for the very things that would make honest-minded men shrink from joining it. The obligation to keep all secrets of a companion, the vows to a negative morality that is absolute license—all these he rolled as a sweet morsel under his tongue. What wonder then, when he saw the imminent danger that threatened his beloved craft, he was filled with rage and fury.

Ways of annoyance are easy enough to find when all one's powers are set in that direction. Bars were mysteriously let down, giving my cattle the freedom of the neighboring cornfield with the result in a heavy bill for damages; an old debt of my grandfather's, paid long before his death, was hunted up and made the basis for a claim on the estate that could only be settled by submitting to the wrong, or by wearisome and costly litigation. And finally an action for trespass was brought against me for laying a new stone wall a trifle outside of what was alleged to be the true boundary line between my own farm and the one adjoining.

"The hand of Joab is in this thing," said Luke

Thatcher, significantly, to me. "They say Fox threatens to drive you out of Brownsville."

Joe happened to be standing by and heard him.

"I've got a small account to settle with Joab first," he remarked, coolly. "I think of going over to-night to see him about it, and taking Sam with me."

"Wall, I reckon ye've let him go about to the end of his tether," Sam put in with a grin, as he whipped the dust from the knees of his trousers with one hand, and give a satisfied thump to the crown of his hat with the other. "It won't hurt him nor nobody else if ye tie him up a grain closer."

For Sam was once more installed as general factotum in and about the house, the same queer, shiftless good-for-naught, whose short-comings had so often roused the ire of the much-enduring Miss Loker. He always alluded to my grandfather with a kind of tender, touching reverence.

"I tell ye the Captain was a Christian. Some folks never care how they treat a hired man, but yer grand-'ther, now, was one of the kind that allus wanted his men to hev as good victuals and drink as he had himself. And when I think about him I like to remember that verse in Revelations about their all sitting down together to the Marriage Supper up above. He'll hev good fare there, no mistake."

O, it is a blessed thing when the poor and lowly keep our memories green after the places that knew us once know us no more forever; when their kindly thoughts follow us like attending angels as we pass into the eternal mysteries of the life beyond.

I have previously mentioned the fact that Darius Fox kept a distillery. It was to this place that Sam and

Joe, when the evening shadows began to gather and the farm chores were over for the day, directed their steps —an ancient, smoke-stained building much frequented by the men and boys of Brownsville, either because they liked the odor of the still, the chance of imbibing stray drops of the sweet liquor through a straw, or for some social charm inherent in the general atmosphere of the place.

Joe sat down nonchalantly on one of the big casks beside old Ezekiel Trull, who was partially deaf; and drawing a small volume from out his pocket inquired in the loud tones rendered necessary by the old gentleman's infirmity—

"Have you seen one of Morgan's books yet, Mr. Trull? I heard Miller had got it out so I sent for one the other day."

"Morgan's book out! the one they murdered him for trying to get up. Dew tell. I'd give a sight to see it," answered the old man, eagerly, fumbling for his spectacles, and speaking himself in that high key natural to the deaf, so that the general attention was attracted precisely as Joe meant it should be.

They crowded round to see the book, some scornful, but all curious. Even Darius Fox drew near with the rest. The thing to prevent which he and so many others had united to murder Morgan had not been prevented after all. Here was the work for which he gave his life, rising phœnix-like from his martyr's grave under the cold waters of Niagara, tenfold more potent through his death. And this was what they in their mad rage against him had accomplished.

He took the book, shuffled the leaves over, then threw it from him with an oath.

"It's just a pack of lies, but they'll do to fool Antimasons with."

"If that is the case it ain't worth swearing about, seems to me," said Joe, coolly, as he stooped to pick up the book, a trifle the worse for the rough treatment it had received. His retort was followed by a laugh from one or two who saw the point. It angered Darius, who fiercely repeated—

"I say it again. The book is a vile imposition. I don't want to see no more of it than I have." And Darius turned away, but not so quickly that he failed to hear Sam Toller drawl out—

"Say, Joe, ain't it a good deal like that book ye borrowed once? Or I dunno as ye 'zactly borrowed it. Kinder fell in yer way, didn't it? Maybe Morgan copied from that."

"If he did he has altered one or two things. That was J. B.; this is B. J.," replied Joe.

"B. J.? That ain't the title of the book, is it?" asked one of the company not posted in lodge lore, while Mr. Fox, trembling at the idea that Joe might be on the brink of revealing what would certainly make him the laughing-stock of the whole neighborhood if it should ever get out, was for once in the unpleasant predicament of not knowing what to do or say. But to make peace with his dangerous adversary, in the words of Scripture, "while he was in the way with him," seemed the only discreet thing to do under the circumstances.

"Sam," he said, "I wish you would help me a minute out here. And you too, Joe, if you will. It's only a hand's turn I want." And Sam and Joe accordingly followed Mr. Fox, who led them into a small, unfinished room in the rear of the building, and pouring out two glasses of his own liquor he presented one to each, saying in an injured tone as he did so—

"This is confounded mean business to go and blow on a fellow after you've given your solemn promise to keep mum."

"Now look here, Mister," answered Joe, scornfully refusing the proffered peace-offering to which Sam, on the contrary, had due respect. "When I heard that you were throwing out hints to the lodge that Leander had been letting out the secrets, I went to you and I warned you pretty plain that the real traitor would be exposed if that talk wasn't all taken back. When Jachin and Boaz tumbled out of your pocket and I picked it up one night when you were going home from the lodge too drunk to know your right hand from your left, I had no thought of making you ridiculous and hurting you in the lodge by telling the story round how I came by the secrets. I only wanted a little fun and I had it, by teaching them to Sam, so that he could pass himself off for a Mason. But now the secrets are all out my little game is up, but I see yours isn't. Because Leander knows that Masons murdered Morgan, and ain't afraid to say so; because he left the lodge like an honest man when he found out what Masonry really is, you've persecuted him every way you could think of. You've used tools and tried to keep your hand hidden, but what is the use when everybody in Brownsville knows as well as I do that you are at the bottom of all this mischief. Now, Mr. Fox, unless you give me your solemn pledge with Sam Toller here for a witness, to have all legal proceedings against Leander dropped, and not to trouble him any more, that story shall be spread all over the neighborhood. And I mean what I say. You had better be careful, Darius Fox, just for your own good. Folks say that you know all about Morgan, and they say some other things that are not exactly to your credit, but I ain't called on to repeat 'em. Just give me that promise. That's all I want of *you*."

Darius Fox stood for a moment in silence, but he had enough good sense to accept Joe's alternative.

"You're too hard on me, Joe. But that matter about the wall—if I can get Joel Barnes to drop it I will. I was only in the way of my duty serving my writ. A sheriff has to act without respect of persons, you know."

"O, yes; Mason or Antimason," answered Joe, sarcastically, as he marched off in company with the chuckling Sam. "Good night, Mr. Fox, I hope you will remember the little talk we've just had and govern yourself accordingly."

One more scene and Darius Fox fades from my story.

CHAPTER XXVIII.

MASONRY REVEALED.—SAM TOLLER'S MASONRY.—THE MYSTERY OF OAK ORCHARD CREEK.

THE appearance of Morgan's book deepened the public agitation and excitement. To many in the Masonic ranks it came like a decree of emancipation. The secrets were out; if not actually proclaimed from the house-tops they were freely sold to the simplest cowan who chose to invest a part of his day's wages in learning the august and sublime mysteries of Freemasonry. Why were they bound to keep secret what was no secret? And some bolder spirits, among whom was Mark Stedman, went farther. Why not tear away the veil that hid the higher degrees?—and show Masonry personating Jehovah in the burning bush, or seated as the All-Puissant on his throne of judgment, thus literally fulfilling the New Testament prophecies of the Man of Sin; show Christ's Holy Supper profaned in horrible burlesque by deacons and drunkards, ministers and libertines—and finally the veil entirely withdrawn, show her swearing her devotees "to crush the head of the serpent of ignorance—a serpent which we detest, that is adored by the idiot and vulgar under the name of RELIGION!"

This will surely be the death-blow to Masonry. So said and thought the band of patriots which met at Le Roy and placed on record for all future time their independence as Christian men and American citizens. So thought every honest man and woman who read or heard their testimony. So thought Joe, who concluded it was time to surrender his secret. And accordingly one day I found a bundle of foolscap laid in convenient reach for my inspection, all written over with the first three Masonic degrees.

"What under the sun have you got here, Joe?" I exclaimed.

"Only something for Rachel to kindle her fire with," was the cool reply. "That is all it is good for now. Say, Leander, do you remember that old book I was looking at the night you joined the lodge?"

"To be sure I do. Now, how did you come by it?"

"Easy enough. I was walking home from Jake Goodwin's party "—

"Who with?" I interrupted, with that teasing freedom in which elder brothers sometimes indulge.

"Come, Leander," answered Joe, coloring, "that is no business of yours. If you ask impertinent questions I shall stop. Of course I went home with somebody, but we had parted company, and I was just coming over the hill there by the widow Tappan's when I overtook Darius Fox coming home from lodge just half seas over. I never saw him really drunk before, but folks say since the Morgan affair happened he's been getting into drinking ways fast."

"I've noticed it myself. Well, Joe, go on."

"His gait was very unsteady, and once he nearly pitched over, and in the jerk he give to save himself, or some way, that book fell out of his pocket. There was a good bright **moon** and I stopped a minute to examine it. The title—Jachin and Boaz—sounded as though it was some kind of a religious book, but that **kind of reading** is not quite in Darius' line, so **I** looked **a little** farther. When **I** see it was something about **Masonry** I slapped it into *my* pocket quick as a wink. 'So ho,' thinks I, 'this is the way you lodge members post yourselves. What is to hinder my learning the **signs** and grips and initiating Sam Toller?' You know **Sam is** always **ready** for a joke, and he was just as much tickled with the idea as I was. But learning **it** by heart was such a job Sam told me I had better **copy** it off. So I bought a quire of foolscap and **we** sat up two whole nights out in the barn to do it."

"I wonder you didn't set the barn on fire, Joe."

"Well, we did come pretty nigh it once," confessed Joe, "**when** we thought we heard Miss Loker or somebody else coming. Sam scrabbled so to hide our light he tipped it over, and I thought for a minute we should be all in a blaze. **When** we got it nicely copied off I **had** a fine chance to return it on the sly. Miss **Loker** sent me over to the Fox place for some kind of **dried** herb **she** wanted, and while Aunt Subrey was rummaging **over** her collections up stairs I clapped the book right back again into the pocket of Darius' coat that was laying **over a chair in** the keeping room—the very same one he had on that night. And the joke of **the matter is,** Darius had **never** missed it, so he never thought *he* was the leaky vessel till I come to blow him **up** for calling you a traitor. You should have seen his face. But I had the staff in my own **hands,** and I've kept it there ever since. **Darius** is like an alligator—

bullet proof except in one particular spot. He don't like to be laughed at. Now I know just as well as I want to that he set Joel Barnes on to make trouble about that wall. And you may just thank me that it has all ended in smoke. And another thing Sam tells me, these men that were going to carry off Mark Stedman bragged that Sheriff Fox would never arrest them. 'He's a Royal Arch,' said one, ' and knows as much about Morgan as anybody except them that pushed him into the river." I'm glad I don't stand in his shoes."

And Joe went off after letting in this flood of light on more than one hitherto mysterious point; among others the sudden stay of proceedings in the before-mentioned trespass case. Though one reason may have been that Darius himself was before long in the grasp of that law which, under guise of administering, he had violated and defied.

At the next sitting of the county court a bill of indictment was found against him for procuring a carriage in which to convey Morgan one stage of his journey and otherwise helping on the work of kidnapping and murder. But the trial was put off on account of some technical irregularity, and the same strange difficulties appeared that had beset the way of justice in the case of at least a score of others, formally indicted, but somehow impossible to convict. The hoodwink over the eyes of Masonic juries blinded them to the clearest evidence of guilt. Witnesses were counselled beforehand by Masonic lawyers to withhold the truth, and when examined the questions were so adroitly put that they could be answered without revealing anything on which to frame indictments or prove criminality. And when most important links in the evidence were wanting, witnesses who had knowledge of the desired facts were strangely spirited off nobody knew whither, thus baffling all efforts to forge a chain of clear and decisive proof.

It was plain to see that the whole Masonic fraternity had an interest in stifling investigation; that it intended the fate of Morgan should remain forever one of those shrouded secrets to which the years only add a deeper mystery as they bear them farther and farther on towards the light of God's great Day of final revealing. But since the time when the earth refused to cover the blood of Abel, there has been a deep-seated belief in the human mind, borne out by many a strange and curious fact, that subtle agencies are continually at work to dog the murderer's steps and drag his secrets into human view—as if the heart of our great Mother Nature herself rose in shuddering revolt to cast it out of her bosom.

On the 8th day of October, 1827, a little over a year from the mysterious disappearance of Morgan, the body of an unknown man was cast ashore at Oak Orchard Creek, and hastily buried after an equally hurried inquest. This fact soon became noised abroad, and the question arose and passed from lip to lip, "What if this unknown man should prove to be Morgan?" The fact that all were Masons who officiated at the inquest, and that as soon as the body came ashore members of the fraternity were on the watch to inter it as quickly and quietly as possible, pointed suspicion.

A second inquest was resolved upon; Mrs. Morgan was notified and invitations sent out to his old friends and neighbors in Batavia to appear and give testimony.

But the story of this second inquest as well as some curious after circumstances which finally led to a third one after the identity of the body was supposed to be established beyond doubt, I can best give in the words of my grandfather's old friend, Mr. Jedediah Mills, whom I came across one day when on a visit to a neighboring town.

I thought Mr. Mills looked thinner and a trifle careworn, but he shook my hand with the same hearty cordiality that had welcomed me to Tonawanda; and a few words sufficed to launch him on a subject which was just then the theme of universal conversation—the strange discovery of Morgan's body and the still stranger circumstances attending the efforts made to identify it.

It's a queer story from beginning to end. If I had read it somewhere in a novel I vow I wouldn't have believed it. You see the river had been dragged to find the body, and I suppose it got started somehow from the weight that held it to the bottom, and floated on top. The water of Niagara River ain't just like common river water; it's clearer and colder. Why, I've known a man that was lost over the falls and when they found him a year after he hadn't hardly changed. Now I ain't any surer that I'm a living man than I am that this was Morgan's body. Mr. Greene was there to the inquest, and Colonel Miller and Captain Davids, and they all said the same thing. And his poor wife, when she come to look at the corpse, she just said, 'My God!' and it seemed for a minute as if she was going to faint dead away. I declare, I felt—I don't know how, to see that poor young thing—pretty as a picture, too, with the tears a running down her cheeks, and thought how she was left all alone in the world with her two fatherless babes. What if it had been my Hannah now! I can't feel reconciled to some things that happen in this world, nohow."

And Mr. Mills pulled out his handkerchief and made vigorous use thereof, while I echoed inwardly, "Poor young thing!" hardly older than Rachel, yet called to such a baptism of suspense and anguish; mocked in her perplexity and distress by the very men who had taken her husband's life, as related in the words of her simple and touching affidavit. Verily there are things that make us wonder at the patience of the Infinite; but among the promises of Holy Writ is one that shines with that awful glory which is finally to destroy every system of darkness and oppression. Well may the Church herself look to it that she is not in unholy league with a power that persecutes the saints of the Most High and hides in its skirts innocent blood. "The day of vengeance of our God shall surely come; it shall come and will not tarry."

"Mrs. Morgan's testimony was very clear, I understood, about the marks on the body," said I.

"Clear!" echoed Mr. Mills. "There wan't a flaw in it. She testified before the lid of the coffin was opened about the hair—chestnut color, long and silky, and about his having double teeth all around, and told where he'd had one pulled out. And the very doctor that pulled it was there from Batavia and had the tooth with him, and it fitted right into the place. And she told, too, about a scar on his foot made by cutting it with an axe, and sure enough when they come to look there it was plain as day. Oh, there was no getting over such evidence if she didn't tell right about the clothes. But that is easy enough explained to my mind. I believe the Masons changed Morgan's clothes when they had him shut up in the fort."

"You're idea is reasonable, Mr. Mills," said I, after thinking it over for a moment. "They intended in the event of the body ever being found to prevent identification as far as possible."

"Just so. Exactly;" answered Mr. Mills. "Well of course the body was brought to Batavia and buried; and then came the queer part of the story. It begun to be told round among Masons that it was a Timothy Munroe, a man that was drowned in Niagara River a few weeks before that we'd got buried there. So a third inquest was held and this Munroe's wife and son —or a woman and a boy that called themselves by that name—came before the coroner's jury and swore to its being Munroe instead of Morgan."

"What kind of a testimony did the woman give?" I inquired.

"I didn't think much of it," answered Mr. Mills, emphatically. "She told about the double teeth all round, but she couldn't tell to which jaw the tooth that was pulled belonged. She said his hair was short and black, and she didn't know anything about the scar on his foot. But come to the clothes, and she run on as glibly as an auctioneer. She even told of a place in the heel of his stocking that had been mended with yarn of a different color. There was something mysterious about that woman," added Mr. Mills, lowering his voice. "You've read in the Bible, I suppose, about the judgment of Solomon. Well, if I had been Solomon, and that case was brought before me, I should have known mighty quick on which side to give judgment, Morgan's wife or that Munroe woman. I've got my own thoughts about *her* that I don't tell to everybody. I believe she was a man dressed up in woman's clothes."

I stared at Mr. Mills in astonishment. Could it be that the ancient and glorious order of Freemasonry, which treats the whole female sex with such sublime contempt, was actually not above borrowing its dress in an emergency when some little irregularity, entirely Masonic, but which the general sense of mankind strangely enough disapproves of, needed to be covered up?—as for instance kidnapping and murder?

"She kept her veil down over her face," continued Mr. Mills, "so it was her gait and her voice I judged by mostly, but them two things were enough for me. The boy with her was the greenest kind of a fellow that I ever sat eyes on; just the chap to be made a tool of in any such business. And when the affair was over they both disappeared, nobody knew where. But I'll just tell you"—and here Mr. Mills again lowered his voice confidentially, "what my wife's cousin Joshua says about it. He lives in Wayne county, next door to a doctor by the name of Lewis, a Royal Arch Mason, and one that had considerable to do with taking off Morgan. He says the Masons round there were dreadful flurried when they knew Morgan's body was recognized. The doctor give out that he had a very dangerous patient in the next town, and hurried off post haste with his hostler Mike, but instead of going to perform an operation as he said, it was found out afterwards that he had gone in the direction of Batavia. I described the woman and boy as well as I could to Joshua and he just clapped his hands on his knees, and says he, 'I'd be willing to lay you a five-dollar gold piece that Mrs. Munroe and her son was Dr. Lewis and his coach-boy.' It's a queer kind of a world;" and Mr. Mills sighed with that deep-drawn sigh that only comes from the hidden places of trouble, "Now I never thought that in my old age I should be in danger of losing my farm. But the title deed wan't quite right; something put in or something left out, I hardly know which, and I'm here after a lawyer, though I hain't much opinion of lawyers nor courts nuther now-a-days."

It was the old story over again—of persecution and wrong that was to find no redress this side of the grave; of injustice shielded under the sacred form of law; of the wicked laying a snare for the righteous in the secret chambers of iniquity, and saying, "Behold the Lord doth not regard."

CHAPTER XXIX

SUNDRY HAPPENINGS.

THOUGH it still continued in many minds an unsettled question whether or no Morgan's body had actually been discovered, popular excitement was wakened anew. Masons were exultant over the Timothy Munroe story, while the opposite party saw in it nothing but a clever ruse by which to deceive the public and influence the approaching elections. For the whole subject from being a mere matter for the courts to deal with had now come to play an important part in our national politics. In a country where the unbiased will of the people constitutes the only court of appeal it follows naturally that all great moral evils must stand their trial sooner or later before that august tribunal. And Masonry had reached the point sooner for the reason that her haughty defiance of law and justice, as well as her arrogant assumption of an authority superior to that of the State had alarmed all candid and thoughtful men, and fairly forced the question to a political issue.

That the strife as it went on should develop a spirit of heat and acrimony and unfairness even on the side of the partizans of truth, is nothing strange considering the infirmities of human nature. For in every rising of popular wrath against an established wrong or abuse there is a grand intolerance, like an earthquake or a whirlwind that levels indiscriminately; it makes no allowance for possible honesty on the part of some who support that particular evil against which the arrows are for the time being hurled. Timorous Masons cowered before the storm, and withdrew from the lodge in shame and silence, while others of different caliber, roused to a perfect frenzy of bitterness and hate at the threatened downfall of their cherished institution persecuted, with all the weapons malice could invent, those recreant brethren who had testified to its evil works.

Such was the situation in the fall of 1827, a year after the death of Morgan.

Elder Cushing preached on; his congregation, as regarded the male members, almost entirely Masonic, sustained him. But there had been no revival in the church since the period of its first planting, and it was soon apparent to all that the candle-stick was being slowly moved out of its place, especially when a series of religious meetings in the neighborhood had drawn in many of the young people and caused not a few to inquire anxiously the way of salvation. For so deep was the interest manifested that these meetings were continued and formed the seed of a new church, small in numbers but rich in faith, and full of that spiritual life and energy which naturally abounds where most of the members are new converts. It took in Rachel and I and baptized our little one—dear old Methodist Episcopal church whom I shall never cease to love, though

I love the Church Universal better. And though people and pastor alike have in too many instances forgotten the faith of **their** early founders, and turned **aside to a strange** worship, **God** visit them in mercy and **bring them back to** their first love!

The Morgan trials dragged slowly along without reaching any definite result. His murderers, still at large, defied the hand of law to touch them, and before winter was over Brownsville had its sensation in the sudden flight of Darius Fox, against whom new evidence had appeared implicating him still more deeply in the plot, so that another warrant was speedily issued for his arrest.

"They say the officers were after him," said Joe, who brought in the news, "but somehow he got wind of it and cleared out. It wasn't an hour before they came to arrest him that Seth Briggs says he was talking with him about a young horse he wanted to buy. They couldn't seem to come to a bargain, and while they were chaffing he saw Darius look up and grow sort of white about the mouth. 'I'm in a hurry now,' said he, 'we'll let the matter go till another time.' And Seth says he noticed a man come in while they were talking that he is sure gave Fox the Masonic sign. Anyhow he's left Brownsville," concluded Joe, "and I hope his place will be filled by a better man."

In which expression Joe was not alone, but there remained another surprise for the people of Brownsville in the fact that the ex-sheriff had not left his affairs in the confused state which would seem to follow naturally on such a sudden flight. All his property, including the distillery, was soon found to have been secretly purchased—rumor said by the lodge—at a price so far in advance of its real value as to cover all pecuniary loss sustained in his abrupt departure. As it is on record by indisputable authority that the Grand Lodge and Grand Chapter of the State contributed large sums during the time the Morgan trials were pending for the aid and defence of their distressed Masonic brethren it will be seen that their claim to benevolence is not without a certain foundation; but as a band of thieves and murderers would probably be just as benevolent under similar circumstances I will cite one historical instance and let the subject pass.

The following spring, Richard Howard, the midnight incendiary, closely pursued by the officers of justice, entered an encampment of Knight Templars in the city of New York, and there confessed himself guilty of the murder of Morgan. He was helped to embark on board a vessel bound for some European port; and with the wages of sin in his hand, fled his native country, and how or where he died only the Judgment Day will reveal. The two others also escaped the grasp of the law by a flight into what was then the extreme western boundaries of the Union, but who shall say they went unpunished?—that in dreams haunted by the last look of their victim, in the sigh of the wind or the rustle of a leaf instinct with startling messages of fear for their guilty souls God did not vindicate his righteous judgment against all murderers.

Mark Stedman had been appointed on a circuit that came very near the Tonawanda line. For this reason or some other we soon found out by his letters that he was a frequent guest in the family of Mr. Jedediah Mills, whose troubles he was not slow to ascribe to their true origin—the machinations of the lodge.

"They mean to ruin him for the part he played in the rescue of Colonel Miller," wrote Mark. "When a vast secret power like Masonry sets itself against one solitary individual that individual must go to the wall. They mean to ruin Mr. Greene of the Park Tavern, and they are doing it as fast as they can by 'deranging his business' in every possible way. To tell you all the outrages he has suffered would fill a volume. He is making a brave fight, but what avails it against such an enemy? How long, O Lord, shall the wicked persecute? How long shall they bend their bow and make ready their arrows upon the string that they may privily shoot at the upright in heart?"

"Leander," said Rachel, suddenly, "I have heard of Hannah Mills through one of the Lokers. Miss Alvira Loker, you know, has connections in Tonawanda. She calls Hannah a real good Christian girl, and if Mark has taken a liking to her I am glad. He needs just such a wife as she would make him. Mark is all spirit—he forgets he has a body to be taken care of. I saw that plain enough when he was here two months ago. He was pale and thin and had a hacking cough on him. No wonder, catching cold every little while and never taking anything for it. Riding for miles wet to the skin, and then preaching, and then off again to hold another service somewhere else. He wants somebody to see to him, that he don't break down in a consumption before his work is half done; to lecture him every time he forgets to wear an overcoat or tie up his throat; to insist on his taking a hot drink after he has been out in the wet and cold, and see that his flannels are in order, and a thousand and one things that only a wife can do for him—a plain, sensible Christian woman that will glory in his usefulness and share his love for souls, and yet be a practical, common-sense adviser in all the ordinary affairs of life. Mark is all spirituality and ideality and heroism and what not, and I consider it a beneficent arrangement of Providence that such men are usually attracted to their opposites."

"Dear me, Rachel," I said, "you talk as if the whole matter was prearranged. Mark hasn't even mentioned Hannah Mills in this letter."

"Precisely the circumstance that adds weight to my suspicions," answered Rachel, briskly. "If he had mentioned her I should think there was nothing in it. You don't know everything, Leander."

And Rachel, who I must confess had in her secret heart a little of that love of matchmaking not uncommon in happily married wives, smiled with the pleasant complacency of superior knowledge, while I only uttered that sage and safe remark appropriate to all conditions of mortal uncertainty, "We shall see."

At the very time this conversation occurred, Mark Stedman was traveling on his circuit through woods just leafing out with the emerald hues of spring, and thinking over the subject on which he intended to preach when he reached his destination, a lonely school house where meetings were held at stated periods. He rode slowly, occasionally referring to his pocket Bible for some text, a kind of holy rapture filling his soul as he thought of the grandeur of the struggle before him and the joys of that final victory when the kingdoms of this world should become the kingdoms of our Lord and of his Christ—when every refuge of lies should be swept away and that embodiment of Satanic power and malice, the man of sin to which the New Testament writers point in dim and awful prophecy, should be forever destroyed in the brightness of his glorious second coming. For to such a mind as Mark's, things unseen and eternal have a palpable reality impossible to comprehend by any soul that lingers outside the pale of a full consecration. As he rode along intent on the message he was to deliver, earth seemed nothing and less than nothing; God and his eternal truth, everything.

Suddenly a shot split the air fired from the thicket through which Mark was passing. It took effect, wounding him in the arm. Another and another followed in quick succession but the flash and report so frightened his horse that it needed no spurring but broke at once into a furious run, and the second and third balls whizzed harmlessly past.

Providence doubtless ordered that the affair should happen near Tonawanda, and that when his trembling horse finally stopped, reeking with foam, it was close by Mr. Jedediah Mills' gate. His injury proved to be a flesh wound and nothing very serious, but he had to submit to considerable dressing and bandaging for a few days, during which time his resolution was taken to do what he had more than once half resolved upon doing in some of his lonely rides, and then abandoned as too great a sacrifice to require of the woman he loved—ask Hannah Mills if in deed and in truth she was willing to be the wife of a poor circuit preacher who felt it his mission to take side with every unpopular reform, and preach all sorts of unpalatable truths, and whom the world would frown upon accordingly, reserving its smiles for those prophets who prophesy unto it smooth things; who moreover was now engaged in deadly conflict with an unsparing foe sworn to persecute him to the death—would she, knowing all these things, consent to share his lot?

I happen to know Hannah's answer. It came in the words of a certain old Hebrew idyl which has stood for ages and will stand while time lasts as the epitome of that self-sacrificing devotion which shrinks from no trial with the loved one at its side.

And so Hannah Mills became Hannah Stedman, the elder's wife; and in process of time Rachel's wish was realized in that unlooked for way in which our wishes so often become prophecies, by their eventually occupying the very cottage from which we had moved on our grandfather's death.

As for Rachel, she would scarcely have been human if she had never once said, "I told you so."

CHAPTER XXX.

MASONIC SLANDER.—THE ENGAGEMENT.—RATTLESNAKE CORNER.

AS soon as we heard of the attack on Mark I started off for Tonawanda. It was not likely the actual perpetrators of the outrage would ever be known, but there was no reasonable doubt that they were tools of the lodge whose first plot to silence his fearless testimony had so signally miscarried —thanks to Sam Toller.

At one of the stopping places on the way an incident occurred so strongly illustrative of that spirit in Masonry which a distinguished seceder and writer on the subject has justly denominated "infernal," that I cannot forbear transcribing it.

A man well dressed, but with a general mingling of the fumes of whisky and tobacco about his person rather too strong to be agreeable, stood leaning against the bar apparently on the lookout for an acquaintance, which he finally recognized in a thin-visaged, nervous-looking individual with an umbrella and big carpet bag. The latter returned his salute with a rather slight nod and cool "How d'ye do?"—but the other was of a class not easy to snub.

"Going to put up at Greene's?" he inquired, familiarly.

"I was calculating to," responded the one interrogated.

"Maybe it's none of my business," resumed the other, with the air of a person obliged to say disagreeable things at the call of duty, "but if I did as I would like to be done by, I should tell you that Greene's tavern ain't a good place for travelers that have anything valuable about them. If *I* was obliged to put up there I should sleep with one eye open."

The nervous looking man glanced toward his carpet bag as if he saw it already in possession of unlawful hands, and answered in a slow, appalled way, "You don't say so. Why now I had no idea the Park Tavern was such a place, but I guess I'll go on to the next stand; it won't be much further. I declare, there's no knowing who to trust now-a-days." And depositing his umbrella carefully between his legs he sat down in a remote corner apparently absorbed in mournful reflections on the general wickedness of the world.

"Well, now," put in the landlord, who was standing behind the bar, making some entries in his book, "I must say I am surprised to hear that. I always supposed Greene kept a pretty nice house."

"I reckon after you had a bran new ten-dollar horse blanket taken from you as a neighbor of mine did that put up there last winter, you wouldn't think so, landlord. The fact is Greene's tavern is getting to be really a disreputable place to stop at, and I only do as my conscience tells me to in warning any traveler that I happen to know against going there."

It is needless to say that my blood fairly boiled with

indignation while I listened to these base calumnies, knowing so well their foul origin. Should I remain silent and let this thing in human semblance spit out his vile venom without reproof or contradiction? Never.

"I know Mr. Greene to be a Christian and a gentleman;" I said, turning to the man of conscience. "This is the first time I ever heard that travelers' things were not safe at his house."

My words had a somewhat similar effect to poking a venomous snake with a stick.

The stranger reddened with rage, and answered fiercely, "Do you tell me then that I lie?"

"No," I responded. quietly, "I hope you are only misinformed. But I repeat what I said, Mr. Greene has always borne a character above reproach; and it is certainly strange that no stories to the discredit of his house were ever circulated till the Morgan affair happened."

"Good now; I'll go sides with ye," interrupted a voice behind me. "I'd a blamed sight rather be him than the men that will steal their own blankets and then turn round and prosecute him. Or the men either that would take his poor dog, cut its throat from ear to ear and drown it at low water mark. When I get kinder riled up about such doings I pick out a psalm of David and read it—about Doeg the Edomite, or Cush the Benjaminite, or some other of them rascally chaps that he is always praying to be delivered from. There's one verse in particular—'His mischief shall return upon his own head and his violent dealings upon his own pate,' that does me as much good to think of as it ever did to eat my victuals."

And my new-found ally, who proved to my surprise to be the jocular man introduced to the reader on a previous occasion resumed his seat, and taking a jack-knife from his pocket proceeded to coolly pare an apple and cut it in even quarters, which he stowed away in his capacious mouth with the utmost ease.

Physical bulk and strength is something, decry it as we may, for there is a certain class of men who will pay respect to nothing else. The jocular man stood over six feet in his stockings, and had chest and limbs of herculean breadth and power. The other looked as much at a disadvantage as a terrier before a big Newfoundland dog, and did not choose, for prudent reasons, to turn on him in the same threatening, bullying fashion in which he had turned on me. So he contented himself with a few muttered words in reply and sneaked off, probably to play the same small game of detraction and calumny somewhere else.

Nothing was altered at Mr. Jedediah Mill's. The same air of comfort and thrift; the same kitchen with its scoured floor, its flag-bottomed, straight-backed chairs and homely hospitality; the same " best room " with a sampler Hannah had wrought in her girlhood, hanging over the high, black mantle, and such books as Rollins' Ancient History, Watts on the Mind and Baxter's Saints' Rest standing in solemn rows on the shelves of the bookcase, yet over it all rested the shadow of a brooding trouble as a thundercloud overhangs a fair landscape.

It was visible in Mrs. Mill's dejected face, in her husband's whitening hairs and even in the smile with which Hannah greeted me when I came to the door, for it was that pathetic kind of a smile which Old Sorrow and New Happiness are apt to wear before they have had time to make each other's acquaintance. Light and shadow, joy and grief! Wisely has Providence mingled the cup as we shall all know when we reach those love-illumined heights that rise beyond the mists of time and death; as many of us come to realize even here when some thorny trial blossoms into a rich red rose of blessing, and "Thy will be done" grows suddenly easy to say—so easy that we wonder it was ever hard.

For Hannah's parents were well suited with her choice, though in a worldly sense they knew she might have done better. They reverenced the young preacher with his slight frame, his burning ardor and devotion in his Master's cause, almost like an angelic messenger, and the recent assault upon him had naturally intensified the feeling by surrounding him with not a little of that homage with which, reasonably or otherwise, the best portion of humanity are apt to regard one who has come very near being enrolled in the noble army of martyrs.

Good Mrs. Mills, with pleasant garrulousness, told me the whole story of the courtship before I had been in the house twenty-four hours.

"Father has been real down in the mouth since this trouble come onto us about our farm. You see he's a man that won't give up a grain to injustice. He's always said he'd fight it out to the end if it took every dollar he had, for 'if I give 'em an inch,' says he, 'they'll take an ell, and then what am I better off?' It was two or three days after Mark was shot that father was sitting over the fire in one of his low spells, and I was trying to chirk him up a little by talking about the old times before we were married, and asking him if he remembered the first night we walked home from the singing school together, and how he walked in one rut and I in the other because we were too bashful to lock arms; but I couldn't get a smile onto his face. And just then the door opened, and father, he kinder started up, for there was Mark and Hannah, looking as happy as though they had just stepped out of Paradise. And I lay down my knitting, for I see what was coming, and I wondered how father would take it. Hannah stepped up and put her arms around his neck, and give a little sob; and then father seemed to understand it at last. He looked from Mark to Hannah, and says he, ' You know I am a poor man now, I can't give you any setting out.' And then Mark spoke up, and says he, ' We only want your consent and blessing. Hannah's wedding portion is in herself, and its value is far above rubies. I have told her what to expect if she marries me, but she is willing to try it.' And father gave his consent right off and seemed to cheer up wonderfully, so that I told Hannah afterwards, ' I hain't seen your father so like himself since he begun to have this lawsuit.' And though I do say it of my own daughter, Hannah will make a first-rate minister's wife. She is just cut out for it. She'll turn off work, baking or churning or spinning, and you wonder how she gets so much done with so little fuss; and then she will be all ready to go and watch with somebody that's sick. I tell folks she is just like her Aunt Eunice "—

But I forbear, remembering that the reader's interest will not be likely to extend as far as Aunt Eunice.

The marriage was to take place in a few months, for

as Mark said, neither of them wanted a long engagement. They were eager to enter upon their life work together. The time was short at best. Why should they make it any shorter by unnecessary delay?

Of course the reader of either sex who looks upon matrimony as an affair largely made up of bank stocks, diamond rings and elaborate *trousseaus* will have no patience with such an uncalculating young couple; and I fear that no excuse can be made for their verdancy which will be accepted in such quarters.

The fact was, Hannah Mills was not only "cut out to be a minister's wife," but she was cut out to be the helpmeet of a poor and unpopular minister, whose mission led him in the ways of Elijah and Ezekiel, and other old reformers, to the great detriment of his worldly prospects. And when she accepted Mark she simply accepted her vocation.

Mark accompanied me home to Brownsville as the best way to convince Rachel that he had not been seriously hurt, for the report had reached us, as reports generally do, in so exaggerated a form as to rouse all her sisterly anxiety.

He wanted to call at the Park Tavern, however, before he left, and Mr. Mills, having an errand in the direction of Batavia, the latter took us in his farm wagon as far as the outskirts of the village, where he dropped us and we proceeded the remaining distance on foot.

Batavia was now in its normal condition, a busy but seemingly peaceful community. I was thinking of the very different aspect it had worn on my first visit when we heard a confused shout from a rabble of men and boys in the distance that did not sound exactly like "mad dog," though the cry partook somewhat of that character. An instant after a window opened and a woman called loudly to a little tow-head making mud pies underneath: "Charles Henry, come into the house this minute, or you'll get bit."

The alarm, whatever its cause, seemed to spread with electric rapidity. There was a general banging of doors and windows, while frightened women, in all stages of dishabille rushed out frantically calling in their children as if they were menaced by some fearful danger.

"What is the matter?" we stopped to ask of one, the mother of the Charles Henry aforesaid—for that young gentleman was too delightfully engaged to heed at once the maternal call, and was now being dragged unceremoniously into the house in a small skirmish of slaps and kicks.

"Why, hain't you heard about it? It's awful. Twenty or thirty rattlesnakes loose right here in the village! You'd better take care of yourselves."

And so saying she disappeared with her contumacious young scion, while Mark and I looked around us for some weapon of defense. For though rattlesnakes had ceased to be indigenous to the soil of Western New York, they were not infrequently killed in remote or newly settled places, and many an old hunter could tell yarns quite sufficient to make the hair rise on the most unbelieving—how it fascinated its victim with circles of ever-changing light and color, mingling and melting, melting and mingling, with a low, throbbing music, sweet as the song of the Syrens, till the fatal spell was broken at last by its fangs in his flesh and the creeping chill of death at his heart.

Several men and boys ran past us to join the rapidly

nearing crowd, armed with every imaginable weapon from hickory clubs to brickbats and fire-shovels, and we heard the name of Greene mingled with threats and execrations as if he were in some way responsible for the escape of the reptiles.

"This is only another Masonic outrage on Mr. Greene;" said Mark, suddenly, dropping the stout sappling which he was trimming. "I don't believe there are any rattlesnakes about. See, they've stopped at the Park Tavern and are pouring into his yard. Come, Leander; we must see this affair through. I know a back way that we can take so as to avoid mixing with all that rabble."

Accordingly I followed Mark "the back way" and we entered the public room of the tavern just as a part of the mob, their search for stray rattlesnakes in Mr. Greene's yard and outbuildings having apparently been fruitless, carried the hunt into the house, loading its proprietor with every vile epithet. But the latter met them with cool self-possession. He had been under the fire of the lodge too often to show any surprise or trepidation at this new form of attack, and there was even a suppressed humor lurking about his mouth as if he saw a comical side to the affair.

"Gentlemen"—and I remember how his clear, full voice sounded above the uproar; a voice I was destined to hear afterwards from the platform as he told the story of Morgan to listening crowds, and faced mobs with the same calm, heroic bearing with which he now met the daily outrage and insults to which he was subjected—"the snakes are all safe in their box. Whoever said they had escaped spread a false report. I beg you will be content with this assurance and disperse."

"Do you think we will take *your* word for it, you cussed, perjured villain?" responded the foremost one, who seemed to be full not only of the spirit of the lodge but the spirit of whisky, and who as I afterwards learned had done a good deal of false swearing as a witness in the Morgan trials. And he brandished his club threateningly near to Mr. Greene's face, but the latter did not abate one atom of his cool, dignified bearing.

"You are not obliged to take my word for it. I can easily send for the man who asked leave to store the box in my granary. He can certify that not one of the snakes has got loose."

"I've seen the box myself and it is all right;" spoke up the bar-tender. "Do you suppose I would be such a precious fool as to stay here, if I knew any such varmints were crawling about?"

This argument was rather unanswerable, especially as another man, a lodger at the Park Tavern, added his own assurance to the same effect. And after a little more abuse of Mr. Greene the rioters—for such they were—finding their game was likely to be a losing one, departed.

The court was then sitting, Batavia being a county town, and the explanation of this whole scene consisted in the fact that one of the witnesses in a forthcoming trial had a box of rattlesnakes with him which he was taking to a man in New York.

He accordingly asked storage-room for it during the period of his stay at the Park Tavern. This was a grand opportunity for Mr. Greene's enemies of the lodge to spread a general panic through the village and frighten away his custom by a report that the snakes had broken loose.

He greeted Mark and I with a smile as untroubled as if he had just been waited on by some flattering committee who wanted to make him their political nominee; and his only reference to the scene that had passed was in these few quiet words as he took us into a small apartment adjoining the public room:

"You have only seen one specimen of the many ways in which the Masons are trying to ruin my business here in Batavia. I presume they will accomplish their end. My only comfort is that God rules in Heaven; a God of infinite justice, who has promised to hear the cry of the oppressed. To him I submit my cause."

Grand, simple-hearted Christian hero, thy wrongs were never righted on earth, but none the less sure the overthrow of every dark, unrighteous system of falsehood for whose destruction souls under the altar, that have shed their blood in the cause of truth, cry continually, "O, Lord, how long!"

Readers who may desire a proof that I am relating fact and not fiction, know that in the goodly village of Batavia there is a certain locality called by the townspeople to this day in memory of the foregoing occurrence, RATTLESNAKE CORNER.

CHAPTER XXXI.

NEW SCENES AND OLD FACES.

LET the reader imagine me a necromancer whose magic wand, waved lightly over him, has the power of putting him to sleep for about forty years; for though a great many things may happen in that period of time very interesting to the world at large, to say nothing of minor events equally interesting in a smaller way to the individual, none of which would be omitted by a conscientious historian or a careful biographer, I am neither the one nor the other. I am simply telling the story of my experience with Freemasonry; and if, when nearly all the States passed laws prohibiting extra-judicial oaths, and the churches of Christ everywhere disfellowshipped adhering Masons, the institution had actually died down as it feigned to do I should probably make this my concluding chapter, or, what is more likely, not have written any story at all, preferring to let the dead bury its dead in decent oblivion.

But the wounded dragon of Masonry did not yield up its life so easily. At the South, under cover of the night-dark wing of slavery it hid in shame and dishonor, to slowly recover from its grievous hurt, and finally

NEW SCENES AND OLD FACES.

creep forth again into the light—not always under its true name—while brave men and women, fighting with tongue and pen for the freedom of the slave never dreamed what chains were forging in secret, or how in their own free North the time would come when under the intimidating power of the lodge men dared not freely discuss its claims; when editors of religious journals would refuse, in their craven fear of losing patronage, to publish articles against it; and even the Christian ministers, while hating it at heart, should be afraid—Oh, shame!—actually afraid to stand up in the pulpit and speak God's truth concerning it.

But in passing over such an interim of time there must necessarily be many scattered threads, which it behooves me to gather up and knit in one general whole before I proceed further.

Of the scores of persons actually participating in the murder of Morgan or consenting thereto, only five were convicted. Loton Lawson was sentenced to two years' imprisonment, Nicholas G. Cheesboro to one and Eli Bruce, Edward Sawyer and John Whitney to varying terms of one month or more, and this was all that resulted from four years' trials and investigations.

That these men were considered by their brethren of the lodge, not as convicted felons but as martyrs to the Masonic cause may be inferred from the fact that they remained in full fellowship therewith as members in good and regular standing; that they were visited daily while in jail by their Masonic brethren, in many cases accompanied by their wives and daughters; that they were furnished with every luxury money could procure, and when their term was up escorted from prison in triumph. But O, most benevolent Masonry, where were thy bowels of compassion for many an unfortunate brother confined within those very walls, not for kidnapping and murder, but for debt?

Darius Fox came unexpectedly back to Brownsville about a year after his sudden flight—nowise improved by his stay among the wild and reckless characters of the western frontier. Why he chose to run the risk of returning; whether he had been led to believe that all danger of conviction was over, or whether his course was dictated by mere braggadocio, is more than I can say. But he talked swaggeringly about having "come back to stand his trial," and had his small circle of admirers, who surrounded him in store and tavern, and praised and cheered him as if he had done a very brave and plucky thing in returning.

Perhaps he had overlooked the possibility that some of his associates in evil might turn State's evidence against him. A few days after his unexpected appearance in Brownsville one of the men convicted of abducting Morgan gave testimony in regard to his own share in that transaction that would inevitably have consigned him to a felon's cell had he not been found dead the next morning. The cause of his sudden death was said to be apoplexy, though a story never exactly authenticated was whispered about and believed by many in Brownsville that he had really hung himself in a moment when remorse and fear of punishment so acted on a mind unbalanced by drink as to drive him to self-destruction; and his family, to avoid the dishonor attaching to the name of suicide, had attempted to cover up the fact by ascribing his untimely end to a cause which was not the true one.

But whether he met death by his own hand or in the

common orderings of Providence, Darius Fox went to his own place, where, in the course of years, all his companions in crime followed him; into that dim eternity towards which the evil and the righteous are alike hastening, where the deeds done in the body are either angel's wings ever raising us higher in the scale of purified being, or weights sinking us deeper and deeper into the pit of final despair.

For three years the proprietor of the Park Tavern tried to carry on his business in the face of wrongs and outrages that in number and petty malignity fell to the lot of no other Antimason of those days. Hear his own words on the subject:

"My help was hired to leave me; others sent who after being hired would get in debt and prove unfaithful. Sham sales of stage horses would be made to unprincipled drivers who would keep their horses at my house on usual contracts, and when a quarterly bill was presented against the ostensible owner it would be shoved off upon the driver, who was irresponsible and would abscond; or, if sued, pay the debt on the jail limits. Merchants with whom I had dealt would divide my accounts and sue me on each day's trade, causing me to pay unnecessary costs."

Nor did they stop short at personal violence, as witness his further testimony:

"My furniture was injured, and in my attempts to save it from destruction I have been choked in my own house till my family were alarmed lest my life should be taken. All this was done with the avowed intention of tempting me to commit assault and battery, or seek redress by law suit that they might avail themselves of the law to destroy me effectually."

The fight was too unequal. What chance had one man, however just his cause, against hundreds working in secret conclave to accomplish his ruin? Mr. Greene disposed of his business in Batavia, and as a public lecturer did more, perhaps, than any other man to enlighten the public mind on the real nature of Freemasonry.

Undaunted by opposition, undismayed by danger, though he once came very near sharing the fate of Morgan, he kept on his way, lecturing, editing, publishing, side by side with a young man, Lloyd Garrison by name, who had just heard the bugle-call to another conflict which was destined ere long to be the one great absorbing issue that should swallow up all others.

The *Liberator* and the *Antimasonic Christian Herald* were both published in the same building and delivered by the same carrier—but while one waxed and grew the other waned before the new struggle for human rights. And when a terrible punishment was at last meted out to us; when every newspaper was like the prophet's scroll written throughout with mourning and lamentation and woe; when Rachels wept their dead in Northern and Southern homes alike, who saw the secret hands working in darkness and silence to prolong the contest?

Good patriots on the Union side blushed for the cowardice and incompetency that stayed idly in the trenches for weeks and months; that led hosts of brave men to inglorious slaughter or disgraceful flight before the enemy. Could they have known that promotion did not depend on bravery or merit, but on the number of Masonic degrees; could they have witnessed those secret, midnight meetings when Northern generals fraternized with the enemy, they would have had a better understanding of the whole subject. And when the guns of the Rebellion were silenced and the smoke cleared away, could they have seen delegations from Northern lodges on a visit to Southern cities uniting in brotherly union with Knights of the Golden Circle, these same good people would not have been so slow to recognize, grinning under the mask of the Ku Klux, the same old enemy against which Samuel D. Greene so faithfully warned his countrymen.

He died on the threshold of the on-coming struggle —a new struggle with an ancient foe, and saw not its end. Pursued even to the last by the unsparing hatred of the lodge he died as he had lived, boldly testifying to " the truth as it is in Jesus " against every " unfruitful work of darkness," and now translated into that great " cloud of witnesses " perhaps he *does* see the end after all.

Bright, mischievous brother Joe married early in life a fair acquaintance of Brownsville, who I have reason to suspect was the same he accompanied home from Jake Goodwin's party, and emigrated to Kansas in the early stages of its struggle to be a free State, where as a friend and associate of John Brown he participated in more than one stirring scene of that eventful era.

Sam Toller has long since passed from earth, but there is still a circle, slowly narrowing, who hold him in kindly remembrance.

Luke Thatcher has represented his native State in the Legislature and is looked up to by his neighbors as an honest, far-seeing man who is always on the right side of every social and political question.

Mr. Jedediah Mills lost his lawsuit and his farm—a result not hard to predict from the beginning. Anxiety and trouble so wore upon him that he did not live long after, and another name was added to that hidden roll of martyrs to the lodge which God keeps in his secret place against the day " when he maketh inquisition for blood."

Mark Stedman's life has been one of constant warfare with every prevailing and popular form of sin. When the Antimasonic excitement died away and even he believed that the lodge had fallen never to rise again, he turned his attention to the crime of American slavery. At a time when the mere avowal of Abolitionist principles cost more than the present generation can readily conceive, he preached, prayed and worked for the emancipation of the slave. And careless of fine and imprisonment, out of his own slender store he and his good wife Hannah sent many a fugitive rejoicing on their way towards the North Star—a work in which Rachel and I not infrequently had the pleasure of helping, for both families left Brownsville and moved to Ohio about the same time, where we settled in easy visiting distance of each other.

We are a staid, elderly couple now, Rachel and I, with a number of grandchildren to spoil, and one or two grown-up fledglings still lingering about the home nest. But our little David never went forth with sling and stone against any of these moral Goliaths that from time to time have come out from their Philistine fastnesses to defy our American Israel. One bright summer day we laid him under the green grass in Brownsville cemetery, and on another summer day as bright, there came to our home a second little David,

He sleeps in his nameless grave at Antietam. Still another of our boys donned the blue and marched proudly away to die by slow starvation in a Southern prison.

Oh, it is not in hours of joy that hearts knit together the closest and strongest! From that mighty baptism of anguish Rachel and I came forth united in the grand fellowship of suffering without which love is like gold that lacks the test of the crucible.

And now having brought my story down to Anno Domini, 1870 or thereabouts, I take it for granted that the reader is sufficiently interested to wait its further development, first promising that the end is not far off. For with Rachel and I the shadows are beginning to stretch eastward. She sits shelling beans in the porch which commands a view of rich Ohio cornfields basking in the August sun, a gray-haired, placid-browed matron. But the fires of youth flash still from her brown eyes, showing that she has not materially altered from the quick, imperious Rachel of former days.

If any one doubts it let him rouse her indignation by some act of meanness or duplicity, and if he don't have cause to remember that day as long as he lives I am very much mistaken.

CHAPTER XXXII.

THE MYSTERY OF INIQUITY.

RACHEL finished shelling her pan of beans and carried them into the kitchen. Then in obedience to a certain thrifty custom nearly obsolete now but very common with industrious housewives of a former generation who did not choose to allow Satan even so small a vantage ground as a few idle moments between sundown and dark, she took out a half-finished sock on which her needles flew briskly till she had knit about six times around, when her inward musings took shape in this terse sentence:

"I don't see into it."

"Don't see into what, mother?" I asked. For we had now reached that comfortable stage in our matrimonial journey when to address each other by the parental title seems the most natural thing in the world.

"How Anson Lovejoy can be a Mason. Now I really like the man, and always have liked him from the very first. But when I find that he can take part in such ridiculous, blasphemous folly, and be himself actually Master of a lodge, initiating others into it, I—well, really, I don't know what to think except that there is one more fool in the world than I had supposed."

And Rachel knit vigorously several more rounds while I pondered the subject in silence. I too liked Anson Lovejoy in spite of the fact that he was not only a Mason, but held the office of Worshipful Master of Fidelity Lodge, located in the flourishing village of Granby, Ohio; said lodge numbering among its members one or two ministers, a saloon-keeper, one deacon, several notorious gamblers and a general sprinkling of the lowest characters in the place, all " meeting on the level" in felicitous union and fellowship.

" Well, mother," I said, finally, "a man isn't always a fool because he does foolish things. The fact is I've had a little talk with him on the subject of Masonry, and I have come to the conclusion that it isn't the system as it really is that he admires, but an ideal existing only in his own imagination of something it might, could, would or should be if it was only properly understood, and more care exercised in admitting candidates; such delightfully impossible conditions, in short, that I was strongly reminded of the old couplet:

'If wishes were horses beggars would ride,
If 'twas a sword it would hang by your s'de.' "

" Now, father "—and Rachel laid down her knitting in her earnestness—" why don't you put it right to him about the oaths and obligations and ceremonies. You have been through them yourself and know all about it, so you are just the one. What if this man's soul should be required at your hands?"

" I did ' put it right to him.' I told him he had sworn to conceal the criminal acts of brother Masons, to warn them of approaching danger and help them out of all difficulties, no matter what wrong-doing might be the cause. But he had one answer for every objection, and that was that he did not so understand Masonry, and only considered its obligations binding when they failed to conflict with any superior duty that he owed to God or to Government. I asked him if that was the way he explained them to candidates. He assured me it was. I told him flat that such teaching of Masonic obligations was a mistake and a contradiction; that Masonry owns no law and no authority outside of or superior to herself; that when she ceases to be a complete despotism; when she allows her members to put their own interpretation on the oaths and penalties; above all, when she elevates the Bible from a mere piece of lodge furniture on a level with the square and compass to be what the old Westminster divines called it 'the only sufficient rule of faith and practice,' her power has fled. She simply cannot exist under such conditions."

"And what did he say to that?" asked Rachel.

"Well, that fellow Jervish came in just then and broke up our talk. I suppose he thinks me a fool and a fanatic. I consider him an honest, well-meaning man, whose chief mistake is in thinking that he can do what the Scriptures declare impossible—'Bring a clean thing out of an unclean.'"

"Well, I don't understand it," repeated Rachel, decidedly. "There must be something wrong somewhere when a man can't see the plain truth put right before him."

For Rachel was like most practical, matter-of-fact people, not subject to glamours of any sort. When she saw a truth she saw it clearly—a sun-illumined mount of God piercing heaven unclouded by bewildering fogs and mists, and could not understand why any honest mind should fail to perceive it too. But I knew better how men like Anson Lovejoy can be made the apologists and defenders of a lie; how they naturally seek, the first disappointment over, to reconcile the teachings of Masonry with their own standard of human duty, and only succeed by an ingenious system of interpretations that, carried into practical effect, would annul the whole thing. My grandfather so reasoned till the murder of Morgan opened his eyes. But a man like Anson Lovejoy, who belonged to a generation that knew not Morgan—must another tragedy as fearful shock the public mind and rouse in even the dullest that indignation so terrible because it is a dim shadow of the divine wrath against evil doers, before he could be made to see?

This question I silently asked myself while Rachel rolled up her knitting and called to Grace, our youngest, to light a lamp.

"Yes, Mother," answered Grace, and rose promptly from her seat on the back steps, where she was giving his first lesson in astronomy to a favorite nephew named Joe, of whom I can only say that he had already begun to develop a talent for mischief that bade fair in time to cast all the youthful exploits of the original Joe quite into the shade. At the same moment the gate swung open and admitted a female figure with a tin pail.

"Mother, there is Mary Lyman come to borrow some yeast."

"Well, Grace, you can get it for her." And Rachel drew up her chair within the circle of the light and took her sewing, while she invited the new-comer with a kindly smile to sit down.

She was a girl of not more than seventeen—hardly that. Her large blue eyes, regular features and heavy braids of tawny gold hair made her face one of singular beauty. But there was a sad, depressed look about her mouth, and a lack of youthful elasticity in her motions that made her seem older than she really was.

She took her pail of yeast and departed with a murmured word of thanks. Rachel sewed very fast for several minutes till she snapped her thread. Then she broke out—

"I say, it is a shame."

"What now, mother?"

"To keep that girl as they do. I know how it is just as well as if I saw it; drudge, drudge from morning till night. Not a minute in the twenty-four hours she can call her own. No chance for improvement but plenty of chances for everything else. It is too bad, poor orphan child!" added Rachel, who had all the large-hearted instincts of true motherhood, and its capabilities of indignation also.

"Well, I know it is too bad; but she'll be free in a year or so. That's one comfort."

"I wish her time was out now," responded Rachel. "Grace can't keep school and help me much. And I believe if I could have the training of Mary for a while I might make something of her yet."

"What! at eighteen?" I asked, with natural incredulity.

"Yes, at eighteen," answered Rachel, biting her thread with an air of decision. "It is a mistake to think the die for good or evil must be cast at a particular age. It all depends on circumstances. Now this girl makes me think of some tiger-lilies I remember grew behind the barn when I was a child. I don't know how they ever came there, in that sunless corner, but there they were, growing and blossoming in about the same fashion that she is ripening into womanhood. All she wants is a chance to develop herself. If I could give her that I should feel that I had done one good work in the world before I leave it."

"Why, mother; your life has been nothing but giving and doing for forty years."

"Well, I don't know about that, father," answered Rachel, with a little shake of her head. But I could see that her husband's praise was very sweet to her, nevertheless.

The girl of whom we had been speaking was, as Rachel said, an orphan whom fate, personified by the selectmen of Granby, had delivered over to be the victim of a species of white slavery in the family of a Mr. Simon Peck. To scrub floors, feed the hogs, fetch the water and lug a heavy baby about when there was nothing else for her to do, was the routine of her daily life varied by such small tyrannies and exactions from the younger Pecks as the ingenuity of their own minds or the example of their elders might suggest.

It was not strange that all Rachel's womanly feelings had been roused in behalf of the girl. A natural refinement had kept her from assimilating with her rough and coarse surroundings, and she was now growing up to a dower of singular beauty. Who should say whether it would prove a blessing or a curse?

Rachel sewed away in silence for a few moments and when she again spoke it was to recur to our former subject of talk.

"Well, I don't see, as I said before, how such men as Anson Lovejoy can defend Masonry, but I think I understand the reason why I don't understand it."

"What do you mean, mother?"

"Why, it is the 'mystery of iniquity.' We talk about 'the mystery of godliness' that cannot be known except by Christians, but we forget there is something corresponding to it on the other side. There are depths of Satanic craft just as there are depths of Redeeming Wisdom. We can't understand either. They are beyond us. It is the 'deceivableness of unrighteousness,' 'the strong delusion.' Mystery; that is just what it is, the mystery of iniquity."

And Rachel resumed the work which she had let fall in her earnestness, while I pondered over her words, and concluded that she was about right.

CHAPTER XXXIII.

AUGEAN STABLES.

FIDELITY Lodge met in the upper story of a brick building near the center of the village, agreeably to the practice of their ancient brethren who assembled on high places to worship Baal, as standard Masonic authorities confirmed by all the Bible commentaries and encyclopedias, unite to inform us. It numbered sixty or seventy members and to outward appearances was in a prosperous condition. But an examination of the secretary's books would have revealed a tale of disordered finances only equalled by the petty bickerings and out-and-out quarrels that at every meeting of the lodge vexed the soul of the Worshipful Master, who strove heroically to infuse his own high Masonic ideal into the worthy brethren, but never succeeded in quite satisfying himself or anybody else.

It is a melancholy fact that "the good men in the lodge" of whom we hear so much are a practical nonentity beside a few unscrupulous members. Goodness is modest and apt to shrink into the background, but wickedness is aggressive and outspoken. Anson Lovejoy, though he held the highest office in the lodge, did not wield in reality a tenth part of the influence exercised by another member who held no office at all.

This was Mr. Jervish, to whom the reader will remember that I made a rather disparaging allusion in my talk with Rachel recorded in the last chapter. I disliked the man without knowing anything very positive about him beyond what the tongue of rumor asserted—that he was a free-thinker in religion and a libertine in morals. But it must not be supposed that these two trifling circumstances affected in the least his good and regular standing in the lodge, or moved any one of the reverend gentlemen belonging thereto to protest for the honor of their sacred office against such companionship.

It was commanded of old that even the burden-bearers of the temple should be clean from all defilement. Shall they who are separated to a far higher service fraternize in unholy union with men who habitually violate God's code of moral purity, and think to stand with unspotted garments in the pulpit? Can their prayers, their sermons, their breaking of bread in the Holy Supper, be anything but an abomination and a loathing in his sight? O, Church of the living God, how long will you allow such foolish pastors to lay waste your fair heritage? O, Bride of Christ, how long shall your honor be turned to shame by their praises of your harlot rival?

Mark—or, to speak more correctly, Elder Stedman. had lost none of his old hatred to the lodge. He had only relaxed his warfare on the system when he believed that it was down never to rise again from its mortal hurt. And now the fall of slavery had made a silence in which the approaching footsteps of the next great issue were plainly perceptible to "the hearing ear," which Elder Stedman believed ought to be more characteristic of the ministry than any other class of men —an opinion largely based on the Bible account of the old prophets, who certainly took a lively interest in the great moral questions of their day. But a good many people did not share this idea, and when Mark began to level his arrows at Masonry there was the usual number of undiscerning good men outside of the lodge "who thought ministers ought to preach the gospel and let other subjects alone. But the Elder had never been in the habit of reading his marching orders backward. He hadn't the slightest notion that the command, "Cry aloud and spare not," really meant, "Be silent on all popular sins and spare the feelings of sinners as much as possible." And so he preached on, as serenely careless of any disturbance produced by his words as the sun is of all the agitated runnings to and fro in some colony of discomforted beetles suddenly exposed to the light.

Masonry was strong in Granby, and under its shadow flourished Odd-fellowship, and all the kindred secret orders that like mushrooms sprang up in the night of the war to cover the land with their rank, foul growth. It was strong enough to make men who hated the system from the bottom of their hearts shrink from discussing it with that strange fear that only the lodge is capable of inspiring—to strike the whole community with a kind of moral paralysis, an unaccountable apathy that is like a death chill at the heart of all free thought.

"What can the church be thinking of not to wake up to her duty in this matter of Masonry?" said Mark to me one day when he and Hannah had rode over for an hour's cozy chat and a cup of tea together. Above all, what is the ministry thinking of not to see that fellowship with the lodge is spiritual adultery?—the very same sin for which God visited the Jewish church with such terrible judgments. There is a blindness on this subject that is perfectly inscrutable. In many places the churches are so completely dominated and controlled by this foul spirit of secrecy that they are like a hive of bees riddled through and through with moths. There is no spiritual life left in them."

"Well, the fact is, we reformers made a terrible blunder in the old Morgan days, and now our children and children's children must pay for it by fighting the battle all over again. We took it for granted that the lodge was dead and dropped all talking and writing on the subject. Meanwhile Masonry was striking hands with the slave power south of Mason and Dixon's line, and hatching up Odd-fellowship and Good Templarism and a host of other secret orders to keep the way open for its ultimate return to power. Now it is back in its old place with at least a hundred avenues for mischief where it had one before."

"But we've got the old weapons to fight it with," returned Mark. "Thank God for that."

Rachel and Hannah had been indulging in some low-toned domestic confidences. Their attention was now attracted to the conversation and the latter remarked:

"I wonder that so many women, and some of them sisters in the church too, can stand in an apologetic attitude towards the lodge when they know it excludes and treats with contempt the whole female sex."

"Well, I had an experience on that point," answered

Rachel," at our last sewing meeting, Colonel Montfort's wife, Maria Perkins that was—you remember her Hannah—was telling about a Masonic grand ball that she attended somewhere, given in honor of the members' wives; and she stirred me up after a while to ask her how much of their charity fund she supposed went toward the supper and the music, and all the other fol-de-rols. I might as well have talked to a butterfly. There are always enough foolish women with about as much brain as you could get into a thimble, that don't care two straws for the moral side of the question. All they want is flattery and admiration and a good time, and the lodge has found out that a little judicious expenditure of money in that direction pays even if Masonic widows and orphans don't get one per cent. dividend."

"And yet," answered the Elder's wife, thoughtfully, "I believe that one Christian woman who through ignorance, or timidity, or the feeling that it is a subject in which she is not personally concerned, gives the lodge as much as her silent support, strengthens it more than a dozen of the frivolous, pleasure-seeking class. How many times I have heard the remark from good, praying sisters, 'O, I don't know anything about Masonry and I don't care to know anything about it.' They owe all their social elevation to Christ, but when a system of rites and ceremonies that sets him and his atoningwork at nought rises up in our land they talk as though they actually prided themselves on their indifference to the whole thing."

"I can truly say that the sorest wounds I ever received in this warfare have been in the house of my friends," said Mark. Many a time I have had to meet coldness and scorn from professing Christians for breaking my lodge oaths. They pretend to think it wicked to take such obligations, yet with admirable consistency would keep a man bound in Satan's cable-tow forever, rather than praise the power of God in setting him free."

"I suppose Colonel Montfort is a member of the lodge here?" inquired Hannah. "I think I remember hearing that his war record wasn't very good—tarnished by charges of dishonest use of government money or something of the kind."

"That is not a Masonic sin," I answered. "He only cheated poor soldiers. Colonel Montfort has plenty of 'worthy brothers' in the lodge guilty of equal or greater transgressions that ought to send them to State's prison, and would if the laws were enforced as they ought to be. But these men understand the requirements of Masonry better than the Master of the lodge—Anson Lovejoy, who is the most honest Mason I ever knew, next to my grandfather. In spite of the fact that I am a renegade and perjured and altogether a reprobate, Masonically considered, he has unbosomed his perplexities to me pretty freely at one time and another. And I really pity the man. *He* don't rule: he fills the chair, but these men, especially Montfort and Jervish, are the real Masters of the lodge. I'll tell you one thing just for illustration. He was initiating a candidate who hesitated at a certain part of the oath and so he proceeded to satisfy his perplexed conscience by explaining that it only obliged him to help a brother in misfortune but not by any means to shield him in crime. Montfort and Jervish took exceptions to what he said in open lodge—a thing that, Masonically speaking, they had no business to do, for according to all the statutes of Masonry the Master's word shall be law in the lodge. And ever since that affair happened his position has been anything but agreeable. He considers them as dangerous men and they dispute and defy his authority at every turn."

"I wonder he don't resign," said Mark.

"He has wanted to, but the difficulty of uniting under anybody else makes them unwilling to accept his resignation; and the perplexity of choosing a new Master of the lodge might tend under present circumstances to divide or break it up altogether. You see he has a splendid theory of Masonry, and like most theorists he is willing to sacrifice considerable for it. He is naturally high-spirited but he pockets all these affronts and indignities in the hope that he may finally work such a moral revolution in the lodge that unworthy members will be no longer admitted, and the institution become what he claims it should be—simply a moral and benevolent one."

"I understand," said Mark, with a slight smile. "Hercules and the Augean stables over again. But Hercules had to stand outside when he let on the purifying stream, otherwise he would have stood an excellent chance to get smothered."

CHAPTER XXXIV.

ONE MORE UNFORTUNATE.

MR. SIMON PECK'S establishment consisted of a small grocery store with two or three untidy rooms in the rear, where every article in the canon of a good housewife was persistently set at nought. Mrs. Simon Peck was a woman with thin yellow hair done up in perpetual curl papers and a general appearance suggestive of washed-out calico. Of the younger Pecks the less said the better. They were all that might be expected, however, considering their parentage and training.

This man belonged to Fidelity Lodge, and low as was his social standing compared with Colonel Montfort and others of its leading members, he held a very important office therein which was that of general toady as well as a most convenient cat's-paw for any species of dirty work with which the Colonel did not care to soil his aristocratic fingers. This satellitic intimacy with the great men of the lodge had caused Mr. Peck to advance considerably in his own good opinion, for with the usual obtuseness of toadies he never seemed to suspect the real grounds on which it was based, and set on by the powerful clique before mentioned he contrived in a variety of ways—none of which were very agreeable to a sensitive and finely-strung spirit—to throw contempt on the authority of the Master of the lodge by sly, underhand methods of attack, much more annoying than open warfare.

"But were there no good men in Fidelity Lodge?" inquires the reader. Assuredly there were, but of these many had fallen into that habit of non-attendance which certainly has illustrious prestige in George Washington's example, not to mention later worthies to whom the lodge proudly points as "distinguished Masons," while those who remained wielded no influence worth speaking of. Thus it will be seen that Anson Lovejoy in his attempts to mold the lodge after his own high Masonic standard was not a whit better off than if he had stood entirely alone.

It was not often that I patronized Mr. Peck's counter, but one morning I was in a hurry and stepped in there for some article indispensable to the kitchen economy which had been overlooked in making out the usual household list of necessaries.

Mary, who sometimes waited on customers, went behind the counter and weighed out the pound of bread soda for which I called. I could not help noting as she did so her expression of silent misery and dejection. My heart ached for her. Is it possible, I thought, that in the loving providence of the All-wise Father some lives must ever remain like the unsunned tiger lilies to which Rachel in one of those gleams of poetic sentiment that we so often see flash across the most common-sense and practical nature, had likened her? But all I could do was to drop a pleasant word as she handed me the brown paper parcel, little thinking that when I saw that face again the great Eternal Mystery would have set on every feature its awful seal of silence and separation never to be broken by human blame or pity.

I laid the package down on the kitchen table where Rachel stood rolling out pies and superintending the oven from which several comely brown loaves had just emerged.

"I wonder if that Mary Lyman isn't in some kind of trouble," I said. "Her face really haunts me, she looked so wretched. Of course I couldn't say anything to her, but a real good, motherly woman like you might find out what the matter is and perhaps help her."

Rachel filled a pie thoughtfully and ornamented the edges with elaborate care. I felt that there was something behind her silence and waited patiently till the revelation should come. She put her pie in the oven and proceeded to roll out another before she spoke, and then it was to make an inquiry not apparently connected with the subject.

"I have heard you speak once or twice of a certain Mr. Jervish, a friend of Colonel Montfort's. What do you know about him in particular?"

"Well, nothing in particular, but in general I should call him an unmitigated son of Belial. However, he has got policy enough to keep his vices pretty well under the surface, and so he gets admitted freely into good society, as such men usually do, and no questions asked. Why?"

"It may not be true what I have heard, what I suspect, but if it is"—and Rachel stood erect with firm-set lips and flashing eyes—"if it is, I don't want any other proof that the Bible doctrine of everlasting punishment is the right one."

For a moment I felt stunned. Pity, shame, abhorrence of the wretch who had wrought such sacrilegious ruin of one of God's fairest human temples struggled together in contending tides of feeling. They who think it strange that in the Apocalypse the Hallelujahs of God's saints are represented as rising joyous and triumphant in sight of the smoke of eternal burnings have surely never felt as I did at that moment—glad from my very soul that there is such an awful place of retribution where the punishment which society fails to mete out for crimes like this shall at last be visited upon the evil doer.

"As she doesn't happen to be a Mason's wife or daughter," said Rachel, bitterly, "her destroyer will go scot free as far as the lodge is concerned. Ministers of the gospel will call him 'brother' all the same, and when he dies they'll drop their sprig of evergreen into the grave and make a prayer to the Supreme Architect of the Universe, and he'll be all right for the Grand Lodge above. I tell you I'm sick at heart when I think of it."

And Rachel scraped up her dough and put it back in the pan for a Saturday pie, and the clock ticked away in the corner and the sunshine stole in with a fresh breeze to bear it company; and everything went on precisely the same as if the world had no such awful abyss of sin and sorrow as that which had now opened before us.

"But this poor, fatherless, motherless girl," I said at last. "Can't we do anything to help her? We believe in Christ's way of treating the fallen and not in society's way. Let us show our faith by our deeds."

"Well, father," said Rachel, with a softened voice,

"I'm sure I'm willing to try, I've been thinking it over. I don't just see my way clear yet, but I shall, of course; I always do."

Which was no unfounded boast. Rachel's "thinking," as with most persons of her positive temperament, usually resulted in very energetic action. For just as soon as the pies and cakes were out of the oven and cooling on the pantry table she put on her bonnet and stepped across to the Peck's back yard, where a kitchen garden flourished as well as it could under adverse circumstances. Here among trailing vines of cucumbers and tomato and summer squash, Mary was picking vegetables for dinner, and shielded from sight of the house by a long row of bean-poles, Rachel went and knelt down by the side of the surprised girl, and without the slightest circumlocution inquired gently but firmly—

"Mary, I want to know if this story I have heard about you is true? If you say 'No,' I shall believe you and rejoice. But tell me the truth."

Now if Rachel had not been kind in days before—if she had not manifested by word and look that she felt a true womanly interest in the bound girl who lived at the Peck's she never could have taken this poor erring human heart by storm as she did.

Mary looked up quickly, colored and burst into tears.

"Mrs. Severns," she said, wildly, "I am going to drown myself. I thought it all over last night, but I couldn't make up my mind. There is no place in the world for me—there never was—and it is the best thing I can do."

Rachel quietly took the two hands down from the averted face and held them fast in her own cool grasp.

"Don't talk that way, Mary. God has raised you up two friends in Mr. Severns and I. We are going to do all we can for you. Don't add sin to sin by destroying yourself, and remember, another life with your's."

"What is the use of your talking to me?" said the girl, turning in a kind of fierce despair. "Why don't you let me alone?"

"Because I have no right to let you alone, and because there is hope for you yet. Satan may tell you there is none, but don't hearken to his lie. There is a place for repentance—at the feet of Him who said to a sinner of old time who had fallen lower than you, 'Go, and sin no more.'"

So Rachel talked, strong, brave, Christ-like words, till Mary ceased weeping, and it seemed as though a faint, pale rainbow of real hope had begun to span the gulf of her shame and despair. And then Rachel, rising up from her lowly position behind the beanpoles went home feeling as I think one of God's angels must returning from some errand of celestial pity to a sinning soul of this lower world.

"Father," she said, after dinner, "I have been thinking of Aunt Faith. That would be just the place for Mary if I can get her taken in there, and I feel sure I can, so if you will just have the wagon harnessed up I'll go right over and see her this very afternoon."

Now Aunt Faith was an elderly Quakeress, a kind of uncommissioned Sister of Mercy who knew nothing of training schools or any of the organized systems of charity, but worked independently of all these on a system of her own, which, upon critical examination, might be found to be quite as near the New Testament pattern; and here, as Rachel said, was exactly the refuge the poor girl needed; rest from the strife of tongues, shelter for the present and counsel for the future; and more than all else, a living daily manifestation of the great pitiful Christ Heart, breathing in every movement of Aunt Faith's motherly person, every fold of her Quaker gray dress that partook as little of this world's fashions as if it had been a kind of spiritual emanation, like the mantle of meekness and charity made visible to mortal eyes in tangible form and material.

"Don't thee worry, friend Rachel," she said. "The poor soul shall have all needed care. Nor do I want thy thanks. It is for the dear Lord's sake I do it, as thee very well knows."

Rachel had one more task before her, and that was to acquaint Mary with what had been done, and arrange for her speedy departure from the Peck household. Though not remiss in neighborly offices she had never cared to be on visiting terms with Mrs. Peck, and shrank from what she foresaw would be likely to prove a disagreeable interview. It was late when we reached home, but early next morning Rachel went over, feeling that the sooner the business was accomplished the better.

She saw nothing of Mary. Mrs. Peck, with profuse welcomes and many apologies—neither of which Rachel heeded—took her into the dirty, disordered sitting-room. She looked disturbed, but perhaps it was only the perturbation caused by Rachel's unexpected visit.

"I came to have some talk with you about your girl Mary," said the latter. "I don't see her about; where is she?"

"She's gone off. I hain't seen her since last night."

"Gone off! Where to?" asked Rachel, startled with a horrible fear as she remembered Mary's wild words the day before.

"That's more than I know, where to. But she'll never come back here, the baggage," answered Mrs. Peck, flushing with virtuous indignation. "After disgracing herself and all the rest of us as she has I don't want her in my family again.

Now if Rachel had not been so strongly possessed with the idea that Mary had destroyed herself she might have suspected that Mrs. Peck lied in thus denying all knowledge of her whereabouts. As it was, the shock with which she first heard the news gave place to a sudden revulsion of feeling. She felt a real antipathy to the woman, and before leaving the house she emptied several vials of very righteous wrath on the head of Mrs. Peck, who she rightfully averred had taken Mary to be a mere household drudge, had taught her nothing, and was therefore responsible in no small degree for her lapse from virtue.

Mrs. Peck was angry at first, then took the other tack so common with women of her shallow temperament, and cried. But Rachel, sublimely indifferent to both tears and anger, rose up and went her way sick of soul as she saw all her well-laid plans thus suddenly brought to nought.

Why, O why must it be that the good angels are so often thwarted in their blessed ministry by the Satanic wiles of some opposing spirit of evil? Why must the craft and guile of the old Serpent be allowed to drag back to destruction a soul that was almost saved?

Several days passed during which we heard nothing of the unfortunate girl, but the fact that a closely-covered carriage had been seen to stop at the Peck's the night she was missing, and **then drive rapidly off in the dusk was a coincidence remembered by one or two** people when the subject began to be inquired into. And it was believed that she had gone off of **her own** voluntary will. But where? and with whom? Questions which it is reserved for the next chapter to answer.

CHAPTER XXXV.

MASONRY PROTECTING MURDERERS.—VOX POPULI, VOX DEI.

ONE night about a week after these events there was a meeting of two men at a cross road a little way out of the village; which meeting was evidently not accidental, for one of the two had been pacing restlessly back and forth for some time in a state of mingled agitation and expectancy, and now greeted the other with only these three abruptly spoken words:

"*She is dead!*"

His companion started and a quick change passed over his face. To a man accustomed to taking a good position in society and being flattered and smiled on accordingly, the vision of possible arrest at the hands of the law could hardly be an agreeable subject of contemplation; but there is an old saying which tells us to give even the Prince of Darkness his due, and I am willing to believe that Maurice Jervish felt for one instant a real pang of remorse—though only a passing sentiment, quickly overpowered by selfish considerations for his own safety.

"This is a horrible business," he finally answered. "There will be a tremendous fuss made I suppose when the affair comes to be looked into."

"I shall have to lay low till it blows over," returned the other. "So now, Jervish, you must let me have a hundred dollars; I can't go without it; my affairs are in a devil of a fix."

"Haven't got more than fifty by me."

"Then borrow the other fifty, can't you?" said his companion, impatiently. "I must clear out of here to-night or it is a jail matter."

"You forget that this confounded ugly business is likely to get me into a tight box as well as you," said Jervish, uneasily. "But I'm willing to do the best I can. There's a private room in my office. Come down there with me and we'll talk the matter over."

"I know you are thinking of your own skin, but I've got some regard for mine," answered the other, with cool contempt. "And I want you to understand that the sooner I'm off and out of the reach of pursuit the better for you. I might prove a very inconvenient witness before the coroner's jury."

"Oh, come," said Jervish, alarmed at the threat. "What is the use of talking like that. I'll get the money of Montfort or some other member of the lodge. They won't get wind of the affair before to-morrow morning, and that will give you plenty of time for a fair start."

"I've got the night before me, and, luckily, a good fast horse." returned the other, after a moment's reflection. "Perhaps I had better go down to the office, and you can bring me the money there. Only be quick about it."

Jervish handed him the key of his office in silence and the two separated.

While this conversation was going on, in a house that stood a little way back from the road and not far from their place of meeting lay all that was mortal of Mary Lyman. The seal of the death angel was on those fast-closed lids, and the lines of weariness and pain left by the last struggle made the beautiful face look even sadder than in life, as, framed in its rippling abundance of tawny gold hair, it looked up white and silent, bearing mute but awful witness that a deed of murder had been done.

Meanwhile Maurice Jervish, in no enviable frame of mind, was directing his steps toward the house of Colonel Montfort. It was decidedly the largest and most pretentious in the village, for the Colonel was a man of considerable property, gained not so much in lawful business as by certain shady transactions already referred to. Ringing the bell he was soon admitted into a room styled the library, though the Colonel was not a man of scholarly tastes, and spent more time smoking than in reading anything older than the morning newspaper—and proceeded at once to state his business, with which the reader is already familiar.

"The deuce! This is going a little too far, Jervish. Of course the lodge will do its best to bring you off all right, but the truth is we have got about enough to shoulder already. A good many here in Granby are all ripe for an Antimasonic excitement, and a less affair than this would be quite sufficient to kindle one. That infernal seceder, Severns, is capable of turning the whole neighborhood upside down, to say nothing of the Methodist parson, his brother-in-law." And with an amiable wish that he might see us both consigned to regions unmentionable—for I must stop to remark that the Colonel was a man of decidedly profane habits of speech, which is nothing very surprising considering the fact that at one time and another he had taken a matter of several hundred oaths, each one far surpassing in studied insult to Jehovah's name the profanity of an ignorant Irish drayman—he took out his pocket-book with a rather disturbed air and proceeded to count out some bills which he handed to Jervish.

The latter clutched the money eagerly. He had in truth been rather impatient of the preceding lecture and cared little for the possible "Antimasonic excitement" so vividly present to the Colonel's imagination, in the narrower and more personal subject of alarm which now absorbed his thoughts.

The Colonel, left alone, lit a cigar and puffed away uneasily. What was it to him—this foul murder of an unprotected orphan girl? He was sorry the affair had happened. It was really unfortunate. But with all his Masonic degrees of knighthood did a single thrill of indignation at this double outrage on the weak and defenceless, attest to one faint spark lingering within him of the true knightly spirit of old? Did this "Prince of Mercy," who had dared to take at the same profane shrine one of the divinest titles of the crucified Redeemer—a title the most precious to the heart of his church on earth, and his brightest crown of glory among the shining ranks of heaven—feel even a throb of pure human regret or sorrow for the young life whose lamp had gone out forever in such starless gloom?

I trow not. He finished his cigar, sat down and

wrote a few hurried lines, addressed to the village sheriff, also a member of Fidelity Lodge, and having sealed the note, transmitted it by a trusty messenger. He had learned by certain former experiences that it is not impossible to make an affair even more " unfortunate " than this redound to the glory of the lodge by a skillful use of those secret tactics which such men know so thoroughly.

Among the many profane boasts by which Masonry and its kindred order, Odd-fellowship, seeks to " exalt itself above all that is called God or that is worshiped," we hear it sometimes said, " the members of secret lodges hang together better than the church." Now this matter in the light of the above scene, is certainly worth inquiring into. It is a deplorable fact that a band of thieves and murderers will sometimes " hang together " when a party of philanthropists will split asunder over some miserable shibboleth; but the reason for this is not hard to seek. Selfishness is a strong cement of union, and is it strange that with our imperfect human race it is often stronger than the bond of the most disinterested love? Besides, it must be remembered that a band of philanthropists do not need to " hang together " for the purpose of shielding each other's crimes—for this is really all the argument amounts to, though like other pieces of lodge sophistry it palms itself off on many an honest but unreflecting mind for the truth. But how long, oh ye Christian pastors, will you let " the simple perish for lack of understanding?" How long shall these false teachers " bring in damnable heresies," and you, Gallio-like, " care for none of these things?"

The night wore away. Like a queen in gold of

Ophir, all her garments smelling of myrrh and aloes and cassia, rose the fair regal morning without a cloud on its glory; and the light of day fell at last on the white, up-turned face, and slowly the village of Granby woke to the fact that murder had been done.

A coroner's jury was speedily impanneled and a post mortem examination left no doubt of the cause of Mary Lyman's death. The sudden flight of the physician at whose house she died pointed him out conclusively as the guilty tool, and a warrant was at once issued for his apprehension.

A number of men started in pursuit, the majority being good and honest citizens who owned allegiance to no power but their lawful government, and to this circumstance, quite as much as the delay caused by an accident to "the good fast horse" on which he had relied for safety, was due the fact that the doctor was overtaken and brought back to Granby.

His witness before the jury cleared up all remaining mystery about the case. Perhaps he thought it would be better for himself if he made a clean breast of the whole affair seeing that the evidence of his guilt was too overwhelming to be denied, and the result of his testimony was most damaging proof against Jervish, who still stayed about town, knowing that his flight at this particular juncture would only point suspicion towards him as the real author of Mary Lyman's death.

The proceedings were *ex-parte*—the jury's business being simply to obtain evidence against the guilty parties. While we were in session—for, reader, I was on that jury and know whereof I affirm—at precisely the point when this new witness, whose name was Dr. Forsyth, though the name is immaterial as he has no after connection with my story, was about to give his testimony, we were joined by lawyer Burroughs, a practicing attorney of the village and a member of Fidelity Lodge, who apparently dropped in for no other purpose than to kindly aid, with his legal knowledge the examinations of the jury. He was a man whose words were softer than oil and smoother than butter, though at need they could be sharper than drawn swords. A thrill of suspicion shot through me when he entered, but it seemed like a breach of charity to think him actuated by any other motive than the simple desire to serve justice, so intently did he listen to the testimony, so earnest did he appear to have all the facts elicited which had a bearing on the case. But when the closing of the prisoner's testimony left us nothing to do but to draw up a formal warrant for the arrest of Maurice Jervish, the before-mentioned attorney looked at his watch and quietly remarked:

"I need not stay longer now the witness is all in. I see it goes hopelessly against my client, but as I am counsel for Mr. Jervish I felt bound to stop and see it through." And so saying he left the room, unmindful of the indignant surprise which was visible on every face, unless I except the only Masonic member of the jury who sat in a corner busily trimming his nails, from which engrossing occupation he did not take the trouble to lift his head as the door closed behind the retreating attorney.

But another surprise awaited us. The coroner had just penned the warrant, and it only waited our signatures, when information was brought to the jury-room that Jervish had fled, having learned—no doubt through the Masonic lawyer—of Forsyth's arrest and his own danger. Then, and not till then, did we realize in what an impudent and shameless fashion the jury had been sold.

"Just like Burroughs to serve us such a trick, the mean, sneaking rascal!" broke out one of the jurors, ordinarily a quiet man, but just now roused to a perfect white heat of indignant wrath over this example of Masonic double dealing.

"Well, the mischief is done," said another; "the best thing we can do is to sign the warrant right off and get it into the hands of the sheriff as soon as we can."

Quickly each man wrote his name—all but the Masonic juror. Oh, that precious hour and a half wasted in trying to argue with one whose stupidity—if it had been real instead of pretended—ought to have consigned him to an asylum of imbeciles! But I have understood better ever since how one Mason can so obstruct the wheels of law as to cause "truth to fall in the streets and turn justice backward." For that hour and a half was improved to the utmost by Jervish in making his escape.

The next thing was to put the writ in the hands of the sheriff, but in vain we waited to hear news of Jervish' arrest. Sheriff Simonds had his own notions of Masonic duty which agreed very well with those entertained by Colonel Montfort. The latter's note the previous evening had done its work, though my knowledge that he influenced the sheriff to betray his official trust by a reference to his Masonic obligations, and a promise that the lodge would shield him from consequences, as well as other incidents here related, has been pieced out from the various disclosures that leaked out at different times either through legal investigation or the less formal process of hearsay.

Hour after hour passed. Men gathered in knots, excited, indignant, and talked the matter over, indulging in free comments on the shameful inactivity of the sheriff, as well as the conduct of Burroughs in contriving to possess himself of all the testimony against Jervish, and then going straight from the jury-room to warn his client. And as the talk went on it was easy to see that the smouldering fires of popular indignation needed but slight fanning to burst into a fierce flame. There is something awful in such a rising of outraged justice when the people unite as one man to execute vengeance. I know of but one thing more terrible to meet—the face of the Judge in the Great Day of his wrath.

Before the sun set Colonel Montfort and his clique were likely to get such a dose of Antimasonic excitement as they little calculated on.

"The sheriff is a Mason and an Odd-fellow. He don't want to arrest Jervish, that's plain to be seen." I heard remarked in one of these excited groups. Masons and Odd-fellows are bound to stand by each other. That's what they all say."

"Well I don't know much about the Odd-fellows, only they and the Masons seem to be hand and glove together," observed another. "I've heard it said that Masonry was a good thing for some of our men when they fell into the hands of the rebels in the war, but when it comes to secreting and running off criminals there's two sides to the question."

"I've got a story to tell on that point," spoke up a man who wore a soldier's coat. "When I was in the army I used to see a good deal of Masonry—from the outside, I never was one myself. I know one of our colonels that in the battle of South Mountain would have been cashiered for cowardice if he hadn't been a Mason. Somehow the court-martial didn't convict, and not a great while after he was promoted. But that ain't the story I was going to tell. I was in Custer's command and a batch of us were taken prisoners by guerilla General Mosby. He ordered that seven drawn by lot be hung in retaliation for the hanging of seven of his men by the Unionists. Among those that drew the marked ball was a lieutenant that I knew very well. I never saw these men again. They were carried off to a place near Sheridan's headquarters and hung. I and some others got exchanged after a while and about a year afterward I met this same lieutenant alive and well. 'I thought you wan't in the land of the living,' says I, when we came to speak. 'I shouldn't have been,' says he, 'if I hadn't been a Mason; that saved my life.' I tell you I thought Masonry was a mighty good thing after hearing that, and I had a great idea of joining them myself, but there's a sequel to it as they say. When the war was over I fell in with a man that had been a Confederate soldier and knew all about the hanging of these men—saw it done. Well, I asked about the lieutenant. 'He was a Freemason,' says he; 'I saw him give the sign to my colonel and saw him return it. The colonel went off and a little while after he came back with two prisoners of his own that he handed to the officer who had charge of the affair. They were placed on the fatal line instead of the lieutenant, who was set free, and their two lives went for his.''

A thrill of horror ran through the group, which was now considerably enlarged. The soldier's story had only added fuel to the fire. Every minute the excitement deepened as fresh cause in the continued inactivity of the sheriff or some rumor of a new attempt on the part of the lodge to thwart justice, fanned the flame.

Suddenly the cry rose up, at first from a single throat, then caught up and repeated by others, "Tear down Burroughs' office! Lynch the Masonic scoundrel!"

The mob spirit was fast taking possession of the crowd, which, now swelled to hundreds, had gathered about the court-house, when a clear, commanding voice, addressing them from the steps of the building, made a temporary silence.

"These men are acting on their own responsibility and not in accordance with their obligations as Masons. While I utterly denounce the conduct of the sheriff as a most base betrayal of his official duty, I appeal to you, fellow townsmen and citizens, to come to the aid of the law, and allow no deed of violence to be committed which will only obstruct its course. Justice shall be done. I ask your help in ferreting out the murderer, and when he is found rest assured that no lodge obligation, real or fancied, shall screen him from the punishment he deserves."

"The clear, ringing voice penetrated to the farthest edge of the crowd. The speaker himself stood in fair view, his dark eyes glowing like coals of fire under the full, massive brow, his pale face paler by contrast. Everybody knew him—Anson Lovejoy, Master of the lodge.

There is a mighty force in simple sincerity. Not a

man in that excited throng abhorred more intensely the crime which had been committed than did he, or felt a more burning desire to see insulted law avenged in the speedy arrest of the criminal. And when he threw the odium of all this obstructing of justice on the shoulders of individual Masons instead of the lodge itself, there were enough who believed him in the face of their own previous convictions, not to say the evidence of their own senses, to make a perceptible difference in the attitude of the crowd. A more calm and reasonable spirit was succeeding the tumultuous excitement which had threatened at one time to end in mob violence. The advocates of lynch law were silent and under the reaction thus made the throng slowly and by degrees dispersed.

A few hours later I was at home attending to some duty about the farm when Anson Lovejoy came hurriedly up, his face still pale but settled into those grave, determined lines which speak the man whose whole soul is roused to meet a crisis.

"Mr. Severns, I want the loan of your fastest horse. I have just received news that Jervish has left his hiding place where he has been secreted all this time and hired a man by the name of Leach to take him across the river. This Leach is a poor, worthless fellow, who never has any money and is therefore easily bribed."

"What will Masons think of your action in this matter?" I said, as I threw the halter over the neck of the beautiful roan, acknowledged one of the fastest steeds in the neighborhood, and led him out. "Depend upon it, your part in to-day's affair will never be overlooked or forgiven by the lodge."

"I care not," he answered, "I am acting up to my

Masonic obligations as I understand them. God do so to me and more also if I knowingly leave a single stone unturned that is hindering the way of justice."

He spoke with solemn, almost fierce earnestness—then, after an instant's silence, added in his usual tone, "While you are getting the horse ready I will speak with Mrs. Severns a moment," and so saying he stepped quickly across to the open side door where he had always until now met with the ready admittance accorded to a friend and neighbor.

What he was going to say to Rachel I know not, for he was given no chance to say it, but I think a desire to have her God speed in the task to which he had set himself prompted the action.

Rachel met him just as he was entering, with stern face and forbidding gesture. She had not heard his conversation with me or very likely would not have addressed him exactly as she did.

"Not a step farther. No murderer or companion of murderers crosses my threshold."

"Mrs. Severns!" he exclaimed, startled, astonished.

"I mean what I say," she answered, firmly. "You uphold this dark, unclean system of the lodge and thus make yourself a partaker in the innocent blood it has shed. Go!"

The reader must excuse Rachel, unjust as she was, for her very soul was boiling within her, and this passionate outburst was due to a deeper cause than the common feeling of indignation which possessed the community at large. In divine faith that she might yet redeem to virtue and happiness the erring soul which had mistaken a cold, deceiving mirage for the water of affection, and for whom henceforth society would have no use but to cast out and trample under foot, she had planned and labored as only a Christian woman can. And this was the terrible ending! The prey for which she had wrestled with Satan had been basely, cruelly torn out of her hand, and she felt something of the fury of the bereaved lioness when she confronted Anson Lovejoy.

"I assure you, Mrs. Severns," he began again, and again she interrupted him, though this time her voice was a trifle softer, her manner a shade gentler.

"I accuse you of nothing but of being allied to such a system. And that is enough. Shall a man take fire in his bosom and not be burned? No, Mr. Lovejoy, no adhering Mason from henceforth receives a welcome under my roof."

And she turned from him and walked away, leaving the victim of this severe castigation to recover from it as well as he could. And certainly for a moment Anson Lovejoy looked rather dejected. He was without domestic ties, his wife having died in the first year of their marriage, and I well understood, or thought I did, how this sudden closing against him of a home where he had always been a welcome guest, dropping in at any time when his business permitted, thus seeming to find some faint, shadowy compensation for his own buried joys, would naturally affect him.

But he quickly recovered himself, and going to where the horse now stood in readiness leaped into the saddle. As he did so I took occasion to say—

"Rachel has a sharp tongue, but her heart is all right. Some time she will see that she has done you injustice."

"I hope so, Mr. Severns," he answered. "But"—

and he spoke with the grave, slow emphasis of one recording a vow—"if Masonry is what from this day's work I have reason to fear it is, and I remain connected with it an hour longer than I can help, I shall merit the severest denunciations she has heaped upon me."

And he rode swiftly away to join the pursuing party, which had halted at an appointed place of meeting, and were now discussing which of two different roads the fugitive had probably taken. A few outsiders had gathered about, among them the sheriff, who seemed to take an extraordinary interest in the settling of this question considering his previous inactivity.

"I tell you, Lovejoy, if you take the direction of Quipaw Creek you'll miss it," he said, excitedly. "Jervish has gone more south."

"My men are on the right track," returned Lovejoy, composedly, in whose mind the last lingering doubt whether he was really taking the route Jervish had gone was now dispelled by the sheriff's evident anxiety to have him go the opposite way.

"But I tell you," repeated the sheriff in still more excited tones, "a man told me not more than an hour ago that he had met him and Leach on the road."

This piece of information made some of the party waver but had no effect on their staunch leader, who issued his command to set off at once in the direction of Quipaw Creek, at which the sheriff called to his aid considerable profanity, not necessary to repeat, in confirmation of what he had said, provoking from one of the number as they rode away this satirical speech—

"Set the fox to guard the hen-coop, will ye? When I do that I'll take advice from a Mason. If you knew all this about Jervish an hour ago why wan't you off after him instead of loafing about with the coroner's warrant lying idle in your pocket?"

And the discomforted sheriff, who had certainly striven heroically to fulfil his Masonic obligations, retired amid more hooting and jeering than was quite pleasant.

Swiftly, steadily, the pursuers pressed on, and before long came in sight of a common farm wagon apparently loaded with meal-bags. The driver of the wagon was quickly recognized by several of the party to whom he was well known, as the man who had undertaken to aid Jervish in his flight. But Leach sat alone on the seat, driving. Where was his companion?

An order from Lovejoy to search the wagon soon settled this question. The vehicle was found to be so arranged by sticks laid across—the seeming meal-bags, which were in reality stuffed with hay, placed on these, and high enough from the floor of the wagon to make a hiding place for the miserable Jervish, who was now ignominiously dragged therefrom, and Colonel Montfort's friend, the elegant man of society, spent that night in the county jail to the great satisfaction of all worthy citizens of Granby, with whom, now that the chief criminal was caught, the Antimasonic excitement subsided as rapidly as it rose.

CHAPTER XXXVI.

SOME EXAMPLES OF MASONIC BENEVOLENCE AND MORALITY.

HALF a dozen summers previous to the one in which occurred the scenes related in the last chapter, there happened one of those common and yet most sad events, a serious accident to a laboring man with a wife and children dependent upon him for their daily bread. He was a carpenter and fell from an imperfectly built staging, receiving severe internal injuries that resulted in his death after a year of lingering illness.

"The lodge will see to you and the children," whispered the dying man to his weeping wife, whose always delicate health had been shattered by incessant watching at the bedside of her sick husband, and, knowing that his death would leave her without a penny, could not see in the dark night of approaching widowhood the glimmer of a single star of earthly hope. "I've always paid my dues regular till that accident happened. The lodge owes it to me to see that you and the children are well provided for."

"They have given us in all but twenty dollars since you have been sick," answered the wife, who was only a woman and reasoned as women are apt to in such matters. "That is but a fraction of what you have paid them at one time and another. And I am sure we have needed the money."

"I know twenty dollars don't go a great ways, but we've rubbed along. And now I've got pretty nigh the end, so there'll be all the more for you and the children."

His wife was silent. She had her misgivings, but not for worlds would she breathe the shadow of a doubt into the ear of that soul that was passing into eternity, happy in the thought that he belonged to a brotherhood which made the widow and the orphan the objects of its especial care.

That night he died. The lodge buried him with Christless prayers and dirges, and, to do it justice, spared none of the honors to which a defunct "worthy brother" is Masonically entitled. The widow's hopes revived. Surely they who would do so much for the dead would have a care for the living. But the lodge, when applied to for assistance, viewed the matter in a slightly different light. For, to state the simple truth, a number of grand suppers given by the fraternity, sundry bills of cost for regalia, gloves, aprons, etc., to say nothing of a great many extras for wine, beer and cigars, had swallowed up so much of the charity fund as to leave the lodge in no condition to heed her appeal. But it must not be supposed that any such explanation of the case was given to the indigent widow when she asked for further aid. Oh, no. She was coolly told that her husband had not paid his dues for a year, and they had done all that could reasonably be expected of them in giving him Masonic burial.

She could not prove that the lodge had taken her husband's money and paid him back, not counting interest, scarce a fifth part of what was his actual due. The widow struggled along for a while; a few individual Masons contributed to her relief from their own pockets, but as benevolently inclined persons are to be found everywhere and the lodge collectively had nothing to do with these contributions, it may be fair to infer that they might possibly have done the same thing whether Masons or not. It was a hopeless struggle even with occasional aid from private charity. Her health completely broke down at last. Her two children were bound out, while she went to the almshouse as her only refuge, dying there soon after in a quick consumption.

Death, in separating her from her children, however, spared her, as death so often does, the pang of a deeper anguish—for she was Mary Lyman's mother.

It doesn't matter where I gathered these facts. They are true. This is not a statistical book or else I should be tempted to give a few figures that would demonstrate to the most skeptical that the benevolence of the lodge is on a par with its morality—a hollow sham, a whited sepulchre.

Mary Lyman's father was a Mason, but this fact did not save her from ruin and death at the hands of a brother Mason who had solemnly sworn to preserve inviolate the chastity of all women with near Masonic kindred, though with this very convenient little proviso attached, "*knowing them to be such.*"

Women of America, do you hold your purity so lightly that you can afford to countenance such a system as this? Will you, knowing these things, still continue to smile on the lodge and accept its slimy favors? Sisters of the Church of Christ, does it matter nothing to you that Masonry rejects his name from her ritual as "too sectarian and tramples his atoning blood under foot by teaching another way of salvation? that by the testimony of her own writers she traces back her origin to the ancient heathen mysteries with their abominable rites of darkness, and aspires, as we learn from the same unquestionable source, to become finally "the universal religion of manhood?" Can you pray for the speedy coming of Christ's millennial reign and be indifferent to the fact that another kingdom is being set up in which he has neither part nor lot? Will you apologize for such a system? defend it by your silence or worse still "care nothing about it?" As it rejects Christ, so it has no place for woman, and should the day ever dawn when Masonry becomes the universal religion, God help her!

Rachel herself gathered the flowers from her own garden to lay about the dead girl's white, still form. She placed a half-opened rosebud between the closed fingers, kissed the cold forehead, and with solemn words of prayer that seemed in their tender, impassioned earnestness like a personal appeal to that infinite, unchanging Pity which is at the heart of God in Christ, visibly manifested before his eyes—it was Elder Stedman who performed the last services—Mary Lyman was laid away in a corner of the potter's field outside the cemetery to slumber till the resurrection morning.

But before the grave had set its seal of corruption on the statuesque beauty of a single lineament her murderer was released on a writ of *habeas corpus* and admitted to bail!

Elder Stedman, when the funeral was over, came back to our house; but, unheeding the cup of tea that Rachel poured out for him, he paced up and down the room in stern and solemn silence, broken at last by these abrupt words—

"I have been like one of the foolish prophets. I have healed the hurt of the daughter of my people slightly. God forgive me. Henceforth every faculty of mind and body shall be devoted to an unceasing warfare against this dragon of Masonry that stands like his prototype in Revelation ready to engulf and and swallow the church with the devouring flood he casts out of his mouth."

"Why, Mark;" said I, "you do yourself injustice. When hardly a preacher in these parts dares to mention Masonry you have scourged it unsparingly from the pulpit. What can you do more?"

"I tell you, Leander," said Mark, pausing a moment in his agitated walk, "I feel as if I had only tickled the monster by throwing wooden darts at him. Henceforth it must be a hand to hand combat. Only the iron of truth can penetrate between the scales of his armor, for, like Apollyon, his scales are his pride. I must lecture as well as preach on this subject."

"But Mark," I answered, a little startled, "you will only rouse persecution. A good many people seem to think Masonry is like the Giant Pope Christian saw sitting in the mouth of his cave—too old and decrepit to hurt. But I know better. The lodge don't care much for a few side thrusts, but attack it at close quarters and you will find that it can turn with as deadly vengeance as it did in Morgan's day."

"Well," answered the Elder, quietly, "I am old and

gray-headed now, and a few years of life less or more matters little to me. There is a conflict coming and woe unto me if I gird not on my armor to meet it. My old belief comes back to me. This is going to be no ordinary contest. It is the battle of Armageddon, the last great conflict before the final end."

Mark spoke with the same kindling eyes and solemn fervor with which he had dilated on this very same subject forty years before.

"I have had some such thoughts myself," I answered, after a moment's silence. "Organized secrecy seems to be Satan's last and most cunning move. In the old pagan and popery times he tried to conquer the church by sheer open force. Now he is trying to undermine the citadel, and the worst of it is the church won't be roused to see her danger. However, I suppose I can no more keep you out of the battle than I could Job's war-horse. Only have a care of yourself, Mark, for Hannah's sake."

The Elder started as if I had touched a tender chord, for he and Hannah were a lonely couple now. Of their two sons, one had died in the service of his country, the other was a toiling missionary on the far-off soil of southern Africa. But it was only for an instant, then the pole star of his life shone out clear and steady.

"I told Hannah the day she married me that she must take me as the Covenanter John Brown took his wife, Isabel, with the assurance that when she least expected it the hand of violence might part him from her. We have learned to hold nothing back—not even each other."

But while the Elder was thus absorbed in thoughts of that great pre-millennial contest which he believed was approaching, Colonel Montfort was likewise thinking—though on a different subject and with a good cigar to aid the process. Two difficult tasks lay before him; one was the triumphant delivery of Maurice Jervish from the hands of justice, the other was the sacrifice of Anson Lovejoy to violated Masonic law.

The Colonel was not a man of generous impulses, and had there been no other tie between him and Mary Lyman's murderer than mere friendship, he would in all probability have washed his hands of him. He desired to shield Jervish, firstly and primarily, because the honor and glory of Masonry demanded it. What was to become of the fraternity if its members could claim no special privileges over honest men? A vital question to the Colonel, who knew very well that there had been times in his own political and military career when he might have fared badly if the shielding of each other's crimes had formed no part of lodge obligations. However hopeless the situation might appear to un-Masonic eyes, in the light of these encouraging items of his past experience, the Colonel did not despair of bringing off his friend with flying colors. It was over another subject that he spent the most anxious thought, and consumed the greatest number of cigars.

He hated Anson Lovejoy as wickedness will always hate rectitude. He was furious that he had dared to pursue Jervish and deliver him over to the grasp of the law; and as the controlling spirit of the lodge he was well aware how very easily the wrath of the fraternity against him could be made to bring forth its legitimate fruit—murder. Nor is it too much to say of the Colonel that he knew he could at any moment put his finger on the men who would not scruple to dispose of Anson Lovejoy after the most approved Masonic fashion. The possibility however of another Antimasonic excitement was a factor which continually came in and disturbed the Colonel's reckoning, for he was a man accustomed to weigh duly all the pros and cons before committing himself to a course of action which might entail disagreeable consequences. But his hatred of Lovejoy burned with so intense a flame that for once passion overpowered the cool and calculating selfishness which with him as with most men of that peculiar caliber was the governing principle of his life.

The sound of his name spoken in low and cautious tones by some one standing outside broke in upon the Colonel's meditations. He rose and, opening the long window, stepped out upon the piazza. A man stood there in the moonlight, a prominent member of Fidelity Lodge.

"Oh, it is you, Mugford. I suppose all the arrangements are made then; but don't let too many into the secret. Half a dozen would be enough if the affair was managed properly."

"I've talked with Golding and Peck and the others. They will be all ready to do their part when the time comes. But Whitby we can't depend on I am afraid. He hangs back."

The Colonel muttered an oath.

"Well, shut his mouth up some way. If he is disposed to blab give him a hint that we know how to manage traitors. We can deal with one as well as another." And after a little more conversation of like tenor the two conspirators separated.

Masonic murders would be much more common than is happily the case if the brethren everywhere lived up to their obligations; but just as the majority of slaveholders were far more humane than the system which gave them irresponsible power, so Masons as a rule are better than the institution which swears its devotees to bring every traitor to "strict and condign punishment."

Among the hardened and desperate men, the rowdies, gamblers and drunkards who surrounded Colonel Montfort and moved obsequiously to do his bidding, there was one who shrank from the crime of secret assassination. The result was that Anson Lovejoy the next day received from an unknown source a much crumpled note with a rude imitation of the square and compass in the corner, which after correcting some peculiarities of orthography ran as follows:

"Don't go to the lodge to-night. They mean to ask you to resign, then drag you from the chair if you refuse, and murder you in the lodge-room. In the scuffle it will never be known who struck the blow. If you value your life, stay away. A FRIEND AND A MASON."

"How do I know but this is a mere foolish trick to frighten me?" said Lovejoy. "It would look too cowardly to stay away. I can't do it."

"No," I said, earnestly, "this is no trick but a friendly warning. You must heed it."

Lovejoy stood irresolute. I knew he felt as a brave man always does at the thought of saving his life by what seems like cowardly flight from a post of duty.

"I have thought of a plan," I said, after a moment's silence. "Go to the lodge to-night as usual, and your life shall be protected."

"How?"

"Station a guard round the lodge. There are plenty of Antimasons in Granby that would rather enjoy serving in such a capacity. Take your seat in the chair precisely as at any ordinary meeting, and as soon as there is the least attempt at violence, give the signal and we will burst open the door and rush in."

"That will do," he said, after a moment's deliberation. "No better plan could be devised."

And with the understanding that I should as quickly and quietly as possible gather a force sufficient for his protection, Anson Lovejoy prepared to front the men who had secretly banded together to take his life. For what? For violating his Masonic obligations. In other words, for daring to do his duty as an honest, God-fearing citizen of this free Republic, consecrated to liberty by the blood and tears of our forefathers, yet fostering in its bosom a dark and terrible despotism which, when its laws are violated, knows neither mercy nor forgiveness, allows of no appeal from its sentence, and punishes without the form of trial.

Although the tide of popular excitement in Granby had subsided with the arrest of Jervish, it left, as such excitements usually do, a deposit behind it. Firm and settled conviction had taken in many minds the place of ignorance and doubt. Pronounced Antimasons were scarce before; now they were very common. Consequently I found no difficulty in gathering a force sufficiently large to surround the lodge and prevent the threatened attack on Anson Lovejoy.

We allowed the brethren time to assemble, and then marching silently from our place of rendezvous we took our stations around the building, scarcely daring to breathe lest some sound should escape our ears from the upper room where the lodge was meeting.

Meanwhile Lovejoy had seated himself in the Master's chair and gone through the preliminary exercises with outward calmness. He no longer doubted the truth of the warning note. Even before he caught sight of a knife concealed under the coat of one of the members he knew himself to be surrounded by a band of secret assassins, and felt that on his courage and tact in co-operating with those outside his life depended.

Colonel Montfort, as before hinted, was a man that preferred to do his dirty work by means of tools. He meant to keep his hand concealed throughout this whole affair. It was therefore no part of his scheme to open the attack on Lovejoy in person, but to put forward Simon Peck instead, as the mouth-piece of the lodge. Peck was an ignorant and illiterate man, and far from being a good spokesman, but he knew that the demand to resign would be felt by Lovejoy as an additional insult, coming from such a quarter. Peck was the most subservient of tools under his master's eye, and in the present case some personal feeling, mingling with the infuriated hate towards Lovejoy which he shared in common with the other members of the lodge, for so violating his Masonic obligations as to arrest a murderer.

Some writer has said that everybody is well connected in certain directions. So also is the opposite fact true, especially among the heterogeneous elements that compose American society—for Maurice Jervish, the personal friend of Colonel Montfort, was also some connection of the Pecks. It was there he had first seen Mary Lyman, and though he moved in a so much higher social sphere than they, was quite willing to take all the advantage which his relationship to the family gave him in accomplishing the ruin of his victim. Peck had badgered his wife into denying before the coroner's jury all knowledge of the closed carriage that had been seen to stop at their door the night Mary was missing; he had likewise aided in secreting Jervish—it was believed on his premises, which the sheriff, true to his Masonic obligations, refused to search—all at the bidding of Colonel Montfort, who found in Peck just that mixture of bigotry and self-conceit which is so convenient in the underlings of the lodge when their superiors wish to manipulate them for purposes of their own.

Lovejoy listened calmly to the end of the halting, ungrammatical speech, which was really nothing but a low tirade of abuse. He was prepared for this part of the programme. Peck sat down and wiped his forehead, rather exhausted with his effort at oratory, but supremely satisfied therewith. There was an instant's silence, during which Lovejoy's eye looked with eagle keenness over the throng of conspirators which surrounded him like a pack of hungry wolves thirsting for his blood; and then he answered slowly and firmly:

"If I have committed any offence against Masonic law I am willing to meet the charge, and if proved, submit like any ordinary member to the sentence of the lodge. I am denounced as a traitor. To resign the chair under these circumstances would be equivalent to a plea of guilty, and I therefore refuse most decidedly to do any such thing."

This reply was also in agreement with the programme. There was a murmur of rage as Lovejoy finished speaking, and a forward movement from the member who carried the concealed dirk.

"You *shall* resign, you blasted traitor!" he exclaimed, with an oath. "Take your choice, either be dragged from the chair or give it up peaceably."

"I will neither be dragged from the chair nor give it up, coolly answered Lovejoy, who knew that the fatal moment was fast approaching when, according to their pre-concerted arrangement, the whole band of ruffians would be on him. "You have met here to take my life. I know it, and others know it, too. A guard of the citizens of Granby, at least a hundred strong, now surround this lodge, prepared to rescue me from your hands should you attempt violence. I have only to give a certain signal and they will rush in. The result may be a worse Antimasonic excitement than the one you accuse me of heading. Now take *your* choice; give up your plan to assassinate me, or carry it through and take the consequences."

The lion's mouth was fairly shut, for the most infuriated Mason present did not care to provoke the popular vengeance that would have surely followed any attack on Lovejoy. Colonel Montfort, under his concealing moustache, fairly ground his teeth with rage at this unlooked-for miscarriage of his deep and subtle plot. He had rightly calculated that with every member of the lodge pledged to keep Masonic silence over the affair, and Masonic sheriffs and juries to obstruct the course of justice in every possible way, there would not be the ten thousandth part of a chance that the actual perpetrators of the deed would ever be discovered or punished. Nor had it occurred to his mind that Lovejoy, even if he should hear of the plot against him, would take any other measure of self-defense than simply to stay away

"I have one more remark to make on this subject," continued Lovejoy, looking round with unflinching gaze on the baffled conspirators. "You denounce me as being false to Masonry because in the discharge of my duties as a citizen, I arrested a criminal who is also a Mason. If to be true to my lodge obligations requires me to be false to God and my country, then I have had enough of the system, and the world has had far too much; and the only thing that I or any other honest man can do in such a case is to quit it."

I will not transcribe the volley of cursing and profanity which followed this speech of Lovejoy's. It was as if hell had broken loose. Colonel Montfort, who had by this time assured himself that eager ears were really straining in the darkness and silence below to catch the least sound of tumult or uproar in the lodge, was alarmed.

"The brethren forget that this is a meeting for business," he said, with cool effrontery. "We are only wasting time by this useless talk. Our Worshipful Master charges the brethren with a conspiracy to assassinate him. I on my part charge him with un-Masonic conduct in hiring a mob of cowans and eavesdroppers to surround the lodge; with using inflammatory language designed to excite the public mind against the order, besides many other violations of his obligations and duties as a Mason. I therefore move that a complaint be presented to the Grand Lodge of the State against Anson Lovejoy, Worshipful Master of Fidelity Lodge, No. 60., A. F. & A. M., petitioning for his expulsion and removal from office."

Lovejoy listened with calm disdain. To a man who had stood but the moment before face to face with death this was but the firing of blank cartridges. The after proceedings were unimportant, and after an unusually brief and quiet meeting the lodge disbanded, fairly checkmated in its murderous purpose.

The hushed and silent crowd kept vigilant watch till Lovejoy came out; then greeted him with enthusiastic cheers that could be heard half over Granby. He was the hero of the hour, but I fancied that like some other heroes he felt that there was a certain thing lacking to his triumph.

"A Christian should not bear malice, Mr. Lovejoy," I said, as I shook his hand. Give us a call to-morrow and allow Mrs. Severns to congratulate you."

Lovejoy hesitated. He had not crossed our threshold since the day Rachel had forbid his entrance; and I could not blame him if he entertained some rankling remembrance of her harsh and bitter words.

"If you think I shall be welcome—not otherwise," he answered.

"Try it," I said, with a smile. Lovejoy hesitated no longer.

"Thank you, Mr. Severns, I will, if it is only to prove that I 'bear no malice,' as you call it, because your good wife told me the truth. I was a companion of murderers as to-night's events have made me realize. But I am so no longer."

The next day, agreeably to his promise, he came over. Rachel met him with extended hand and a hearty, "Forgive me, I was unjust; but I have found out my mistake."

"I have nothing to forgive, Mrs. Severns," was his equally sincere and hearty answer. "The medicine was harsh, but I am no worse for it."

Verily,
"A curse from the depths of womanhood
Is very bitter and salt and good."

CHAPTER XXXVII.

HISTORY REPEATS ITSELF.

THE community at large looked upon the speedy conviction of Jervish as a matter of course; and when the time arrived for the court to sit on the case the public mind had quieted down from its state of excitement to one of comparative apathy. Against such overwhelming evidence what possible chance for any verdict but guilty?

Anson Lovejoy thought otherwise.

"The lodge is bound to clear Jervish," he said to me one day when the subject of the approaching trial happened to be mentioned. "*And they will do it.*"

Even I, who knew so well what Masonic craft and guile is capable of in the way of perverting justice, was surprised at the positiveness with which he spoke.

"Impossible!" I said. "No plainer case of guilt ever came before a jury."

"That may be," answered Lovejoy with a little touch of satire," but you will find that when a fourth or even less of the jury wear Masonic spectacles to assist their understandings the plainest cases have a faculty of growing strangely involved. Colonel Montfort and the other members of the lodge have a personal stake in this affair quite outside of any particular interest they may feel in Jervish. **It is a kind of a** test question. They want to prove to **the** world and to themselves that Masonry is strong enough to spread its protecting wing over the vilest criminal and then defy the hand of the law to **reach him.** My word for it, Sheriff Simonds will fill out the jury with Masons and Oddfellows to a man; with possibly one who is neither Mason nor Odd-fellow, but whose sympathies or connections are all with the lodge, put in simply for a **blinder** to the public—nothing more."

I started, for this was the same dodge that had been played **so** often and so successfully in the Morgan trials forty years before. What should hinder its working equally well in the present instance?

The wide-spread notoriety of the case attracted an **unusually** large number **to hear** the trial, and each day **of the** proceedings **a crowded court room** attested to **the** interest it had **excited. The** witness against Maurice Jervish was clear and conclusive; the testimony in his favor slight **and** open to **serious doubt** from the character of the witnesses or **the** suspicion that lodge influence had been at work, especially with Mrs. Peck, who swore positively to having no knowledge where **Mary Lyman went** on the night she left the **house, or in** whose company; but was believed by every **candid person to have** perjured herself under terror inspired by her husband, who **knew very well** how to use **the peculiar** arguments **of the lodge with** most impressive effect on his weak-minded partner.

Lovejoy's prophecy had proved **true to** the letter in relation to Sheriff **Simonds, who** filled out the jury with **four** Masons and **one Odd-fellow,** together with a sixth **who was** neither **a Mason** nor an **Odd-fellow, but a** warm personal friend **of the** prisoner! And so the **case** proceeded—a great deal of tedious quibbling and impudent brow-beating of witnesses from the Masonic lawyer who was counsel for the accused, and did his best, though signally failing in the attempt—for there are some things beyond even the power of Falsehood—to represent the whole affair as a malicious persecution of his client. And then, the evidence all being in, the departure of the jury to render their decision—guilty or not guilty.

I remember with what hushed expectancy we waited for the verdict; how in the stillness of the court room the jury's returning footsteps after their brief absence sounded painfully loud. And I remember, too, the half-stunned, half-sick feeling that came over me, as if I saw Justice stabbed to the heart and was forced to stand by when the death-blow was struck as the foreman pronounced their decision—

"Not guilty!"

The lodge had triumphed. Mary Lyman's murderer was free.

Astounded, indignant, almost questioning whether my ears had heard aright, I listened to the giving of the verdict, which was followed by loud applause from Colonel Montfort's adherents, who closed around Jervish and bore him away like a conquering hero. It was the same scene with which the court rooms of western New York grew so familiar in 1826 and the four years succeeding. It was history repeated, a Masonic jury setting aside the plainest evidence for testimony that bore the stamp of perjury on its very face; law helpless under the heel of the lodge, and the same exultant rallying around the murderer.

Rachel was silent for a moment after I told her the result of the trial; then she bowed her head on her clasped hands with a sound that was half a groan, half a sob.

"Mother!" I said, gently.

"I can't help it," she answered. "Shall secret iniquity triumph forever? I feel as if I could call upon God as the prophet did to rend the heavens and come down."

"But there is a day of reckoning coming, you forget that, mother."

"No, I don't forget it, but it seems such a great way off. What my heart cries out for is justice now. It will be a satisfaction to the universe no doubt when this wretch gets his deserts at the Day of Judgment, though it be a million years hence, but thinking of that will never reconcile me to his going free of punishment here. His acquittal is a standing menace to the peace and virtue of every home. If the lodge can defy law at one time and in one place it can at other times and in other places—and what is more, it will."

"Well," said Anson Lovejoy, who had come in to talk over the result of the trial, "Colonel Montfort and his party triumph openly and shamelessly in the fact that they have cleared Jervish. At this very moment some of the jury are over at the tavern having a grand drinking fuddle in honor of their victory. Colonel Montfort, I understand, is preparing a garbled report of the affair for a Chicago daily, in which he will represent Jervish as a cruelly attacked victim of a malicious Antimasonic persecution, winding up with a glowing account of his triumphant vindication before the jury. I am rather glad he is going to do so for it will give me a chance to reply. The real facts of the case should be placed before the people and signed by competent witnesses, so that every honest man and woman who reads it shall be convinced on which side the truth lies."

"That is a good idea if you can get such an article inserted," I answered, with a vivid remembrance of the times now grown so distant and shadowy, when from one end of the land to the other scarce a paper dared to print an account of Morgan's abduction; when, deaf alike to the appeals of outraged humanity and violated law, editors almost everywhere resolutely closed their columns to the whole subject, presenting that saddest of spectacles in a land of freedom—an enslaved press.

"Oh! I think there will be no difficulty about that," returned Lovejoy. "After publishing one side of the affair they couldn't for decency's sake refuse to publish the other."

"How is your trial before the Grand Lodge coming out?" I inquired.

"I hardly know yet, I sent my defence in writing, for I could not spare the money to go in person, and besides I have ceased to consider myself as being under the jurisdiction of the lodge. They appointed a committee of three to investigate the charges against me and report to the Grand Master. As this committee was composed of an ex-Governor and two ministers I naturally supposed that I should receive gentlemanly treatment from their hands—at least courtesy and common fairness. But this was not the case. They refused to hear any testimony but that of my accusers, and conducted the investigation, which was the merest farce from beginning to end, more in the spirit of examining members of the Inquisition than anything else. I presume they reported adversely; I neither know nor care. Nor shall I wait for the decision of the Grand Master; I have already sent in my renunciation and my reasons for doing so which are substantially these—'I find that every Mason is under obligation to conceal a brother Mason's crime; that the greater the crime the stronger the obligation to conceal it; that the lodge has the power of life and death over its members; and that if any member knows of his intended assassination he has no right to use any other means of safety than his own physical force or keeping out of the way.'"

Lovejoy spoke with slow, solemn emphasis. He had learned at last the lesson that Mark and I learned two score years before from a page stained with martyr's blood and blotted with the tears of the widow. The iron had entered into his soul.

Elder Stedman had already delivered one or two Antimasonic lectures without encountering any very serious opposition. Another was advertised to be given in the Quipaw Creek school house on Thursday evening of this same week.

The party at the tavern had a chance to see the notice, which was put up in a conspicuous corner of the public room, and make their own peculiar comments thereon. But remembering that my reader's ears are unaccustomed to vulgarity and profaneness, I shall only transcribe that part of their talk which is of immediate interest in view of the events that are to follow.

Colonel Montfort himself was pledged to settle the score, and under the pleasant stimulus of this recollection there was a general drinking to the health of the gallant Colonel.

"Come boys, now for a rouser," said the leader, as he again filled up his glass. "Here's to Maurice Jervish, the brave and innocent."

The toast was responded to with drunken enthusiasm and in nauseating triumph every glass was drained.

Reader, when the lodge has reached what it takes a good deal of pains to inform us through its orators on St. John's day and other appropriate occasions, is its ultimate aim and object; when it rules the whole of our beloved country from New England to the Sierras;

when it elects all our public officers from President and Governor downwards; when it pulls the wires at every political convention and caucus and controls every town meeting; in those palmy days a man may do that which is right in his own eyes; he may seduce, murder, rob, cheat, commit all the crimes in the decalogue, only provided that he has first had the foresight to learn a few Masonic signs and grips, and has likewise had the discrimination to select his victims entirely from the ranks of cowans and outsiders. A possibility that by that time so many will join the lodge from motives of self-protection as to seriously limit the field of operations would seem at first a slight obstacle in the way of this cheerful prospect. But all the difficulty rises from a superficial view of the subject. There will always be the cowan in the land; men too poor or too shiftless to pay the lodge dues; men too independent to surrender their liberty to a secret despotism; humble followers of the Lord who refuse to bow to anti-Christ; besides cripples and minors, to say nothing of the whole female sex barred out by circumstance or accident from the tender charities of the lodge.

Now, as the above mentioned classes, taken together, form, at a moderate estimate, considerably more than two-thirds of the world's population it will be readily seen that the time is not likely ever to arrive when Masonry shall be restricted in its operations by too narrow a field outside.

But we will leave dipping into the future and go back to the party gathered at the tavern who had been drinking just freely enough to be primed for rowdyism.

"I say, let's go over to Quipaw to-night and shut the mouth of that confounded Methodist parson," proposed one. "The old rascal needs a lesson. Why don't he stick to his business and let other things alone?"

"That's so," was the ready response of another. "He ought to be treated to a coat of tar and feathers, ranting up and down the country, making trouble in the family and setting wives against their husbands. Now my wife hates Masonry like the devil, and ever since she heard that confounded fellow lecture she's been worse about it. Now I say that Masonry ain't a part of a preacher's business. He ought to stick to the Gospel. That's what ministers are for."

It is astonishing, reader, the unanimity of opinion that sometimes exists between two very opposite classes of men. The drunken rowdy who gave utterance to the above edifying sentiments was of exactly the same mind with the Rev. Dr. Easy, who was at that very moment expressing to one of the deacons of his church his sorrow that Bro. Stedman should leave his legitimate business of saving souls to attack such a respectable institution as Freemasonry, with which so many worthy men were connected.

Meanwhile the Elder was lifting up his heart in prayer for strength to stand firm against the enemies of the truth; for a spirit of meekness and charity towards all who should oppose; for the presence of Jesus Christ to go with him in might and power, directing the battle to a glorious victory over the hosts of Baal for the honor of his precious name and the hastening of his day of Millennial triumph.

The Elder rose from his knees and walked to the place appointed, calm as the summer sunset. He would have been calm if he had known that he was to encounter a raging mob ready to tear him in pieces. Into that eternal fortress where the righteous run and are safe, his soul had entered. Girded from Jehovah's celestial armory, with the sword of truth in his hand that forty years of constant warfare had only whetted to a keen edge, why should he fear the face of mortal man?

He began his lecture, which was on the relation of the Christian religion to Masonry, in comparative quiet. It was a rather miscellaneous audience; a few earnest, intelligent men and women met to learn what they could about a system which pretends to hold in its keeping ineffable secrets impossible to be discovered by profane gaze, yet with curious inconsistency binds all its members under awful oaths never to reveal the unrevealable! A few drawn by curiosity; and a considerable number, among whom was the party from the tavern, whose only design in coming was to disturb the meeting and mob the lecturer.

In the course of his argument he first described in a few brief, fitting words, the nature and essence of true religion, on which followed naturally a counter description of Masonry. Here the Elder began to tread on dangerous ground. So long as he kept to generalities they could afford to listen with tolerable equanimity. They could even bear to be told that the lodge was an emanation from the smoke of the bottomless pit; a low, cunning caricature of Christianity, a revival of the worship of Baal and Tammuz, and every other heathen deity mentioned in Scripture. But when in order to prove these statements he began a rapid review of the lodge ceremonies, the stripping, the hoodwink, the cable-tow, and the mock killing and raising to life again of the widow's son, they felt that it was high time to rally to the support of the ancient and venerable handmaid thus ruthlessly despoiled of all that borrowed attire in which her heart delighted.

"You are perjured!" shouted a voice in the audience.

"In what way?" mildly inquired the Elder.

The man was about to answer, "By telling our secrets," but the liquor he had drank had not so far muddled his brains that he did not bethink himself in time, and as he had not taken the precaution to "fill his mouth with arguments" beforehand, having filled his pockets instead with another kind of argument very much in vogue with the opponents of unpopular reform, he contented himself with simply reiterating, "You are perjured," and sat down.

The Elder, however, was armed cap-a-pie against all such attacks.

"I am perjured, then, because I tell the truth about Masonry. If I was telling falsehoods it wouldn't be perjury. Now," added the Elder, turning to his audience, "this man who has just interrupted me is sworn 'ever to conceal and never reveal' the secrets of the order; but he has just revealed them by the very act of applying to me such a term. Which of us, then, is perjured? I speak as to wise men. Judge ye."

But at this point the speaker's voice was drowned in a storm of hissings, hootings, stampings and yellings, while showers of rotten eggs bespattered him liberally from head to foot. The wild elements were let loose. Raging waves of the sea, foaming out their own shame, is no wrapt description of the scene that followed.

The Elder, after a vain attempt to continue speaking, dismissed the audience as well as he could, and the respectable part dispersed. He himself remained behind to gather up his books. This gave time for a crowd of infuriated Masons to close about the platform, and surround him like a cordon of wild beasts, with cries of "Bring a rail, egg him, feather him, shoot him." But their most outrageous demonstrations of insult and violence did not cause a ripple in that heavenly calm which pervaded the Elder's soul.

To long to suffer for the truth's sake is in some souls almost a natural instinct. It was so with Mark Stedman. He was born with those qualities that make a martyr—dauntless courage and intense loyalty to his convictions. And if we add to this the fact of all those long years of service for his Master, deadening every ease-loving, self-interested fibre in his nature; but quickening in the same ratio every heavenly impulse of his soul, till the ordinary motives that sway men had scarcely more influence over him than if he had been a glorified spirit, it will be readily seen that if their object was to frighten the Elder, he was about the worst possible subject they could have selected for such an experiment.

"My friends," he said, mildly, "you see that I am powerless; you can do with me what you choose. You can take my life, but God rules in Heaven, and the truth will triumph all the same—perhaps quicker. My soul is in his keeping; you cannot harm the truth, and you cannot harm me."

The mob was silent for an instant, overawed by the meek daring of this servant of God; then their rage broke out anew in redoubled yells and fresh threats of violence. Suddenly a man among the crowd whose features were partly concealed by a hat that he wore, either by accident or design, pretty well over his eyes, leaped on the platform, and with one quick movement extinguished the lights. The same friendly hand seized on the Elder. who, by the diversion thus made, and with the aid of his unknown helper, managed in the darkness and confusion to make his escape.

It was Anson Lovejoy, who had seen the notice and made up his mind to attend the lecture, half surmising that there might be trouble. By mingling with the mob as if one of them. he had executed his bold maneuvre, and the Elder went home unharmed in person and not a whit discouraged in soul.

"The wrath of man shall praise him, and the remainder he will restrain," said Mark, in talking over the affair a few days after. "Outrage and violence never really hinder the progress of the truth. I believe more Antimasons were made by that lecture than by the two others that passed off quietly."

"And it would make still more," said Lovejoy, "if the press were not so completely dominated by Masonic influence that the most daring attempt to suppress free speech passes unnoticed. That Chicago *Journal* has actually refused to publish the contradiction to Colonel Montfort's article, though signed by candid, intelligent men who were on the coroner's jury and knew all the facts of the case."

"Well," said I, "editors and ministers are, of all men, most timid about touching anything that savors of reform. The lodge has pretty much the same argument for both. Editors don't want to displease their Masonic patrons and lose thereby a part of their bread and butter. Ministers don't want to preach an unpopular reform and so run the risk of losing a slice off their salaries. And considering what a poor, weak concern human nature is, even at its best estate, I can't say I much wonder at it."

"Do you know that a professed minister of the Gospel was foremost in the riotous demonstrations the other night?" said Lovejoy. "I tell you while ministers and church members support Masonry, the system will stand. And furthermore, so long as ministers and church members who are not Masons 'think it is a good institution, so long as they will excuse and defend it, so long it will be impossible to overthrow it."

"I have been thinking of bringing up the subject before our next Quarterly Conference," said the Elder. "If the church is ever to cast this viper out of her bosom it must be through agitation from within. If reform does not begin at the house of God, judgment surely will."

CHAPTER XXXVIII.

UNDER THE JUNIPER TREE.

THERE is a certain exaltation of spirit which overcomes the weakness of the flesh when we engage in a stern wrestle with any kind of moral evil. Hence it is that reformers in every age have gone through life with the step of laurelled victors moving to the sound of triumphal psalms. Yet God has so constituted the human soul that it cannot always keep stretched to this heroic tension. The Elijahs who climbed the nearest heaven on those heights of sublime daring for truth's sake generally find their juniper tree somewhere in the way.

Mark Stedman had encountered threats, obloquy, persecution, with unfaltering heart. He expected nothing else. He was renewing the battle at double odds, for while the murderous spirit of Masonry remained unchanged, as evidenced by the attempted attack on Lovejoy, there was not now, as in the Morgan days, an awakening public sentiment to back up its opposers. To rouse that slumbering public sentiment, to lift up his voice like a trumpet and show the house of Judah their sin he conceived to be one of his peculiar duties as a sentinel of Zion; and he made no account of possible difficulties in convincing of her guilt a lukewarm church that had forsaken her first love.

"Really, brother Stedman," said the first of his brother ministers in the conference to whom Mark addressed himself, "I gave you credit for being a man of more sense than to run a tilt against Masonry at your age. You might as well try to throw Gibralter into the sea."

"Amen," returned the Elder, while his dark eye kindled and his thin face flushed. "Every false worship has been called impregnable. But the God I serve is a God of the hills as well as a God of the valleys; and moreover I have Christ's promise, "If ye have faith as a grain of mustard seed, ye shall say unto this mountain, be thou removed and be thou cast into the sea, and it shall be done.'"

"These are not the days of miracles," returned the other, rather curtly. "And to tell the truth I don't think it is Christian charity to indulge in such wholesale denunciations of Masonry when four-fifths of the ministers in our conference belong to the lodge."

"Counting yourself, I see," dryly answered Mark, who had just caught sight of a Masonic pin gleaming under the coat of his charitably-disposed clerical brother.

The latter looked a trifle embarrassed, not to say ashamed, at the discovery.

"You see I don't wear it out in open sight. If I was all wrapped up in the institution like Elder Chadband, I should. I joined the lodge a few years ago because I thought it might increase my influence as a pastor. You know St. Paul became all things to all men that he might save a few."

Mark rose to his feet, stern and solemn.

"I have one question to ask: Was it to save men or to gain more hearers, and, as a consequence, more popularity and more money that you joined an order whose badge you are ashamed to wear openly? You need not answer it to me. Answer it to God and your own soul."

And having launched this keen arrow of truth Mark went his way with an inward prayer for this self-deceived shepherd of the flock, who after all was not so blameworthy as his elders in the ministry who had lured him by their example into such a path of hypocrisy and time serving.

Elder Chadband was an altogether different subject to deal with. Far from being ashamed of Masonry he gloried in the many degrees he had taken, and sounded the praises of the handmaid at every funeral and corner-stone laying at which the fraternity figured, far and near.

He saw with alarm the serious trouble that Mark's fanatical views were likely to make in the conference, and he felt warranted in using almost any measure that might rid that body of his undesirable presence. But he believed in trying a little diplomacy first, and to this end he sought an interview with Mark, who, on his part, had rather avoided any discussions with the Elder, considering him as being too much in the situation of the Scriptural Ephraim to warrant the hope that any good might arise therefrom. He was therefore proportionately surprised when the Elder thus urbanely began the conversation:

"While I am sorry that you feel it your duty to oppose such an excellent thing as Freemasonry, my dear brother Stedman, a system that in its leading points is drawn from revelation and teaches in such an admirable manner so many important moral truths, I must say that your sincerity and earnestness, however misdirected, is above praise. And I wish that there was more of that spirit in the church. We need a fresh baptism of the old-time zeal. There is too little of it —altogether too little of it now-a-days." And the Elder sighed as if deeply impressed with the melancholy truth just uttered.

Mark opened his eyes. What did it mean? Was Saul also among the prophets?

"Now, I believe in the largest Christian liberty," continued the Elder, not waiting for an answer, "and no doubt one important use of having so many different sects is to make that liberty possible. I have been seriously thinking, my dear brother Stedman, that in some other church holding similar views on the subject of Masonry, you could preach those views without offense, and thus labor with more freedom and a greater prospect of usefulness. Of course we should be sorry to lose one of our most valuable preachers; but our loss would be the gain of some other denomination, such as the United Brethren, for instance. We will give you letters of recommendation to that or any church you may prefer."

Mark's eye flashed. He had been unsuspicious, hitherto; now he saw through the whole thing. Elder Chadband had been playing to perfection the part of a boa constrictor, which slimes its victim over before swallowing it, and I am afraid that Mark's reply to his proposal had less than the usual savor of Gospel meekness.

"Is this Christian liberty—to be able to declare the whole counsel of God, not freely in any part of the church universal, but only in a few sectarian by-ways and corners? No, Elder Chadband, while I have Christian fellowship with all who walk in the truth, by whatever name they are called, the church of the Wesleys is the church of my adoption. It was there my first vows were paid, and until she casts me out of her communion I will join no other."

This outburst rather startled Elder Chadband. He had hoped for a different result, not calculating that there was still some unquenched fire under Mark's meek countenance and threadbare coat.

"Really, brother Stedman"—and there was a decided dropping of the Elder's urbane tone—"I am grieved that you should take a mere kindly hint in such a spirit. We are commanded to separate ourselves from such as cause schism and offense, and to tell you the truth, many in our conference consider you liable to that charge. So in the truest spirit of brotherly love I have pointed out to you a course that will prevent all necessity for such a painful and disagreeable step."

"It seems, then, that you are willing to recommend me to some unsuspecting church as 'a brother beloved for his work's sake, while all the while I am lying under a grievous charge of 'causing schism and offense.' You would have me act a lie by representing that I seek another church from personal preference, when I do it to avoid the 'painful and disagreeable' notoriety of being forcibly ejected by the one I go from. Is this Christian charity or lodge dissimulation? If truth, faithfully preached, causes schism in any church, the worse for that church. Elder Chadband, in the day of Christ's appearing, how will you answer before him for your connection with a system that points out to man another way of salvation than through his atoning cross? How will you bear to stand at his judgment-bar with the blood of souls clinging to your skirts that the lodge has deluded and destroyed? Woe unto you Masonic pastors, for ye shut up the kingdom of heaven against men. Ye neither go in yourselves, and them that are entering in ye hinder."

And having thus delivered his righteously indignant soul, Mark left Elder Chadband in a more disturbed state of mind than Masonic philosophy would seem to warrant, and more than ever confirmed in his opinion that brother Stedman was a dangerous man to remain in the ranks of the Methodist ministry.

Now Elder Cushing's church in Brownsville, was Baptist, and though, as Mark truly said, the church of the Wesleys was the church of his adoption, he always felt in the hidden depths of his soul a yearning impulse of affection towards that particular chamber in Zion where he had been cradled. So when a certain Baptist minister came in his way a little while after, who "had never joined the lodge, and considered all secret societies at variance with the spirit of the Gospel," Mark began with considerable hopefulness to urge upon him his duty as a Christian minister to express those views in the pulpit.

"I have very few Masons in my church; I could count them all on my finger's ends," said the Baptist pastor, looking a trifle disturbed at this very direct application of his principles. "It would hardly be worth the while for me to leave the saving doctrines of the Gospel to preach on a side issue."

"You acknowledge that Masonry is an evil thing," returned the severely logical Elder. "Then if you have one Mason in your congregation his soul is in danger, and you can no more neglect to warn him without incurring guilt than if there were fifty or a hundred."

The Baptist minister was silent for a moment and then answered coldly:

"You were once yourself in the Masonic order I understand."

"It is true that I have worn the mark of the beast," quietly answered the Elder, "and for a short time I rendered him faithful service. But Christ's own blood washed away that mark long ago."

"Well, everybody has his own ideas of duty, Elder Stedman. Now for my part I couldn't take the solemn obligations that are required of all who become Freemasons and then feel right to break them afterwards. The just man, we are told, sweareth to his own hurt and changes not. So we must agree to differ on the other question. I think hobbies should be kept out of the pulpit—reform hobbies as much as any."

This was the taunt that sent Mark under his juniper tree—that is to say, into his plain, bare little study, where he paced back and forth for a while, his whole soul in one of those wild tumults to which only the still, small voice can speak peace. But the earthquake and the whirlwind must go before. Where he had a right to expect understanding and sympathy, he had received a stone—nay, worse; a stinging scorpion. His heart writhed under the injustice and cried out in the bitterness of its agony. Why must he ever lead a forlorn hope? Why must he be the one to always stand in the breach? How could he hope to batter down this grim fortress of secret iniquity single-handed? Had he not been very jealous for the Lord God of Hosts when every pastor around him was either openly committed to the worship of Baal or preserving a cowardly and shameful silence? Surely he had battled long enough. Death seemed better than life; an ignominious retreat better than to continue a hopeless struggle with the church and the world against him.

But God never leaves his servants under the juniper tree without sending an angel to strengthen them. And even now his angel was on the way to strengthen the poor, discouraged Elder who, to spiritual weakness, was beginning to add bodily faintness; though when there came a tap at his study door, which he took for a call to dinner, he only answered:

"I think I won't come down to-day, **Hannah**."

Hannah was used to her husband's frequent seasons of fasting, and it did not strike her as anything unusual. So she only replied: "There is a stranger waiting below who wants to see you. He didn't give me his name."

"Tell him I will be there in a moment."

As soon as Hannah closed the door Mark threw himself on his knees and tried to pray; but the moment passed in a wordless trance of pain; and, rising, he went wearily down stairs to greet his unknown visitor.

That the rough-looking stranger in blue jean trousers, tucked into very muddy boots, who shook his hand with such awkward warmth, was just as divinely appointed to bring him help and comfort as any angelic messenger that ever appeared to patriarch or prophet in the Old Testament times, was an idea that never dawned, in even the most indistinct fashion on the Elder's mind.

"I'm glad ye didn't get no hurt the other night, parson," was the first greeting of the unknown.

"Thank you, my friend," replied the Elder. "The Lord is truly a shield and buckler to them that fear him."

"Well, I went fifteen miles to hear that lecture, and I tell you, parson, I was just thundering mad at the way you showed us up; so I was as ready as any on 'em to bear my part when the rumpus begun. But you had a kind of look as you stood there with the rotten eggs flying about that made me think of my old Methodist mother when dad used to curse and swear at her about her religion and threaten all kinds of things if she didn't leave off her singing and praying. And arter all I don't know but I was more glad than sorry at your getting off so slick when that chap blew out the lights and left us groping in the dark, like the Syrian army that was sent to take the prophet Elisha. You see I stumbled right on that ar passage when I was hunting up the eighth chapter of Ezekiel. I was bound to find out if there was really anything in the Bible about Masonry; and for all it was two o'clock when I got home, I raked up the fire and went at it. And I tell you, parson, that ar chapter in Ezekiel is a stunner. It just knocked me flat to think I'd been worshiping the sun like any heathen. And now I've come out from the lodge for good and all. I don't want no more of it. The Lord has come into my heart and taken all the Masonry clean out of me. I hate it worse'n pizen, I do; and now, parson, I want a lecture in our parts as soon as you can come and give one. My name is Timothy Bundy, and I live at Bundy's Flats, just over the river. Maybe you know the place?"

The Elder had heard of Bundy's Flats. He knew it was a hard locality, but at that moment though a legion of devils had beset his way he would have gone all the same. Surely God had spread a table for him in the desert and riven the rock at his need, and his fainting, discouraged soul mounted up as on eagle's wings in exulting triumph over all the powers of earth and hell.

It is in the fiery furnace that a form appears like the Son of Man. Scorn, contempt, persecution, still beset the Elder's path, and he saw no reason to hope for anything else till he reached the end of his mortal journey. But a spirit of divine joy in doing and suffering for the grand eternal cause of Truth just as long as that cause needed him, now possessed his soul. Was it not an earnest of victory that he had been allowed to convert even one soul from the worship of Baal to serve the only living and true God?

"Praise the Lord, Mr. Bundy, for bringing you out of darkness into his marvelous light," he said, as he grasped the stranger's rough hand. "I will gladly give a lecture in your place at any time you may set."

And having consented to an arrangement for Friday night of the following week and seen his visitor off, the Elder rose up from under his juniper tree and did the most sensible thing he could do, which, we are told, was the course followed by Elijah in somewhat similar circumstances—he did eat and drink.

CHAPTER XXXIX.

A FORETASTE.

MR. TIMOTHY BUNDY was a specimen of a particular class of men once common in Ohio and the bordering States. He had been a hunter and trapper in his youth, was of Herculean frame and corresponding strength, and there was a legend current in the lodge that he had proved a very troublesome member to initiate, for instead of allowing himself to be knocked down quietly and buried in due form under a pile of rubbish at the east gate of Solomon's Temple, he had taken the farce for a literal attack and pitched his assailants right and left to the imminent danger of breaking their bones.

Elder Stedman fulfilled his appointment and lectured at Bundy's Flats, to a small but more quiet and well-behaved audience than he had any reason to expect after his late experience at Quipaw, which was in comparison quite a center of civilization and refinement. But truth often has the freest course in seemingly most unpromising places, and nowhere were the Elder's labors more signally blessed of the Lord than at Bundy's Flats. The two dollars given him at the close of the lecture was certainly meagre pay, but the Elder was satisfied. Not so Mr. Bundy, who took him aside at parting with a rather mysterious air.

"Now, parson, I want to tell you your life ain't never safe. One month ago if I had been picked out by the lodge to cut your throat, *I should have done it.*"

This revelation did not startle the Elder. He knew too well what a terrible power the oaths of the lodge have over an ignorant and blinded conscience.

"Thank the Lord, Mr. Bundy, that he has given you a better mind," he calmly answered, "and pray that his grace may work the same blessed change in others."

"I know we orter pray and not to faint, but grace don't do its work all in a minit, you'll find. Now, parson, this ere is a fust-rate revolver, brand new, and I'm going to make ye a present of it. You ain't obleged to let it be known you kerry one, bein' a minister, and you ain't obleged to use it—I mean on any ornary occasion; but it's a good plan to have some sich thing about ye jest for a scarecrow, to scare off folks as might want to meddle with ye to your hurt sometimes."

The Elder remembered Peter, and his answer to this warm-hearted but ignorant disciple had a decided savor of mild rebuke.

"The Lord has wonderfully preserved my life hitherto from all the snares evil men have set for it, and would you have me begin to distrust him now by relying on anything else than his own mighty arm for protection? 'Cursed be the man that trusteth in man and maketh flesh his arm and departeth from the Lord.'"

Mr. Bundy stood irresolute. Almost without physical fear himself, all the more did he realize the dangers which beset the Elder. His sudden conversion had generated a spiritual force and fervor that had as yet developed in the active rather than the passive line of direction, for like most men of his peculiar physique the animal in him having the start to begin with, was not immediately subdued by days or even weeks of this new, controlling spiritual force which had arrested him like Saul of old, "breathing out threatenings and slaughter," and bent him by the power of its mighty mysterious will to confess and forsake his false worship. Still he felt a strange reverence come over him for the meek and fearless Elder. Far back in his rough boyhood he remembered a timid, shrinking woman who, nerved with the same divine courage, had patiently borne threatening and abuse for Christ's sake; and though for long years her spirit had walked, palm-crowned, the heights of Paradise, Timothy Bundy wiped his eyes on his coat sleeve as the vision passed before him.

"I don't know but you're in the right on it, parson," he said, finally, laying back the revolver on the shelf. "Anyhow, take this," and he pressed some bills into the Elder's hand. "It was what I've been saving up to pay my lodge dues with, and if you don't need it for yourself jest take it to help on the work in some place where they are poorer than they be at Bundy's Flats."

The Elder took the offering with a heart of grateful joy. To him there was a peculiar preciousness in this first fruit of his labor. Gladly should it all be laid on Christ's altar; oh, how gladly!

"God bless you, brother Bundy," he said, "and fear not what man's rage can do. He hath preserved me in six troubles; yea, in seven there shall no evil touch me."

The Elder rode home in a state of calm, exultant happiness. There are times when to the soul of every sufferer for God's truth he gives a glimpse, as it were, of the final victory. And to Elder Stedman came another such experience of joy and triumph as he remembered having once before when the shot of the secret assassin rang through the still, green woods, and but for the hand of protecting providence would have terminated his career on its very threshold. The years that stretched behind lay bathed in the sunlight of divine goodness; he remembered not one hard place in his pilgrimage, no Slough of Despond, no Hill of Difficulty, no Valley of the Shadow of Death. And over the days that lay before glowed that same mellow Indian summer light. Many or few, what mattered it? Sooner or later he must fall in this strife and another take his place, as full of youthful strength and ardor as was he when he first stepped into the ranks. But he was willing, nay, joyful, to die on the field with no huzzas of victory ringing in his death-dulled ears, for only a little while and the end would surely come for which the whole creation groaneth and travaileth in pain—the end of every wrong, the triumph of eternal right in the world-wide reign of the Lamb. Welcome persecution, welcome revilings, welcome the martyr's crown if so be it actually glittered for him over those turbid waters that rolled so dark and chill this side of the heavenly Canaan! Living or dying he was more than conqueror.

The Elder roused himself from his reverie and spoke a cheery word to the patient steed on which his old love of animals now found its chief outlet and center. The intelligent beast responded thereto by breaking into a brisk trot, probably accelerated by certain equine considerations of the snug stable and feed of oats waiting for him at his journey's end.

But the Elder's lecture had not failed to rouse the baser elements at Bundy's Flats as well as at Quipaw Creek. A few nights afterwards Mr. Bundy was roused by a rap at his door. A little barefooted child stood without, weeping bitterly, and in response to that worthy man's astonished inquiries, sobbed out:

"You won't let them do anything to that good Elder, will you, Mr. Bundy? He come to our house and talked and prayed with ma, and she says he seemed just like one of the angels of God, only when she said so before pa it made him swear."

"They shan't do anything to him if I know it. Come in, Bub, and tell me what you mean," said Mr. Bundy, who recognized in the child the little son of a consumptive woman who lived about a mile away, and whose husband was both a Mason and a hard drinker.

"I heard pa and some other men talking about the Elder," said the child in a frightened whisper. "I was in bed and they were talking and drinking down below. And they said such awful things of what they would do if they should catch him in the dark. And they are going to burn his house down, Mr. Bundy, I heard them say so. I kept still till I thought they were gone and then I jumped out of bed and run over to you; I thought you could stop their doing it."

"Now look here, Bub," said Mr. Bundy, after staring for an instant at the wee mite who, with a courage beyond his years, had braved all the terrors of the darkness to avert the danger that threatened the Elder. "Here's a prime turkey I shot to-day. I've been reckoning to send it to your ma. Come over to-morrow and you can have it. But now run home, sonny, and get into bed as quick as you can, and don't forget to say your prayers. I reckon the good Lord above will take care of the Elder."

The child departed somewhat comforted. Mr. Bundy hastily dressed himself, drew on his boots, saddled his horse and was soon galloping through the night with one hope in his heart—that the warning had not come too late and he should get the start of the incendiaries.

He never stopped to question, as one ignorant of the nature of secret organizations would be very likely to, the credibility of the child's warning; whether it were not possible that one of such tender years might have mistaken the real tenor of the talk he had overheard. A man who, according to his own confession to the Elder had been so thoroughly enslaved in conscience by his Masonic obligations that he would have taken human life at the command of his superiors and thought he was only doing his duty was not very likely to doubt the existence of men in the lodge who would have no scruple about committing arson at a similar bidding.

"But the men who do such things are the scum of the community as a rule," objects one of those would-be defenders of the lodge, whose name is legion, and whose sole knowledge of the Masonic system is based on whatever fact or fiction any Mason in the plenitude of his wisdom may kindly vouchsafe to impart.

Were the men who murdered Morgan the scum of western New York? Were the Ku-Klux Klans with their midnight reign of desolation and terror the scum of the South? And, granted this assertion to be a fact, why does not the lodge skim off a little of the aforesaid "scum" by denouncing the acts and expelling the offenders? But, instead, it elevated Morgan's murderers to higher honors and fraternized with the secret orders of the South, their hands still crimson with the blood of hapless negroes and unoffending Union men.

What is the language of facts like these.

It is true that in the present case a drinking, profane fellow, who had as little regard for Lindley Murray as he had for the Ten Commandments, had been talked and fuddled by his fellows of the lodge into thinking not only that the safety of the craft had been imperilled by the Elder's late lecture, but also that it was an imperative Masonic duty to teach him a lesson on minding his own business—a subject on which it will be remembered that the lodge had remarkably clear ideas—and that he, the individual above mentioned could do the job more scientifically than anybody else.

But did this catspaw for lodge iniquity who, though worthless and degraded, was no fool, undertake such a business without knowing that he was backed up by the oaths of the whole fraternity, ministers, judges and officers of the law not excepted, to keep his crime forever a secret? Then where should the responsibility be laid? I leave it to the honest, candid reader who has followed me in my story thus far, to say.

It was a night partly clear, partly cloudy, with a few stars peeping out, and a brisk wind blowing. The elder lived about a mile the other side of the river from Bundy's Flats.

Mr. Bundy urged his horse through the stream, and, just as he emerged on the opposite shore a tongue of flame shot up, reddening the night heavens. It was in the direction the Elder lived, and with a smothered exclamation he put spurs to his steed and dashed forward towards the scene of the conflagration.

The barn had caught first. The Elder, awakened by the glare flashing across his eyes, and not conscious as yet that the same insidious foe was beginning to wreathe in serpentine rings the framework of the house itself, roused his sleeping wife and rushed out intent on rescuing, if possible, the faithful horse that had borne him so many long miles in his Master's service. But it was too late. The fire had made too great a headway, and the Elder himself, in his vain attempt to rescue the poor animal, ventured too far, for as he turned to retreat, driven back by the smoke and flames, he was struck by a timber from the burning building and felled to the ground.

Rough but kindly hands instantly dragged him to a place of safety and dashed cold water over his face and hands. Mr. Bundy's prompt appearance on the scene had saved the Elder's life, but none of his worldly possessions beyond a few valuables hastily snatched from the burning house, which in ten minutes was one sheet of hissing, crackling flame, and in ten more a smouldering ruin.

The Elder's injuries proved serious. For days and weeks it seemed to himself and to others as if his work on earth was done. But he rallied slowly. His manner of living, temperate as an anchorite's, was in his favor, and when spring again returned he was lecturing and preaching with all his old-time zeal and not a whit profited by his woful experience.

Nobody doubted that Masonic vengeance had fired his buildings. At the same time Mark received that meed of sympathy so freely given to persecuted reformers in the anti-slavery times: "It is too bad, such a good man as Elder Stedman is—but why can't he let Masonry alone?"

CHAPTER XL.

THE VICTORY OVER THE BEAST.

A VERY old, and, in his day, unpopular reformer has thus summed up his personal experience: "Persecuted but not forsaken, cast down but not destroyed, chastened but not killed;" thus epitomizing for all future ages the experience of those elect souls who stand out from among their fellowmen with a prophet's commission of rebuke and warning, and with too often a prophet's fate of being misunderstood and rejected by the generation to whom they are sent. To Mark Stedman the Apostle's paradox seemed no strange thing. Ever since that hour of bitter discouragement and unlooked for lifting up he had never lost the consciousness of a victorious divine power working in him and through him, turning sorrow into joy and defeat into triumph, and making his pathway always radiant with the light that streams from the Paradise of God. But there was one more cup of trial for him to drink. He had seen it looming dimly in the distance ever since his talk with Elder Chadband—the same cup which has been pressed to the lips of many a devoted servant of God. The church he loved, in whose service he had grown gray, was about to cast him out, and for no other reason than because he loved her too well and served her too faithfully to tolerate the secret iniquity she cherished in her bosom.

"The fact is," said Mark, when Rachel and I, having heard some hint of this new trouble, rode over to see him, "it has long been a preconcerted thing between Elder Chadband and some other members of the conference to expell me from the Methodist church if they possibly can. And now they think the time is ripe. The charges are frivolous and unfounded, but they will cast me out whether the evidence sustains them or not. I have no reason to expect anything else."

"Oh, Mark!" exclaimed Rachel, indignantly; "when you have been such a faithful shepherd of souls, a preacher after Wesley's own heart, instant in season and out of season; never thinking of gain or ease like others—now to turn round and kick you out of the ministry. It is shameful, abominable!"

"I think I shall have to talk to you as I do to good brother Bundy," answered Mark, smiling on his excited sister. "Ever since his wonderful conversion from Masonry to Christ he has stood out against the threats and persecution of the lodge as bold as a lion. I shall never forget how he came to my help once in the sorest soul strait I ever knew, like one sent of God; or how nobly he has stood by me ever since. But I must confess there are times when I find the old Adam in him very troublesome, and the late action of the conference has stirred him up to such a degree that I could hardly talk him into anything like calmness. He is a genuine son of thunder. If he had his way he would call down fire from heaven on all the lodges in the land and burn them up like the cities of the plain. But he is a great, grand, large-hearted disciple nevertheless."

"It is hard," said the Elder's wife, who had been silent hitherto; "very hard that Mark should be turned out of the ministry in his old age for the crime of being too faithful to souls. And I must say that at first I felt a good deal like sister Rachel. I couldn't be reconciled. But now I feel differently. They who would live godly in this life must suffer persecution. It is not the church which is doing all this to Mark; it is that terrible spirit of anti-Christ which has taken possession of the church. God give us strength to 'withstand in the evil day, and having done all to stand.'"

So spoke the Elder's wife, who had not forgotten her girlhood's terrible experience with this same spirit of the lodge. It had persecuted her father to his death in like manner as it was now persecuting her husband. But this plain-faced, quiet-looking woman had as truly the martyr's seed within her as any of those worthy women of old times who receive such glowing mention in the Epistle to the Hebrews.

There was a moment's silence and then the conversation turned to family matters, for only the week before the last of our home-birds had flown in a mist of white muslin and orange blossoms. Anson Lovejoy, though a staid, elderly man, had not found his superior years any bar to winning Grace. And thus Rachel and I were again left—I was about to say as in the first year of our married life, alone with each other—but there was one very important difference in the fact that no lodge oath now came between us to part asunder those whom God had joined together.

But as Mark and I stood by the open door talking over the matter of the approaching church trial, I suddenly noticed how aged the Elder had grown. Yet never had he seemed more like the Mark of old times— with the intense ideality and enthusiasm that had once led him such a fool's chase through the swamps and fogbanks of error when he mistook a deluding *ignis fatuus* for the guiding star of truth—the brave loyalty, the burning devotion that had characterized his first surrender of every worldly ambition at the call of Christ, not one whit abated, he was the same Mark Stedman who sat on the back stoop, in the glow of that far away spring sunset, when we talked together about joining the lodge.

"It has been a hard warfare, Leander," he said, "but I would not wish to enter Heaven with one honorable scar the less."

"Well, Mark," said I, "I must say I don't feel easy at the risk you are constantly running. There is an Old Country proverb that 'the pitcher that goes often to the well gets broken at last,' and in spite of the assertion lodge men sometimes make that 'they have stopped killing since Morgan's day,' I know the last martyr has not yet been sacrificed to the implacable spirit of the lodge."

"Well, Leander, I have always said that if the cause of truth requires the sacrifice of my life, I am willing to be offered. But it seems to me that I already see—whether in prophetic hope or positive reality I can hardly tell—the first feeble beginnings of a great reform which is destined to sweep the church and nation. Intelligent freemen cannot long resist conclusions forced upon them as they have so lately been forced upon the people of Granby. And when once this question is carried to the ballot box, the lodge will see the handwriting on the wall."

I was about to answer, but Mark suddenly turned pallid, and sinking into the nearest chair covered his face for a moment with his hands.

"You are ill," I said, in alarm. But Mark only made a deprecatory gesture.

"Don't call any one. Hannah knows nothing of these ill turns and I don't care to have her know, for I think they are some after result of the accident that happened to me last spring, and I am hoping will pass entirely off when I gain my full health and strength. Thank God that it only affected my body and not my mind. I can deliver as sturdy blows for the truth as I ever did."

I was not quite satisfied, but my mind was too fully possessed by other fears to attach much importance to a passing indisposition which he himself treated so lightly, knowing as I did that he had gone to work long before his health was entirely recovered. I saw him beset by mobs or waylaid in his solitary journeyings; but I did *not* see that his brave, noble heart was breaking in a martyrdom slower but not less sure than if the knife or the bullet of the secret assassin had been permitted to wreak their deadly vengeance.

As Mark needed me for a witness I attended the meeting of the conference, but I will not trouble the reader with any wearisome details of the proceedings. Suffice it to say that the specifications read by Elder Chadband really amounted to but two:—"Speaking to the injury of his brother ministers and neglecting his proper work on the circuit to lecture against Masonry."

To these charges Mark pleaded not guilty, and a cross-examination of witnesses elicited nothing farther than the fact that on several occasions, when his spirit had been especially stirred within him by the lodge idolatry of some of the leading members of the conference, he had denounced them freely as "hireling shepherds" who fed not the flock, and consequently had not the smallest business to be in the ministry at all. As to neglecting his proper work to lecture on Masonry, it was clearly proved that he had held on an average as many preaching services as any other member of the conference; and it was also clearly proved that the leading prosecutor, Elder Chadband himself, had been known more than once to neglect his regular ministerial work to participate in the ceremonies at some Masonic gathering. But what avails innocence against inquisitorial power? They could tolerate no longer the rebuke of Mark's presence among them, and were bound to cast him out. or, to use Elder Chadband's expression, "put him where he could do the least harm."

Mark had no counsel and made his own defense before the conference.

"Brethren," he said, "I stand among you accused of serious offenses, which the witness against me has utterly failed to prove. You, in your secret hearts, know that the real ground of the accusation is my uncompromising hostility to Freemasonry. That hostility will never abate. It will only grow stronger with every breath I draw. I boldly declare that the Rules of Discipline faithfully carried out would expell every Masonic pastor in this conference. There are no less than sixty-nine different oaths in the first seven degrees of Masonry. And this, in the face of that part of the Discipline which forbids 'all vain and rash swearing,' and any taking of oaths 'save when the magistrate may require in a cause of faith and charity, so it be done according to the prophet's teaching in justice, judgment and truth.' Is there justice, judgment or truth in these obligations with their fiendish penalties, their terrible trifling with Jehovah's name?

"I charge Masonic pastors everywhere with the sin of Balaam. They cause God's people to err, they deny the Lord that bought them, and will surely, unless the

Spirit of the Lord leads them to repentance, bring upon themselves swift destruction. 'Woe be unto the pastors that destroy and scatter the sheep of my pasture, saith the Lord.' Shall I, by keeping silent, incur their doom? Nay, ten thousand times better be shut out not only from the Methodist church but from every church in the land.

"I have offended in no point the rules of the Discipline. I have ever striven to go in and out among you with a conscience void of offense and in a spirit of meekness and charity towards all men. The Lord judge between us and lay not to your charge the sin of casting me out for no other reason than because I refuse to bow the knee to Baal."

Mark sat down. Once more he had flung his gage of defiance at the Beast.

The after proceedings did not seem to interest him. He sat with a strange look on his face, a high celestial expression, as of one who had fought his last battle and conquered his last foe, and was waiting in serene silence the moment of palms and shouts of victory, and lifting of triumphal gates.

The committee retired and in a little while made their report, which was to the effect that they had found all the charges against Elder Stedman sustained and therefore adjudged him suspended from the ministry of the church and all church privileges.

The Elder started up as if to rise and speak, but sank back in his chair with a groan. The medical man who was hastily summoned could do nothing more than pronounce his verdict—a case of heart trouble induced by the accident which befell him on the night of the fire and suddenly developed to a fatal result by the excitement attending the trial.

Mark Stedman had borne his last testimony against

the lodge. Shut out from the church militant he had entered the ranks of the church triumphant.

"*And I saw as it were a sea of glass mingled with fire, and them that had gotten the victory over the beast, and over his image, and over his mark and over the number of his name, stand upon the sea of glass having the harps of God.*"

My story is ended. It is the experience of one man and must necessarily fail in giving a complete picture of that terrible secret system which binds men's souls in a network of oaths and obligations to do—they know not what. But such as it is let the facts here given— for they *are* facts which can be indisputably proved— speak for themselves.

Freemen of America, I appeal to you. Will you bow your necks to wear the yoke of the Secret Empire? or will you waken to the danger before it is too late? It has no respect for human rights. It is monarchical, despotic, inquisitorial. It breathed its first breath under the shadow of throned corruption and priestly rule. It is as alien to the principles of a free republic as light is to darkness. And on you depends the question, Which shall rule this fair land, the few or the many; the spirit of caste or the spirit of equality? The weal or woe of future generations hinges on your answer.

Churches of America, God has a controversy with his American Zion. In your midst is a horrible thing—a gigantic religious system which ignores his Son and proposes to do the Holy Spirit's work of regeneration for men—a system as dark, cruel and unclean in its principles and teachings as the ancient Moloch, tolerated and worshipped! Christian ministers officiating at its altars, wearing its dress and sounding its praises!

Is it strange that the ways of Zion mourn? that the bright gold is dimmed and tarnished? The Lord our God is a jealous God. He will not give his glory to another. He speaks now in the still, small voice of warning and entreaty. How soon he may speak in the whirlwinds of judgment who can tell? Before it be too late heed His voice who walketh in the midst of the seven golden candlesticks. "Repent, or else I will come quickly and will fight against thee with the sword of my mouth."

Members of the Masonic order, honest men, kind-hearted, lovers of truth and justice—for I know there are many such among you—who secretly loathe the iron yoke of your slavery, to you I make appeal. Assert your God-given manhood. Deny the power of the lodge to bind for a moment what He has forever loosed. Your country needs you, but she wants freemen, not slaves. God needs you in the great warfare of these latter days against anti-Christ, but He wants men with the martyr spirit who have overcome the Beast through the blood of the Lamb and gained the victory over his mark.

On which side will you take your stand? Will you be the slaves of the lodge, HOLDEN WITH CORDS of secret iniquity, or Christ's freemen? The issue lies before you. If the Lord be God follow him, but if Baal then follow him.

THE END.

www.ingramcontent.com/pod-product-compliance
Lightning Source LLC
Chambersburg PA
CBHW030345230426
43664CB00007BB/536